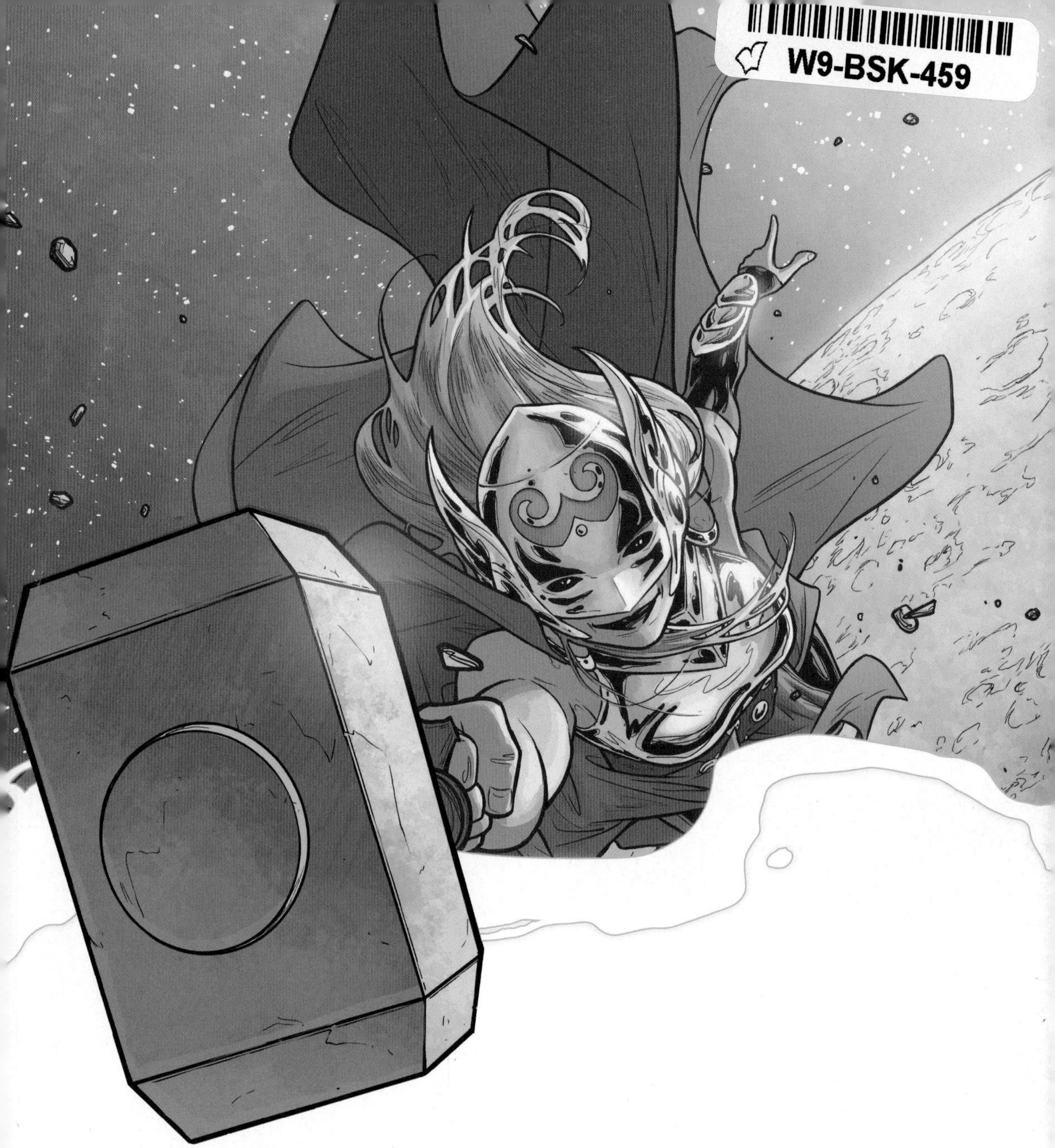

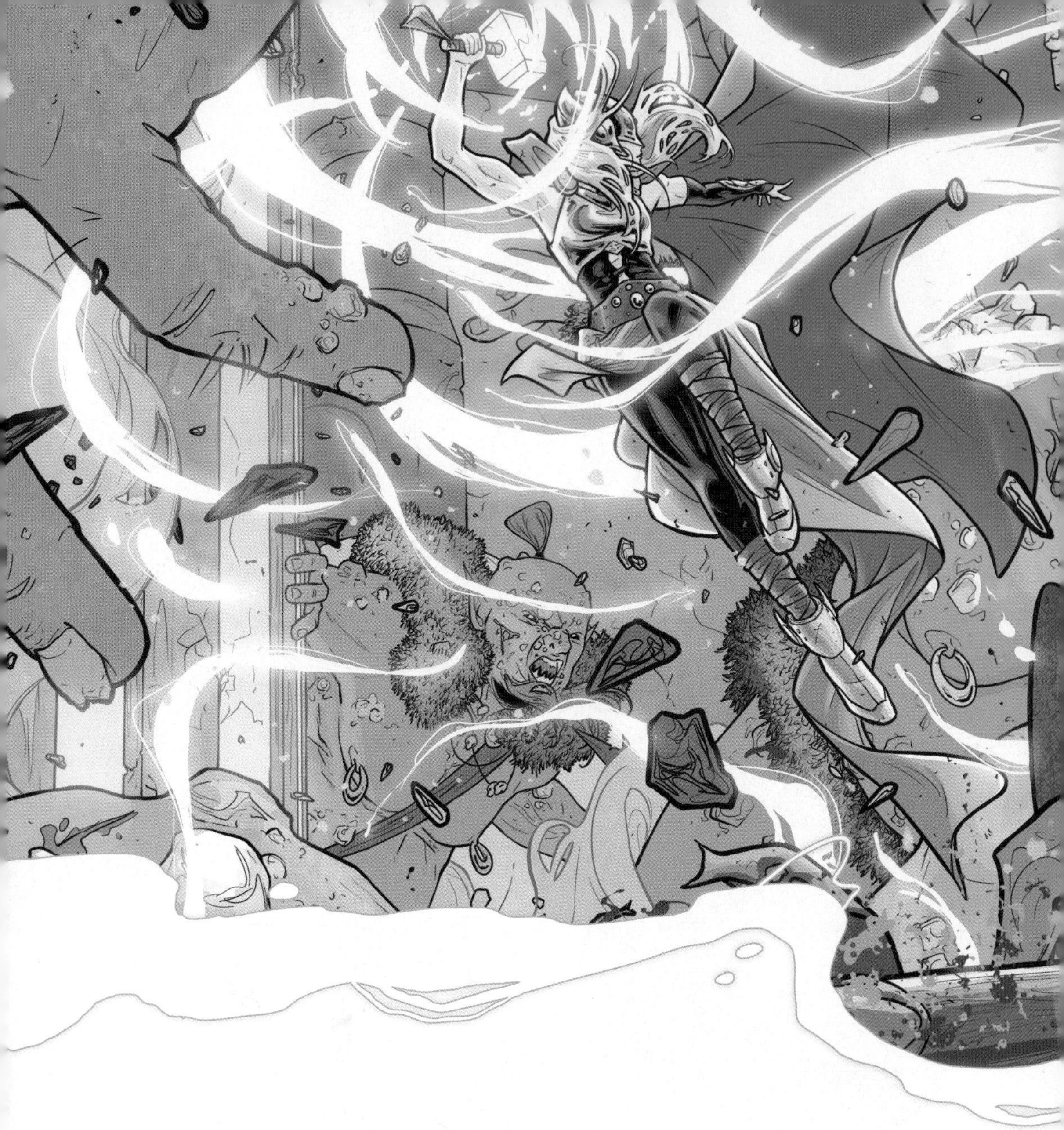

COLLECTION EDITOR: **JENNIFER GRÜNWALD**
ASSISTANT EDITOR: **SARAH BRUNSTAD**
ASSOCIATE MANAGING EDITOR: **ALEX STARBUCK**
EDITOR, SPECIAL PROJECTS: **MARK D. BEAZLEY**
SENIOR EDITOR, SPECIAL PROJECTS: **JEFF YOUNGQUIST**
SVP PRINT, SALES & MARKETING: **DAVID GABRIEL**
BOOK DESIGNER: **JEFF POWELL**

EDITOR IN CHIEF: **AXEL ALONSO**
CHIEF CREATIVE OFFICER: **JOE QUESADA**
PUBLISHER: **DAN BUCKLEY**
EXECUTIVE PRODUCER: **ALAN FINE**

THOR VOL. 1: THE GODDESS OF THUNDER. Contains material originally published in magazine form as THOR #1-5. First printing 2016. ISBN# 978-0-7851-9239-8. Published by MARVEL WORLDWIDE, INC., a subsidiary of MARVEL ENTERTAINMENT, LLC. OFFICE OF PUBLICATION: 135 West 50th Street, New York, NY 10020. **Printed in the U.S.A.** ALAN FINE, President, Marvel Entertainment; DAN BUCKLEY, President, TV, Publishing and Brand Management; JOE QUESADA, Chief Creative Officer; TOM BREVOORT, SVP of Publishing; DAVID BOGART, SVP of Operations & Procurement, Publishing; C.B. CEBULSKI, VP of International Development & Brand Management; DAVID GABRIEL, SVP Print, Sales & Marketing; JIM O'KEEFE, VP of Operations & Logistics; DAN CARR, Executive Director of Publishing Technology; SUSAN CRESPI, Editorial Operations Manager; ALEX MORALES, Publishing Operations Manager; STAN LEE, Chairman Emeritus. For information regarding advertising in Marvel Comics or on Marvel.com, please contact Jonathan Rheingold, VP of Custom Solutions & Ad Sales, at jrheingold@marvel.com. For Marvel subscription inquiries, please call 800-217-9158. **Manufactured between 11/27/2015 and 1/4/2016 by R.R. DONNELLEY, INC., SALEM, VA, USA.**

10 9 8 7 6 5 4 3 2 1

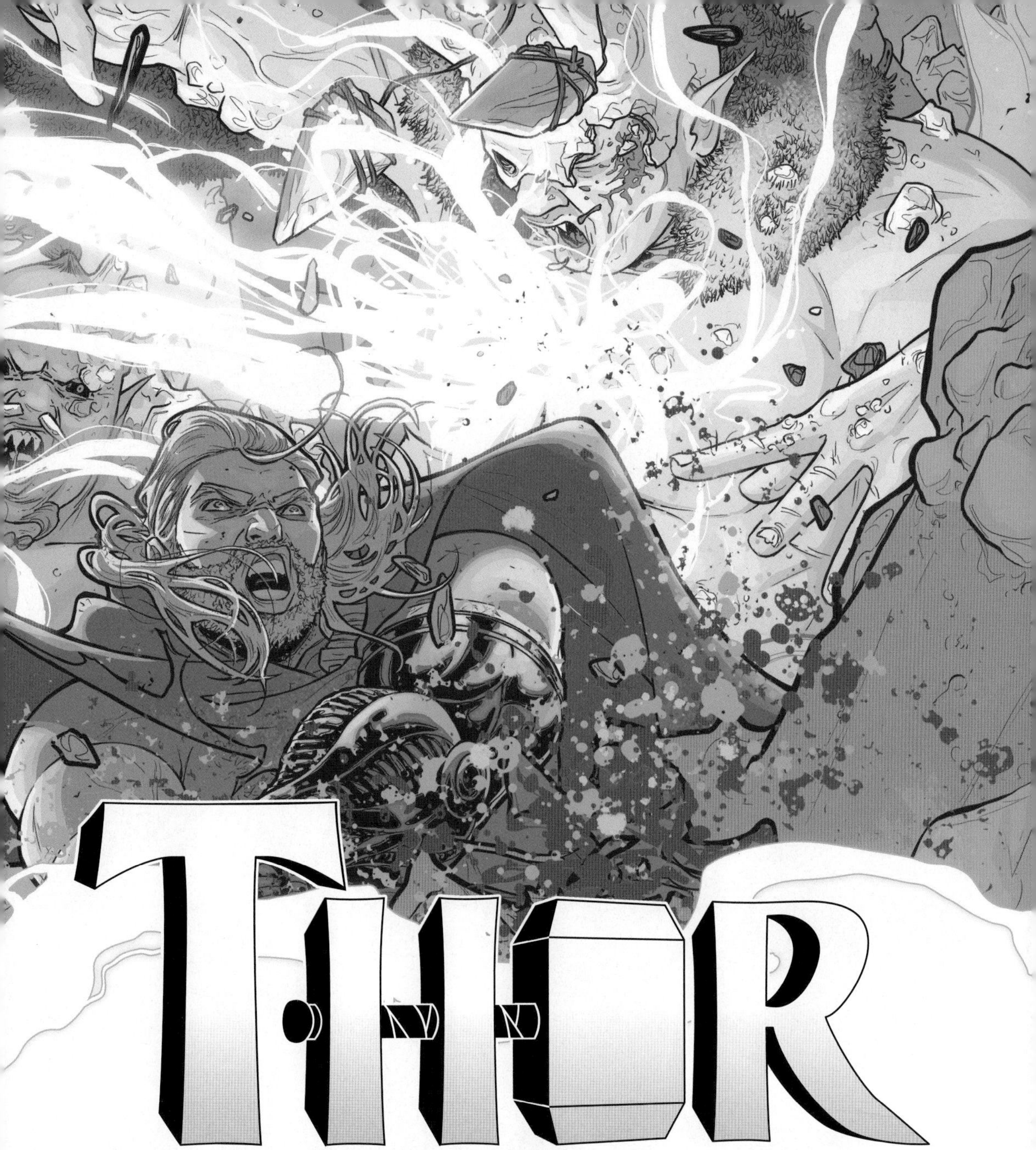

THOR

THE GODDESS OF THUNDER

WRITER
JASON AARON

ARTISTS
RUSSELL DAUTERMAN (#1-4)
& JORGE MOLINA (#5)

COLOR ARTISTS
MATTHEW WILSON (#1-4)
& JORGE MOLINA (#5)

LETTERER
VC'S JOE SABINO

COVER ART
RUSSELL DAUTERMAN
& FRANK MARTIN

ASSISTANT EDITOR
JON MOISAN

EDITOR
WIL MOSS

THOR CREATED BY STAN LEE, LARRY LIEBER & JACK KIRBY

1

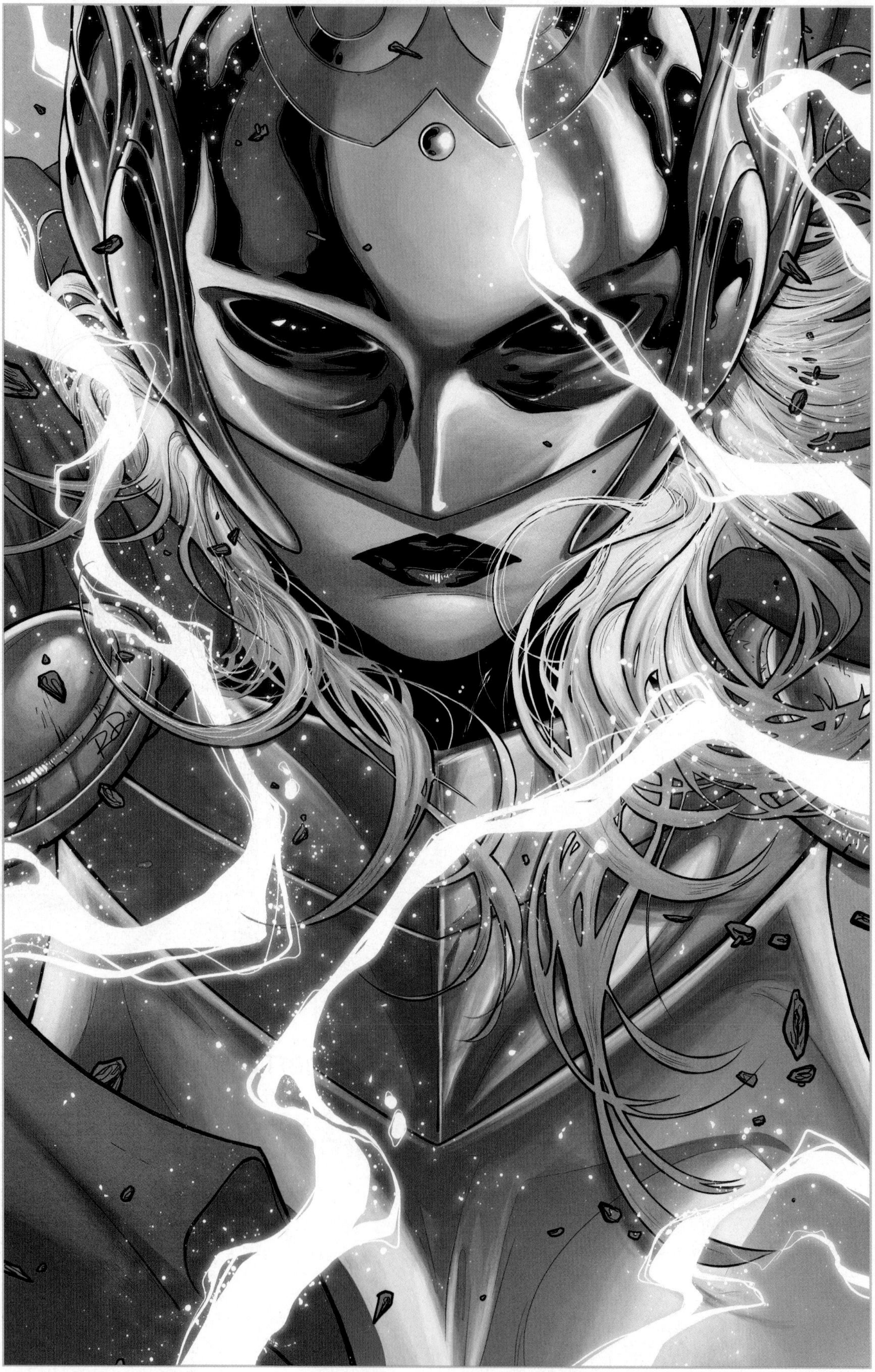

IF HE BE WORTHY

THE NORWEGIAN SEA.
HOMEBASE TO SUBMERSIBLE: WE READ YOU AT 2000 FATHOMS AND DESCENDING. YOU SHOULD BE COMING UP ON THE SEABED ANY SECOND NOW.
YOU SEEING ANYTHING DOWN THERE, GUYS?
JUST A WHOLE BUNCH OF BLACK.
ROXXON
HOMEBASE, THIS IS LOOKING LIKE A WASTE OF TIME. WE'RE AT THE COORDINATES FOR THE ANOMALY, BUT OUR SENSORS ARE READING NOTHING. MUST'VE BEEN A MALFUNCTION ON YOUR PART.
OUR TECHS SAY NEGATIVE ON THAT.
THERE WAS DEFINITELY SOMETHING BIG HAPPENING THERE A FEW MINUTES AGO. THE ENERGY READINGS WERE OFF THE CHARTS!
WELL, THERE'S NOTHING HERE NOW. REQUEST PERMISSION TO--
JERRY, YOU MAY WANNA CHECK YOUR SPEED. SONAR'S SHOWING A SERIES OF RIDGES UP AHEAD.
RIDGES? THERE AREN'T ANY RIDGES ON MY CHARTS.
LOOK AT THAT. JEEZ, IT'S LIKE A WHOLE MOUNTAIN RANGE. FULL STOP ON ALL ENGINES.
SUBMERSIBLE, WE ARE READING POSSIBLE SEISMIC ACTIVITY IN YOUR REGION. WHAT'S HAPPENING DOWN THERE, FELLAS?
UM, JERRY... IS IT JUST ME OR... DO THOSE MOUNTAINS LOOK LIKE THEY'RE MOVING...?

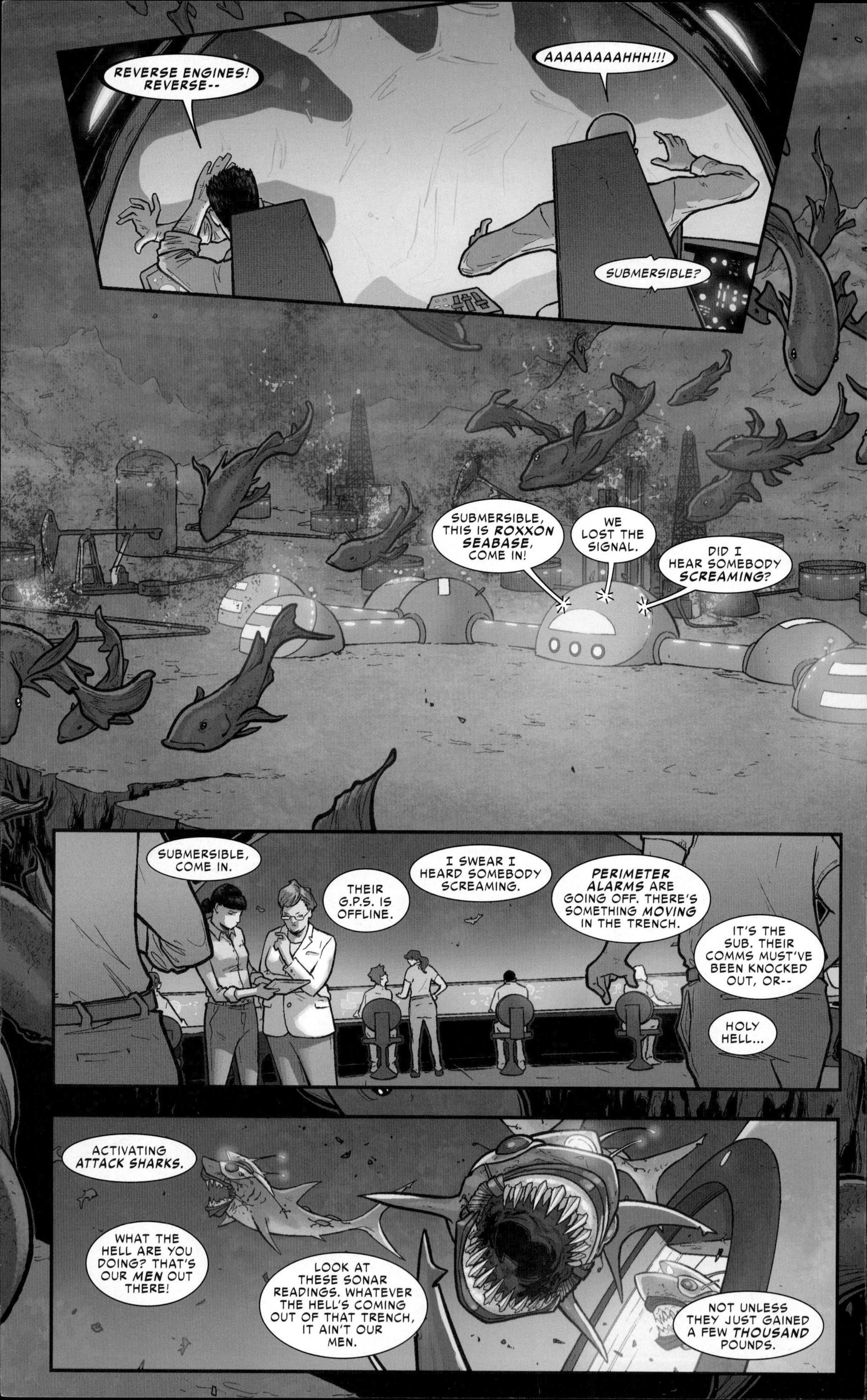
REVERSE ENGINES! REVERSE--
AAAAAAAAHHH!!!
SUBMERSIBLE?
SUBMERSIBLE, THIS IS ROXXON SEABASE, COME IN!
WE LOST THE SIGNAL.
DID I HEAR SOMEBODY SCREAMING?
SUBMERSIBLE, COME IN.
THEIR G.P.S. IS OFFLINE.
I SWEAR I HEARD SOMEBODY SCREAMING.
PERIMETER ALARMS ARE GOING OFF. THERE'S SOMETHING MOVING IN THE TRENCH.
IT'S THE SUB. THEIR COMMS MUST'VE BEEN KNOCKED OUT, OR--
HOLY HELL...
ACTIVATING ATTACK SHARKS.
WHAT THE HELL ARE YOU DOING? THAT'S OUR MEN OUT THERE!
LOOK AT THESE SONAR READINGS. WHATEVER THE HELL'S COMING OUT OF THAT TRENCH, IT AIN'T OUR MEN.
NOT UNLESS THEY JUST GAINED A FEW THOUSAND POUNDS.

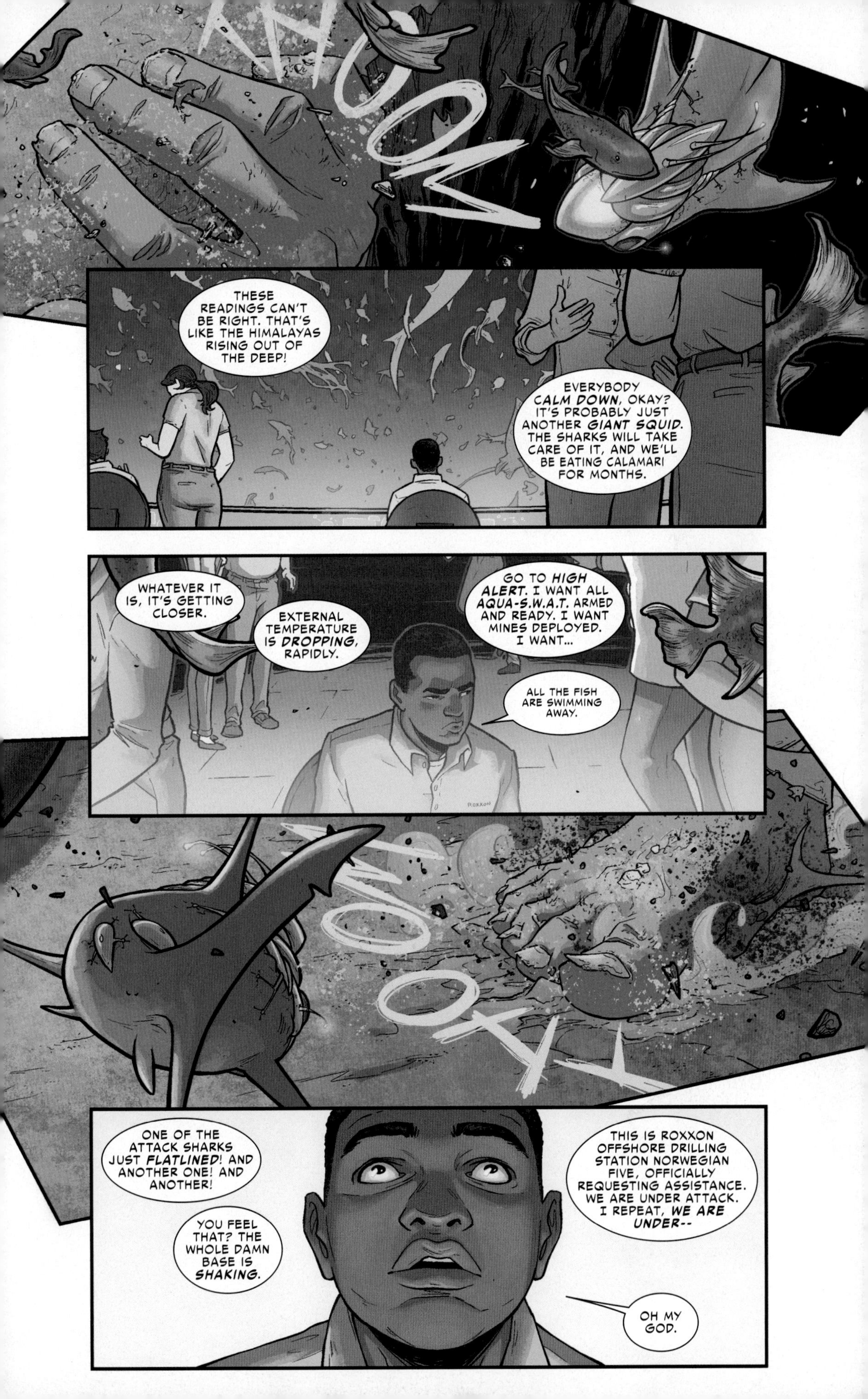

THESE READINGS CAN'T BE RIGHT. THAT'S LIKE THE HIMALAYAS RISING OUT OF THE DEEP!
EVERYBODY CALM DOWN, OKAY? IT'S PROBABLY JUST ANOTHER GIANT SQUID. THE SHARKS WILL TAKE CARE OF IT, AND WE'LL BE EATING CALAMARI FOR MONTHS.
WHATEVER IT IS, IT'S GETTING CLOSER.
EXTERNAL TEMPERATURE IS DROPPING, RAPIDLY.
GO TO HIGH ALERT. I WANT ALL AQUA-S.W.A.T. ARMED AND READY. I WANT MINES DEPLOYED. I WANT...
ALL THE FISH ARE SWIMMING AWAY.
ROXXON
ONE OF THE ATTACK SHARKS JUST FLATLINED! AND ANOTHER ONE! AND ANOTHER!
YOU FEEL THAT? THE WHOLE DAMN BASE IS SHAKING.
THIS IS ROXXON OFFSHORE DRILLING STATION NORWEGIAN FIVE, OFFICIALLY REQUESTING ASSISTANCE. WE ARE UNDER ATTACK. I REPEAT, WE ARE UNDER--
OH MY GOD.

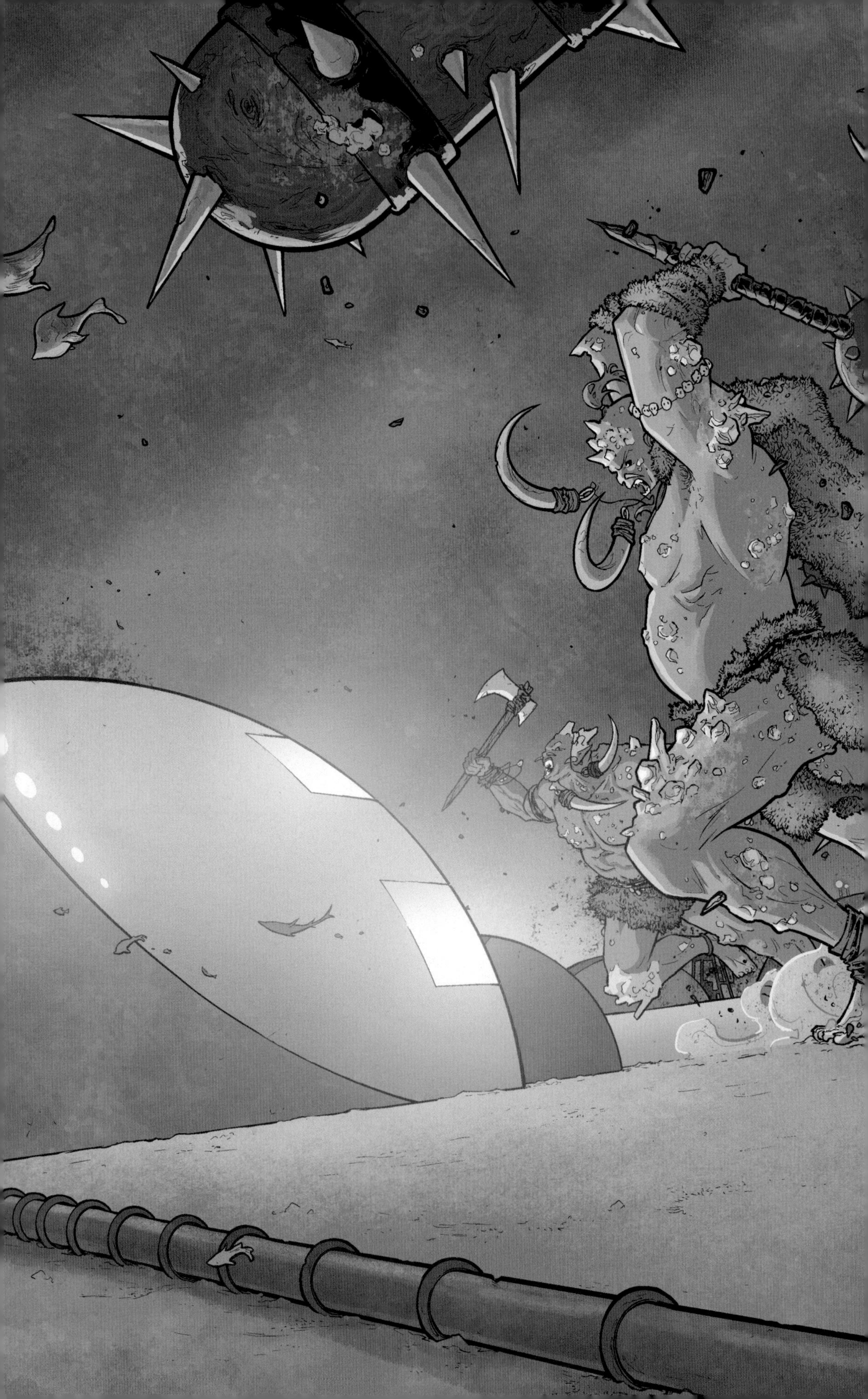

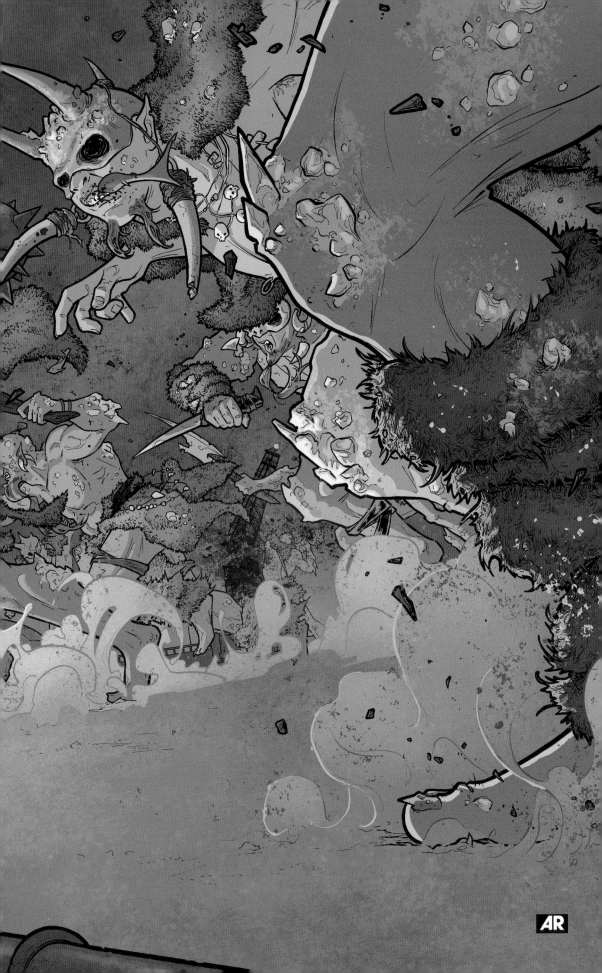

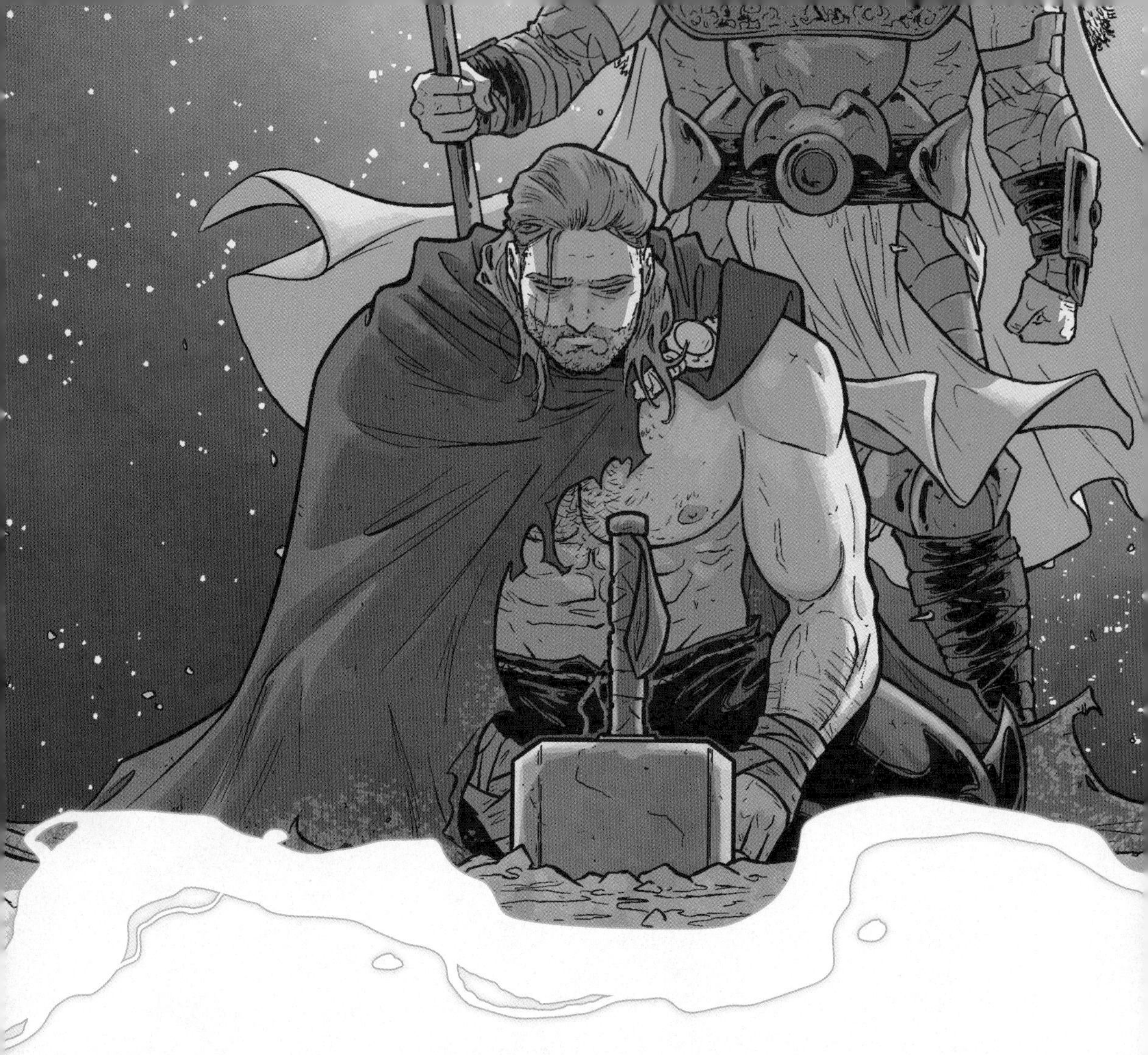

CHANGE HAS COME TO ASGARD.

After a self-imposed exile, Odin the All-Father has returned to his former kingdom (now called Asgardia). But his wife Freyja, who had been ruling Asgardia in his stead as the All-Mother, has no intention of letting things go back to the way the were before Odin left.

The biggest change, though, is that their son, Thor, the God of Thunder, now finds himself no longer worthy of wielding Mjolnir, his enchanted hammer. In a recent battle on the moon, superspy Nick Fury — empowered with secrets he stole from the Watcher — whispered something that caused Thor to drop Mjolnir to the moon's surface, where it has remained ever since. No matter how hard he tries, Thor cannot lift it.

With the leadership of Asgardia uncertain and Thor now in a severely weakened state, it is only a matter of time before enemies of Asgard strike, bringing doom to both the fabled realm and Earth itself.

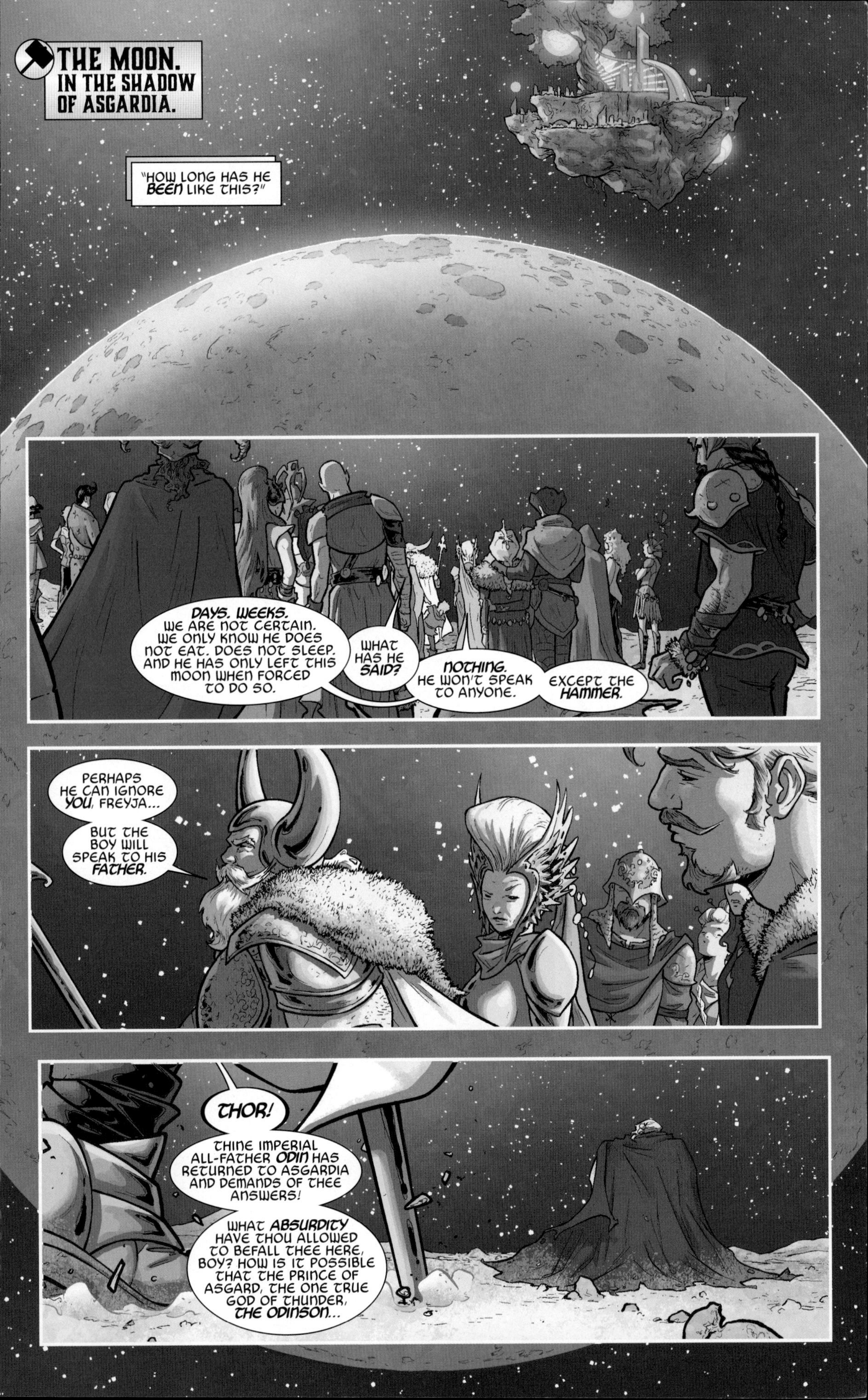
THE MOON. IN THE SHADOW OF ASGARDIA.
"HOW LONG HAS HE BEEN LIKE THIS?"
DAYS. WEEKS. WE ARE NOT CERTAIN. WE ONLY KNOW HE DOES NOT EAT. DOES NOT SLEEP. AND HE HAS ONLY LEFT THIS MOON WHEN FORCED TO DO SO.
WHAT HAS HE SAID?
NOTHING. HE WON'T SPEAK TO ANYONE.
EXCEPT THE HAMMER.
PERHAPS HE CAN IGNORE YOU, FREYJA...
BUT THE BOY WILL SPEAK TO HIS FATHER.
THOR!
THINE IMPERIAL ALL-FATHER ODIN HAS RETURNED TO ASGARDIA AND DEMANDS OF THEE ANSWERS!
WHAT ABSURDITY HAVE THOU ALLOWED TO BEFALL THEE HERE, BOY? HOW IS IT POSSIBLE THAT THE PRINCE OF ASGARD, THE ONE TRUE GOD OF THUNDER, THE ODINSON...

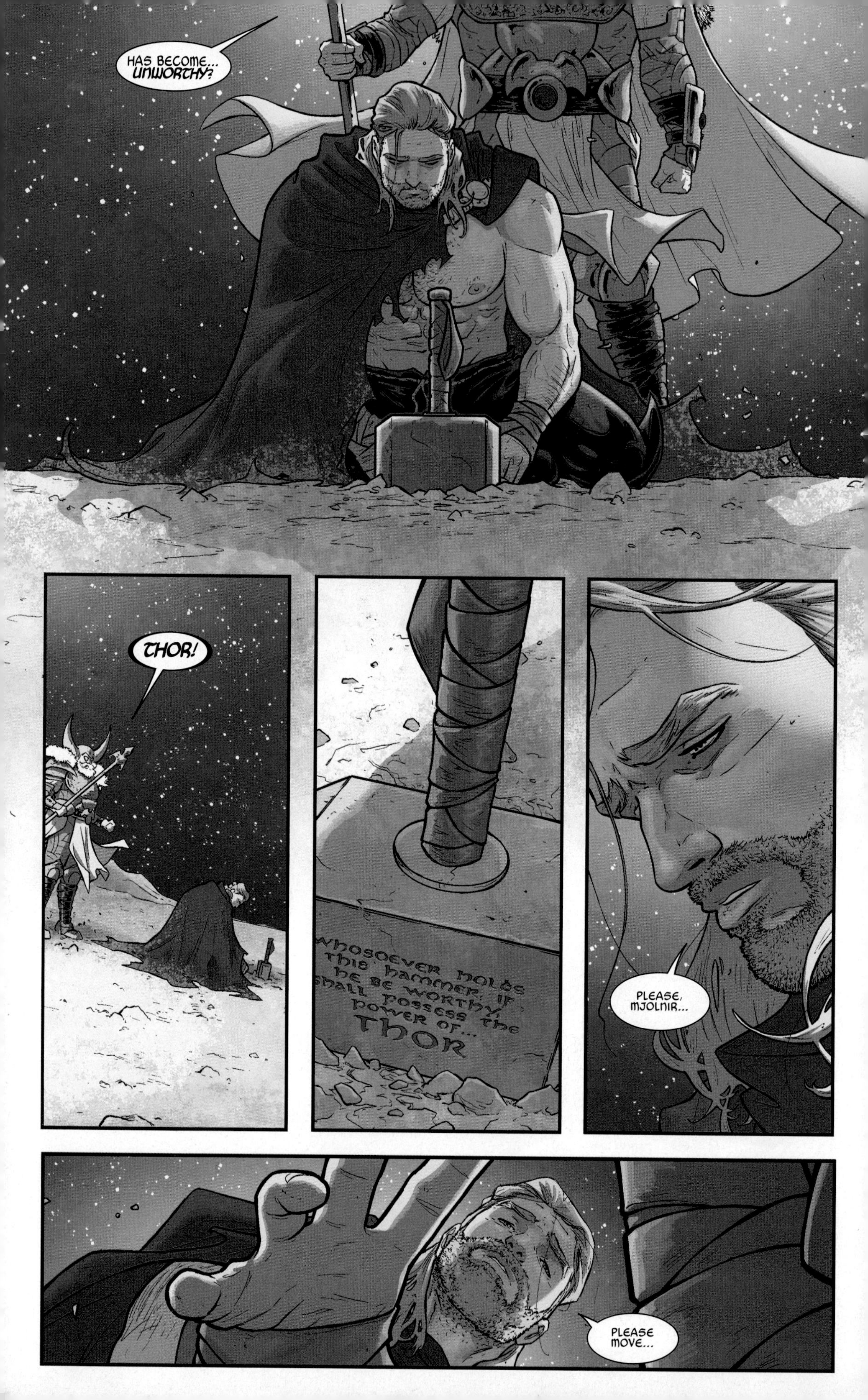
HAS BECOME... UNWORTHY?
THOR!
WHOSOEVER HOLDS THIS HAMMER, IF HE BE WORTHY, SHALL POSSESS THE POWER OF... THOR
PLEASE, MJOLNIR...
PLEASE MOVE...

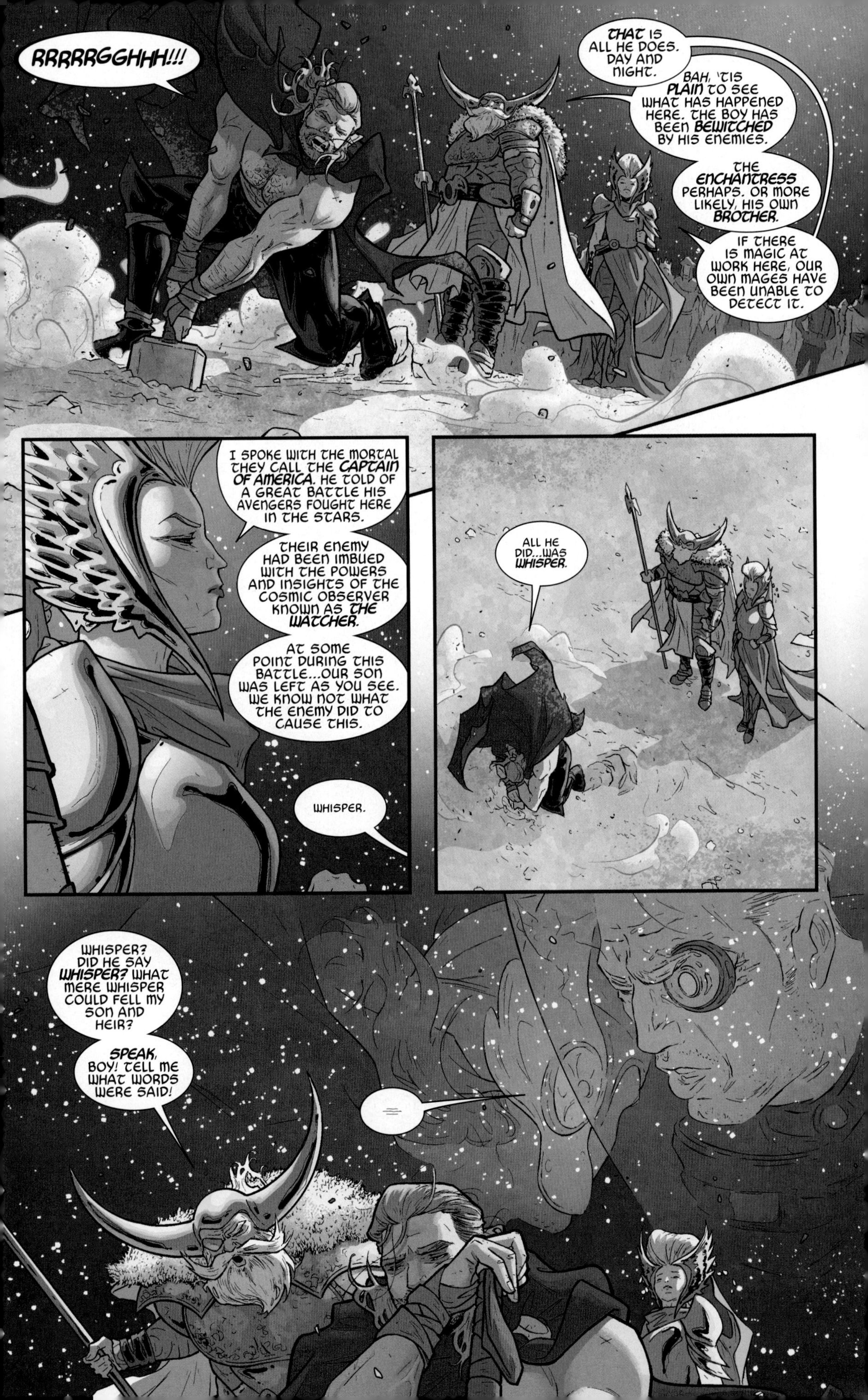
RRRRRGGHHH!!!
THAT IS ALL HE DOES. DAY AND NIGHT.
BAH, 'TIS PLAIN TO SEE WHAT HAS HAPPENED HERE. THE BOY HAS BEEN BEWITCHED BY HIS ENEMIES.
THE ENCHANTRESS PERHAPS. OR MORE LIKELY, HIS OWN BROTHER.
IF THERE IS MAGIC AT WORK HERE, OUR OWN MAGES HAVE BEEN UNABLE TO DETECT IT.
I SPOKE WITH THE MORTAL THEY CALL THE CAPTAIN OF AMERICA. HE TOLD OF A GREAT BATTLE HIS AVENGERS FOUGHT HERE IN THE STARS.
THEIR ENEMY HAD BEEN IMBUED WITH THE POWERS AND INSIGHTS OF THE COSMIC OBSERVER KNOWN AS THE WATCHER.
AT SOME POINT DURING THIS BATTLE...OUR SON WAS LEFT AS YOU SEE. WE KNOW NOT WHAT THE ENEMY DID TO CAUSE THIS.
WHISPER.
ALL HE DID...WAS WHISPER.
WHISPER? DID HE SAY WHISPER? WHAT MERE WHISPER COULD FELL MY SON AND HEIR?
SPEAK, BOY! TELL ME WHAT WORDS WERE SAID!

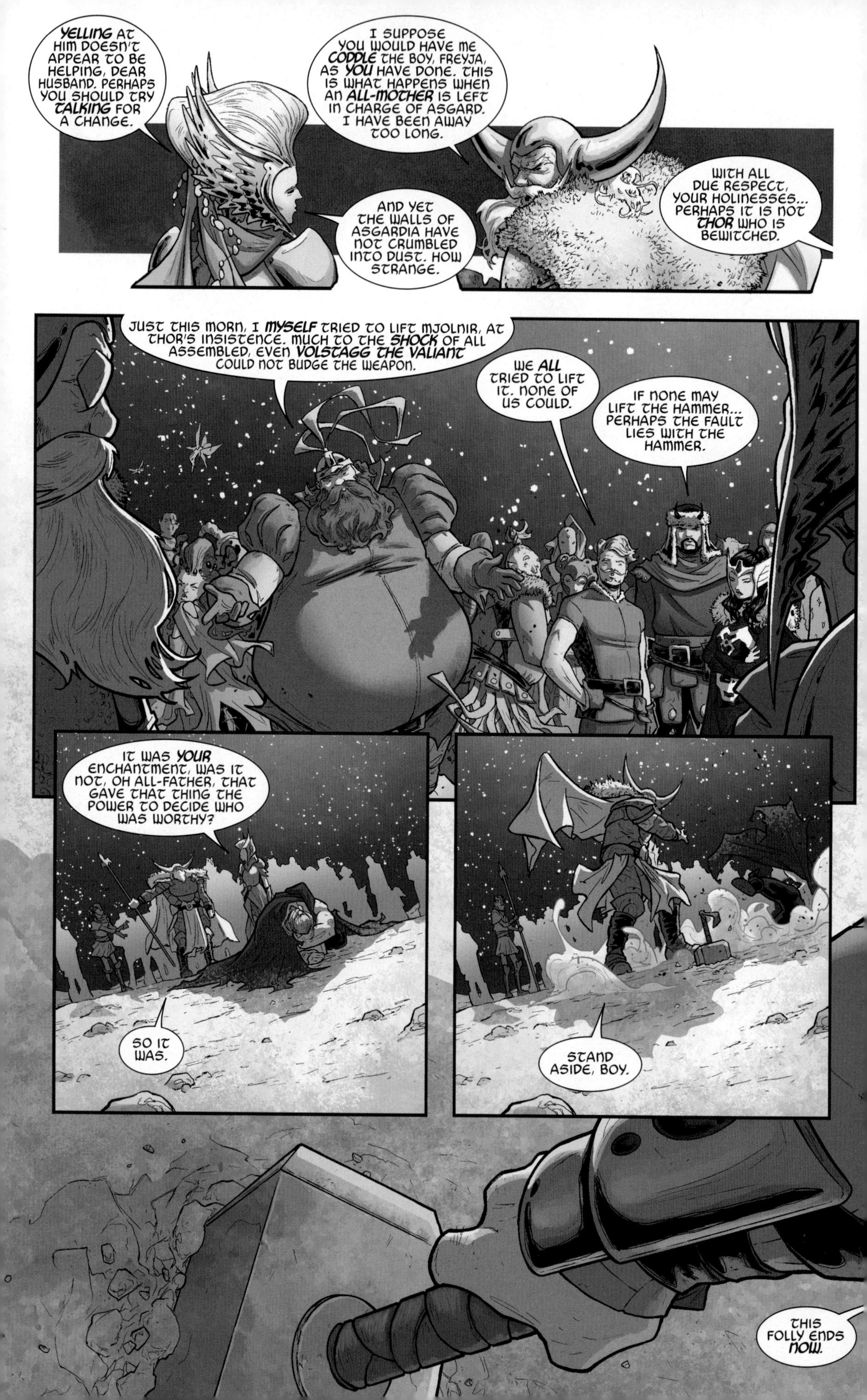
YELLING AT HIM DOESN'T APPEAR TO BE HELPING, DEAR HUSBAND. PERHAPS YOU SHOULD TRY TALKING FOR A CHANGE.
I SUPPOSE YOU WOULD HAVE ME CODDLE THE BOY, FREYJA, AS YOU HAVE DONE. THIS IS WHAT HAPPENS WHEN AN ALL-MOTHER IS LEFT IN CHARGE OF ASGARD. I HAVE BEEN AWAY TOO LONG.
AND YET THE WALLS OF ASGARDIA HAVE NOT CRUMBLED INTO DUST. HOW STRANGE.
WITH ALL DUE RESPECT, YOUR HOLINESSES... PERHAPS IT IS NOT THOR WHO IS BEWITCHED.
JUST THIS MORN, I MYSELF TRIED TO LIFT MJOLNIR, AT THOR'S INSISTENCE. MUCH TO THE SHOCK OF ALL ASSEMBLED, EVEN VOLSTAGG THE VALIANT COULD NOT BUDGE THE WEAPON.
WE ALL TRIED TO LIFT IT. NONE OF US COULD.
IF NONE MAY LIFT THE HAMMER... PERHAPS THE FAULT LIES WITH THE HAMMER.
IT WAS YOUR ENCHANTMENT, WAS IT NOT, OH ALL-FATHER, THAT GAVE THAT THING THE POWER TO DECIDE WHO WAS WORTHY?
SO IT WAS.
STAND ASIDE, BOY.
THIS FOLLY ENDS NOW.

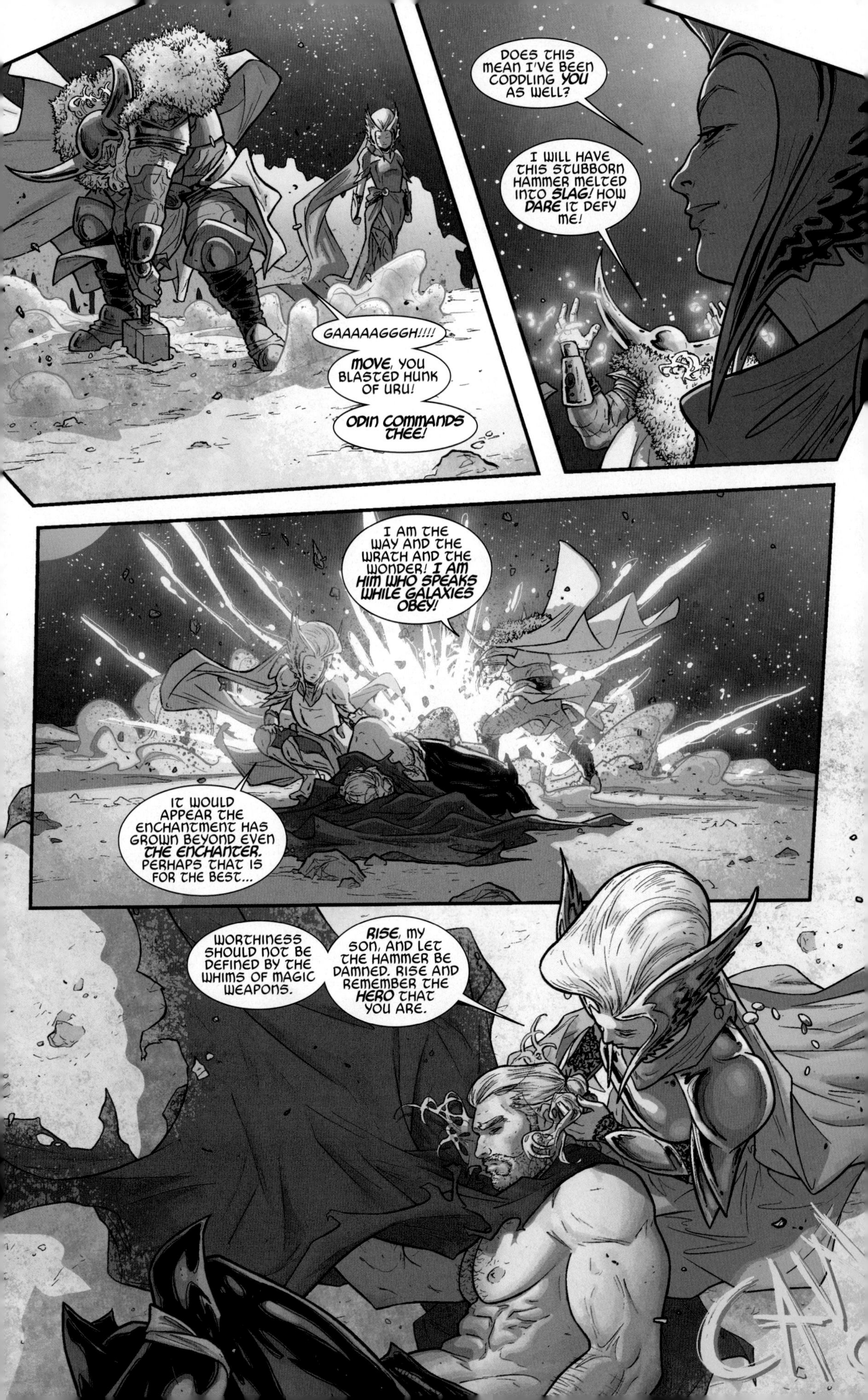
GAAAAAGGGH!!!!
MOVE, YOU BLASTED HUNK OF URU!
ODIN COMMANDS THEE!
DOES THIS MEAN I'VE BEEN CODDLING YOU AS WELL?
I WILL HAVE THIS STUBBORN HAMMER MELTED INTO SLAG! HOW DARE IT DEFY ME!
I AM THE WAY AND THE WRATH AND THE WONDER! I AM HIM WHO SPEAKS WHILE GALAXIES OBEY!
IT WOULD APPEAR THE ENCHANTMENT HAS GROWN BEYOND EVEN THE ENCHANTER. PERHAPS THAT IS FOR THE BEST...
WORTHINESS SHOULD NOT BE DEFINED BY THE WHIMS OF MAGIC WEAPONS.
RISE, MY SON, AND LET THE HAMMER BE DAMNED. RISE AND REMEMBER THE HERO THAT YOU ARE.

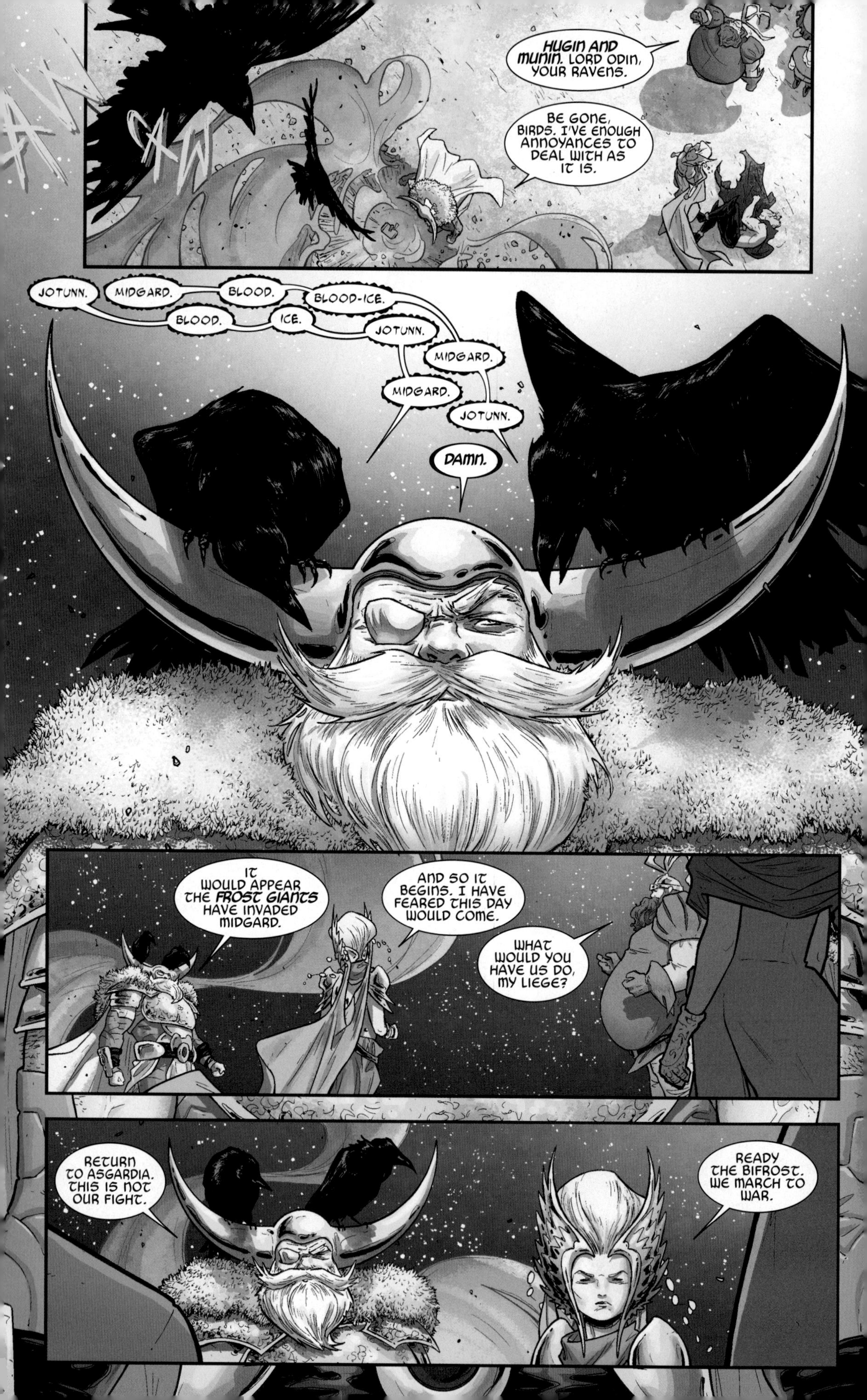

AW
AW
HUGIN AND MUNIN. LORD ODIN, YOUR RAVENS.
BE GONE, BIRDS. I'VE ENOUGH ANNOYANCES TO DEAL WITH AS IT IS.
JOTUNN.
MIDGARD.
BLOOD.
BLOOD.
ICE.
BLOOD-ICE.
JOTUNN.
MIDGARD.
MIDGARD.
JOTUNN.
DAMN.
IT WOULD APPEAR THE FROST GIANTS HAVE INVADED MIDGARD.
AND SO IT BEGINS. I HAVE FEARED THIS DAY WOULD COME.
WHAT WOULD YOU HAVE US DO, MY LIEGE?
RETURN TO ASGARDIA. THIS IS NOT OUR FIGHT.
READY THE BIFROST. WE MARCH TO WAR.

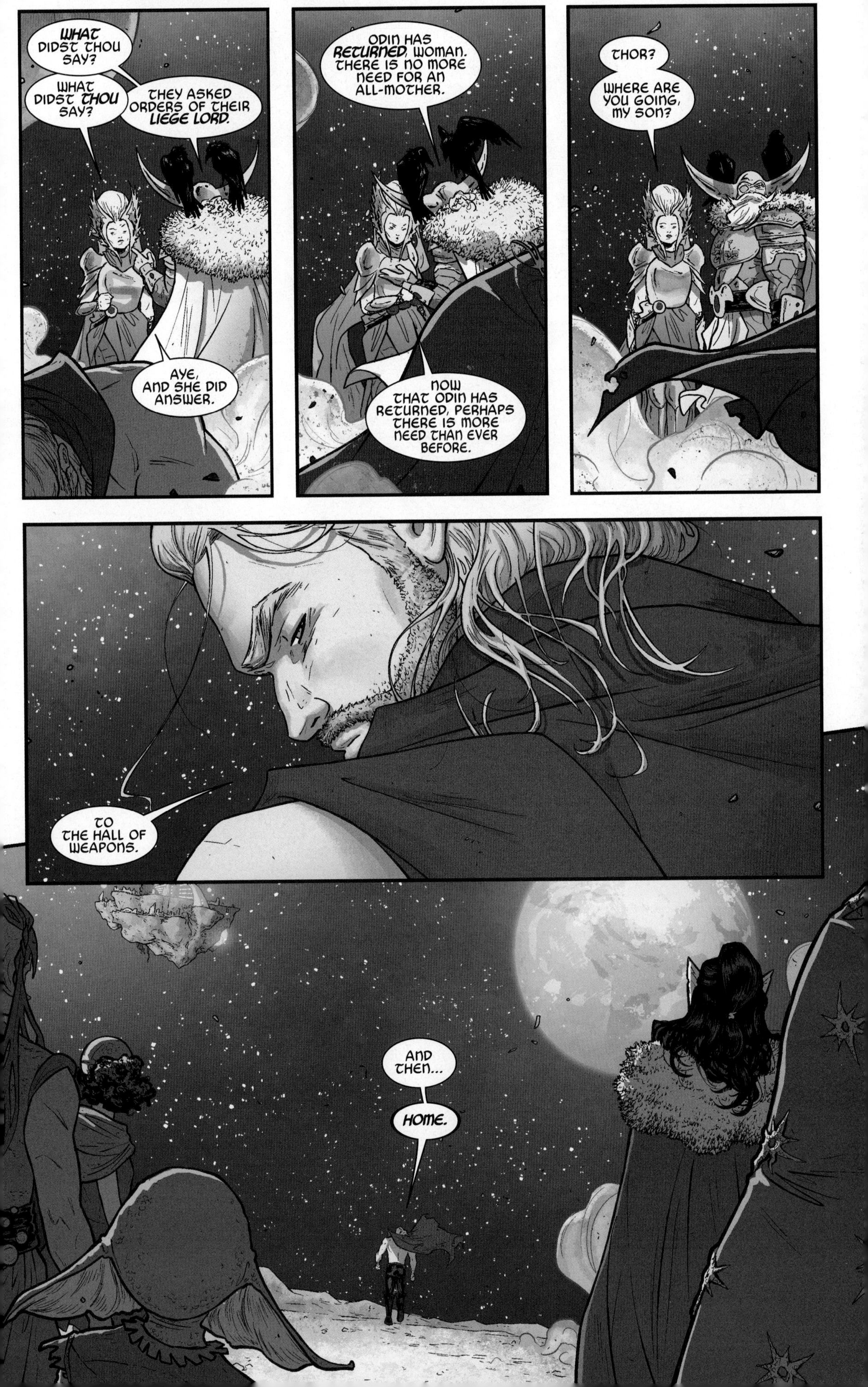
WHAT DIDST THOU SAY?
WHAT DIDST THOU SAY?
THEY ASKED ORDERS OF THEIR LIEGE LORD.
AYE, AND SHE DID ANSWER.
ODIN HAS RETURNED, WOMAN. THERE IS NO MORE NEED FOR AN ALL-MOTHER.
NOW THAT ODIN HAS RETURNED, PERHAPS THERE IS MORE NEED THAN EVER BEFORE.
THOR?
WHERE ARE YOU GOING, MY SON?
TO THE HALL OF WEAPONS.
AND THEN...
HOME.

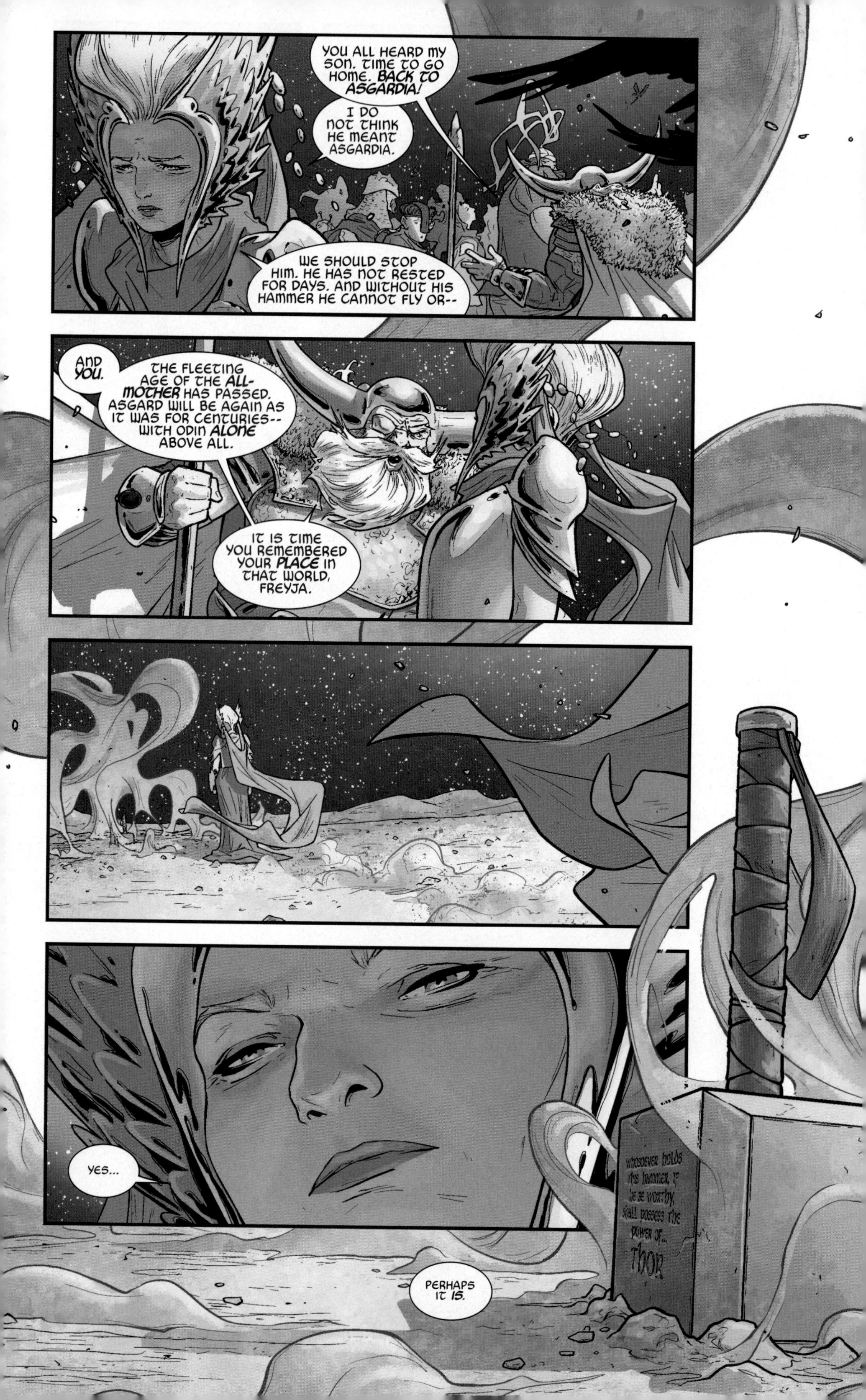
YOU ALL HEARD MY SON. TIME TO GO HOME. BACK TO ASGARDIA!
I DO NOT THINK HE MEANT ASGARDIA.
WE SHOULD STOP HIM. HE HAS NOT RESTED FOR DAYS. AND WITHOUT HIS HAMMER HE CANNOT FLY OR--
AND YOU.
THE FLEETING AGE OF THE ALL-MOTHER HAS PASSED. ASGARD WILL BE AGAIN AS IT WAS FOR CENTURIES-- WITH ODIN ALONE ABOVE ALL.
IT IS TIME YOU REMEMBERED YOUR PLACE IN THAT WORLD, FREYJA.
YES...
Whosoever holds this hammer, if he be worthy, shall possess the power of... THOR
PERHAPS IT IS.

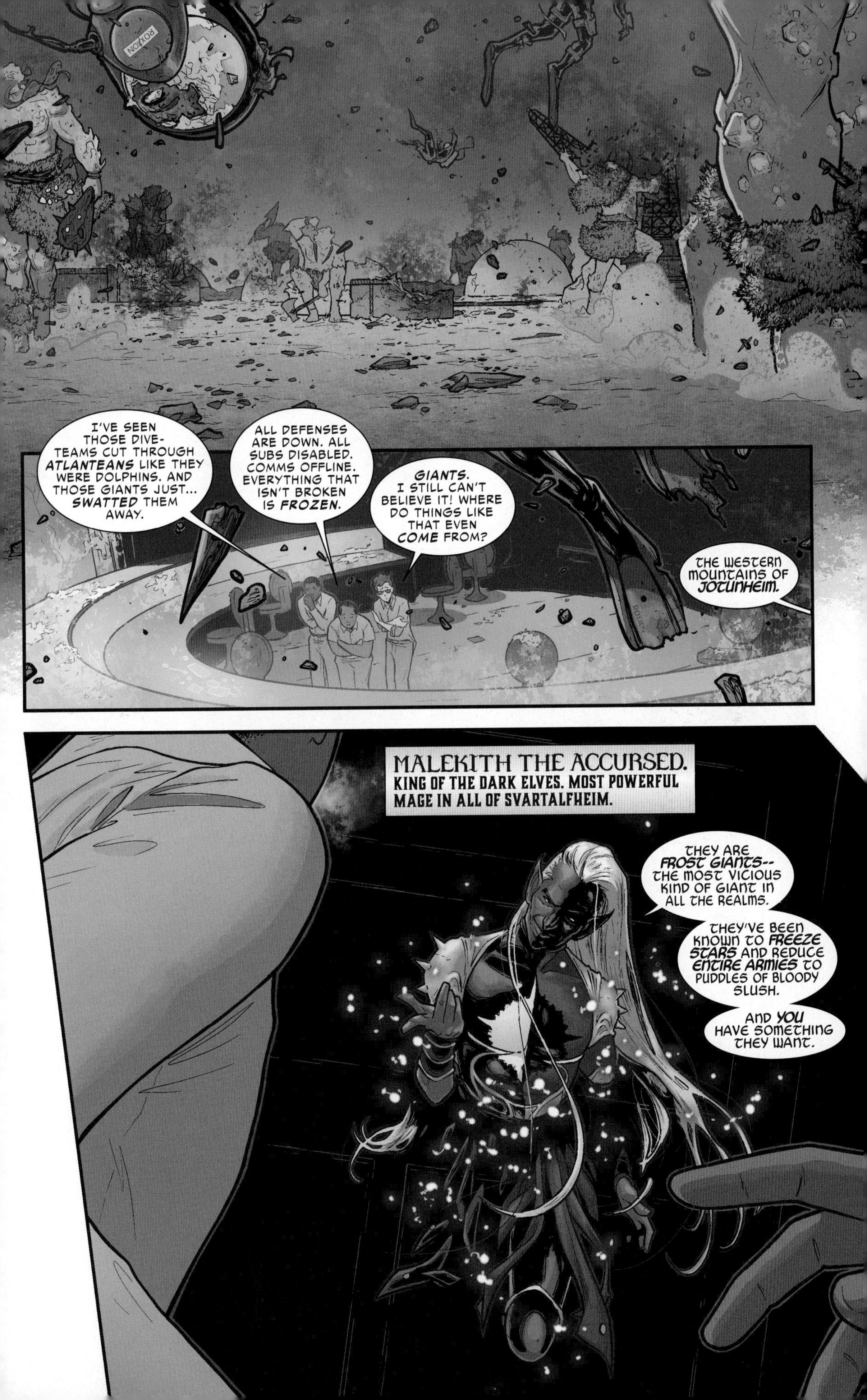
I'VE SEEN THOSE DIVE-TEAMS CUT THROUGH ATLANTEANS LIKE THEY WERE DOLPHINS. AND THOSE GIANTS JUST... SWATTED THEM AWAY.
ALL DEFENSES ARE DOWN. ALL SUBS DISABLED. COMMS OFFLINE. EVERYTHING THAT ISN'T BROKEN IS FROZEN.
GIANTS. I STILL CAN'T BELIEVE IT! WHERE DO THINGS LIKE THAT EVEN COME FROM?
THE WESTERN MOUNTAINS OF JOTUNHEIM.
MALEKITH THE ACCURSED.
KING OF THE DARK ELVES. MOST POWERFUL MAGE IN ALL OF SVARTALFHEIM.
THEY ARE FROST GIANTS-- THE MOST VICIOUS KIND OF GIANT IN ALL THE REALMS.
THEY'VE BEEN KNOWN TO FREEZE STARS AND REDUCE ENTIRE ARMIES TO PUDDLES OF BLOODY SLUSH.
AND YOU HAVE SOMETHING THEY WANT.

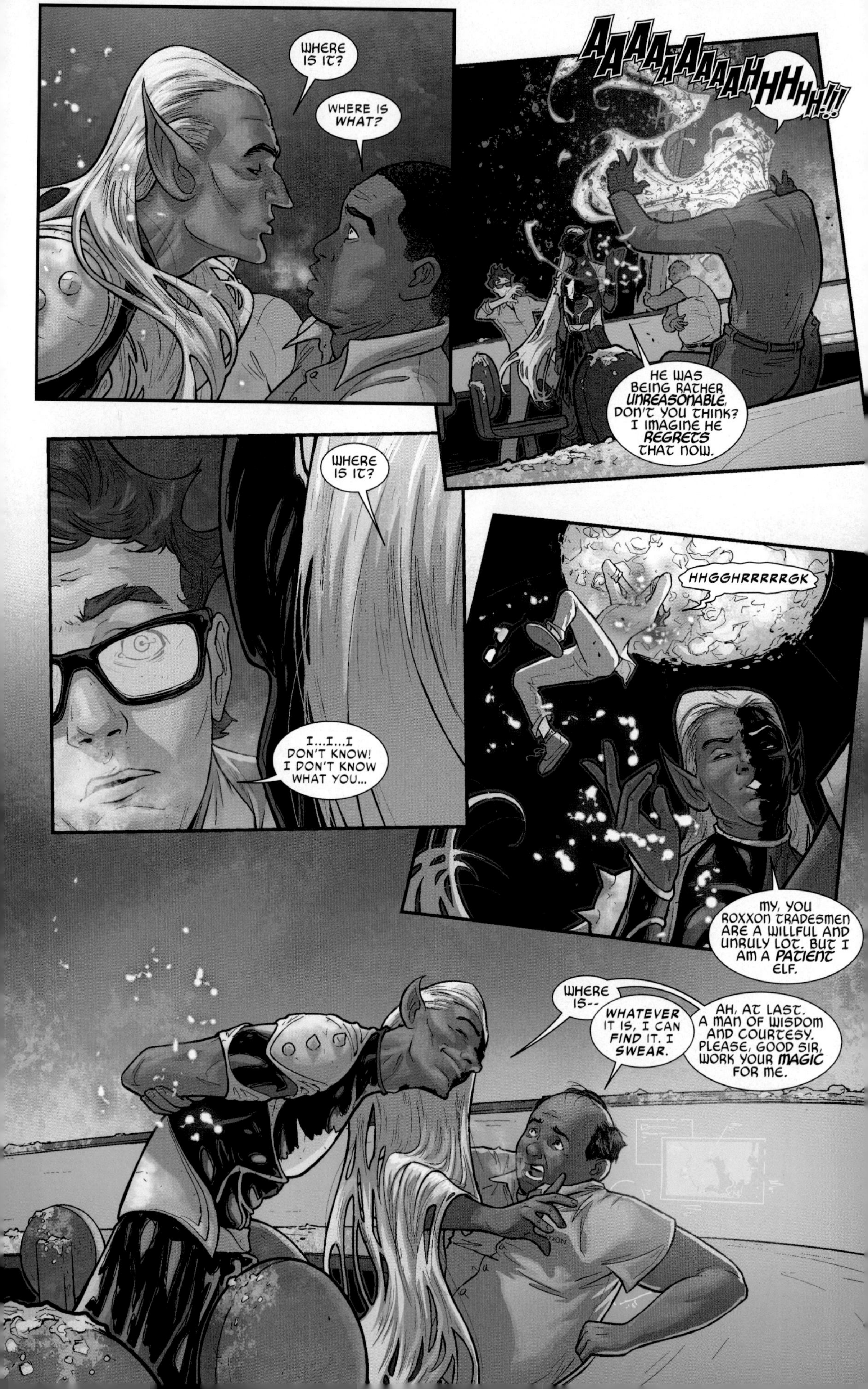
WHERE IS IT?
WHERE IS WHAT?
AAAAAAAAAAHHHH!!!
HE WAS BEING RATHER UNREASONABLE, DON'T YOU THINK? I IMAGINE HE REGRETS THAT NOW.
WHERE IS IT?
I...I...I DON'T KNOW! I DON'T KNOW WHAT YOU...
HHGGHRRRRRGK
MY, YOU ROXXON TRADESMEN ARE A WILLFUL AND UNRULY LOT. BUT I AM A PATIENT ELF.
WHERE IS--
WHATEVER IT IS, I CAN FIND IT. I SWEAR.
AH, AT LAST. A MAN OF WISDOM AND COURTESY. PLEASE, GOOD SIR, WORK YOUR MAGIC FOR ME.

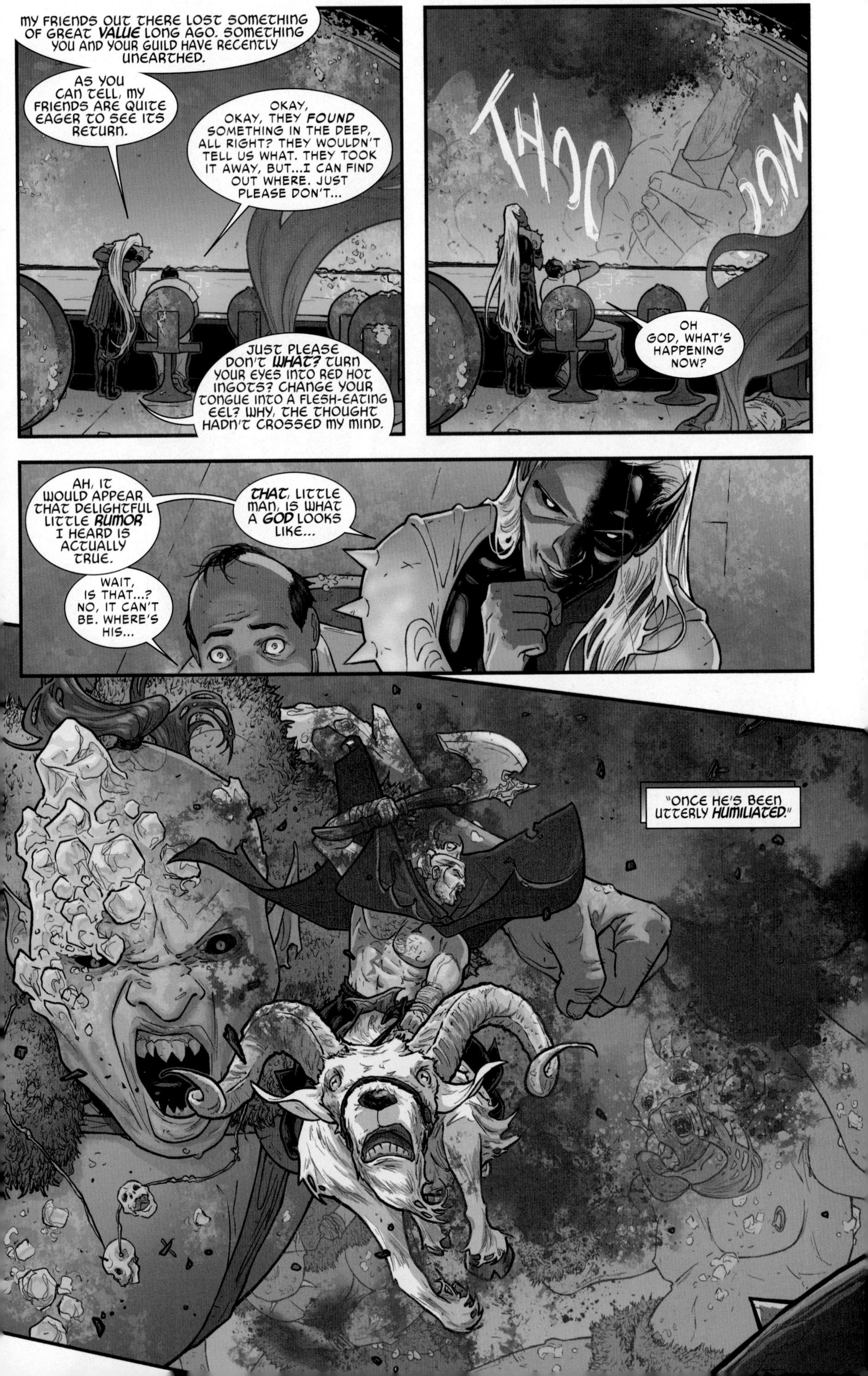
MY FRIENDS OUT THERE LOST SOMETHING OF GREAT VALUE LONG AGO. SOMETHING YOU AND YOUR GUILD HAVE RECENTLY UNEARTHED.
AS YOU CAN TELL, MY FRIENDS ARE QUITE EAGER TO SEE ITS RETURN.
OKAY, OKAY, THEY FOUND SOMETHING IN THE DEEP, ALL RIGHT? THEY WOULDN'T TELL US WHAT. THEY TOOK IT AWAY, BUT...I CAN FIND OUT WHERE. JUST PLEASE DON'T...
JUST PLEASE DON'T WHAT? TURN YOUR EYES INTO RED HOT INGOTS? CHANGE YOUR TONGUE INTO A FLESH-EATING EEL? WHY, THE THOUGHT HADN'T CROSSED MY MIND.
THOOOM
OH GOD, WHAT'S HAPPENING NOW?
AH, IT WOULD APPEAR THAT DELIGHTFUL LITTLE RUMOR I HEARD IS ACTUALLY TRUE.
THAT, LITTLE MAN, IS WHAT A GOD LOOKS LIKE...
WAIT, IS THAT...? NO, IT CAN'T BE. WHERE'S HIS...
"ONCE HE'S BEEN UTTERLY HUMILIATED."

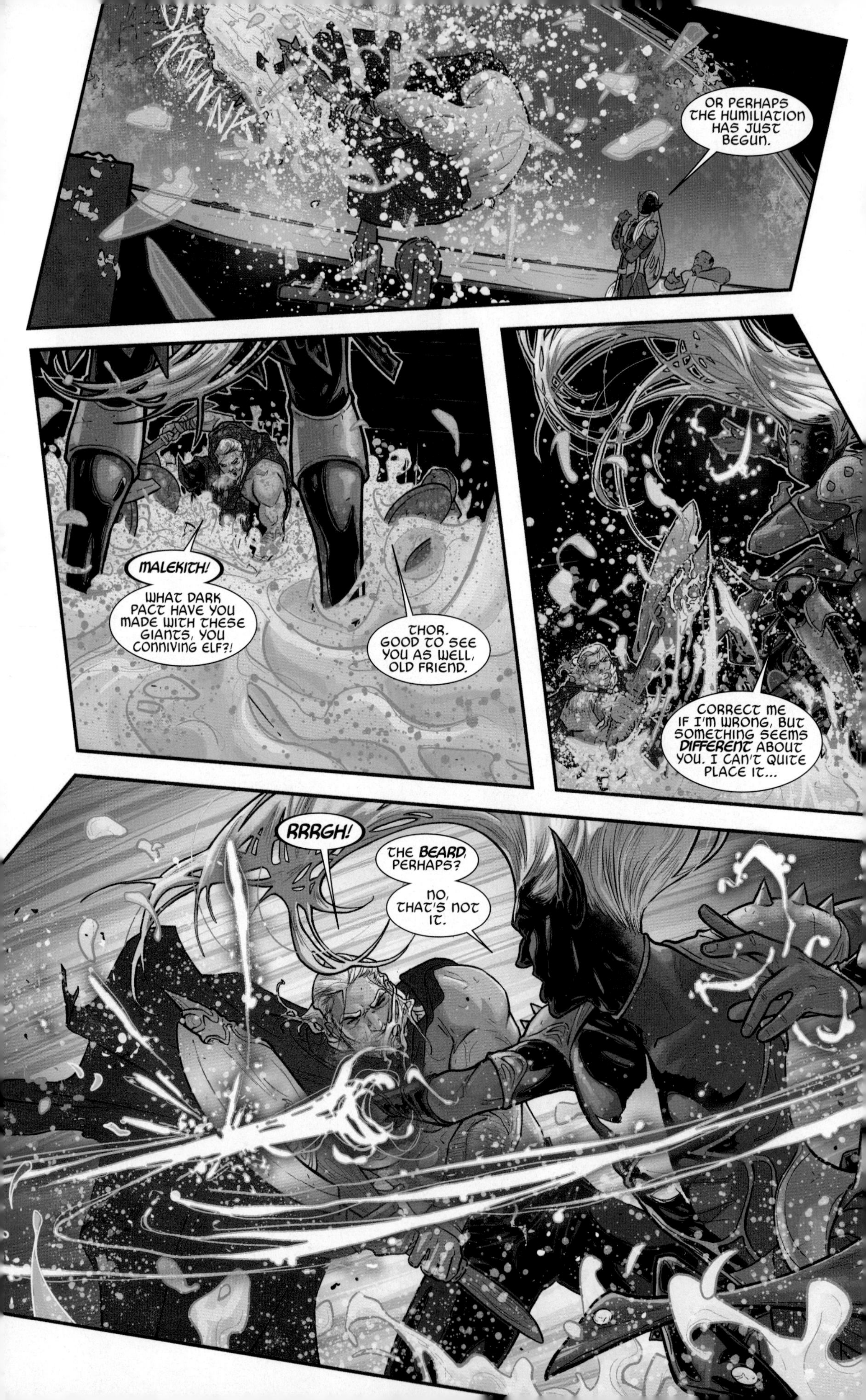
OR PERHAPS THE HUMILIATION HAS JUST BEGUN.
MALEKITH!
WHAT DARK PACT HAVE YOU MADE WITH THESE GIANTS, YOU CONNIVING ELF?!
THOR. GOOD TO SEE YOU AS WELL, OLD FRIEND.
CORRECT ME IF I'M WRONG, BUT SOMETHING SEEMS DIFFERENT ABOUT YOU. I CAN'T QUITE PLACE IT...
RRRGH!
THE BEARD, PERHAPS?
NO, THAT'S NOT IT.

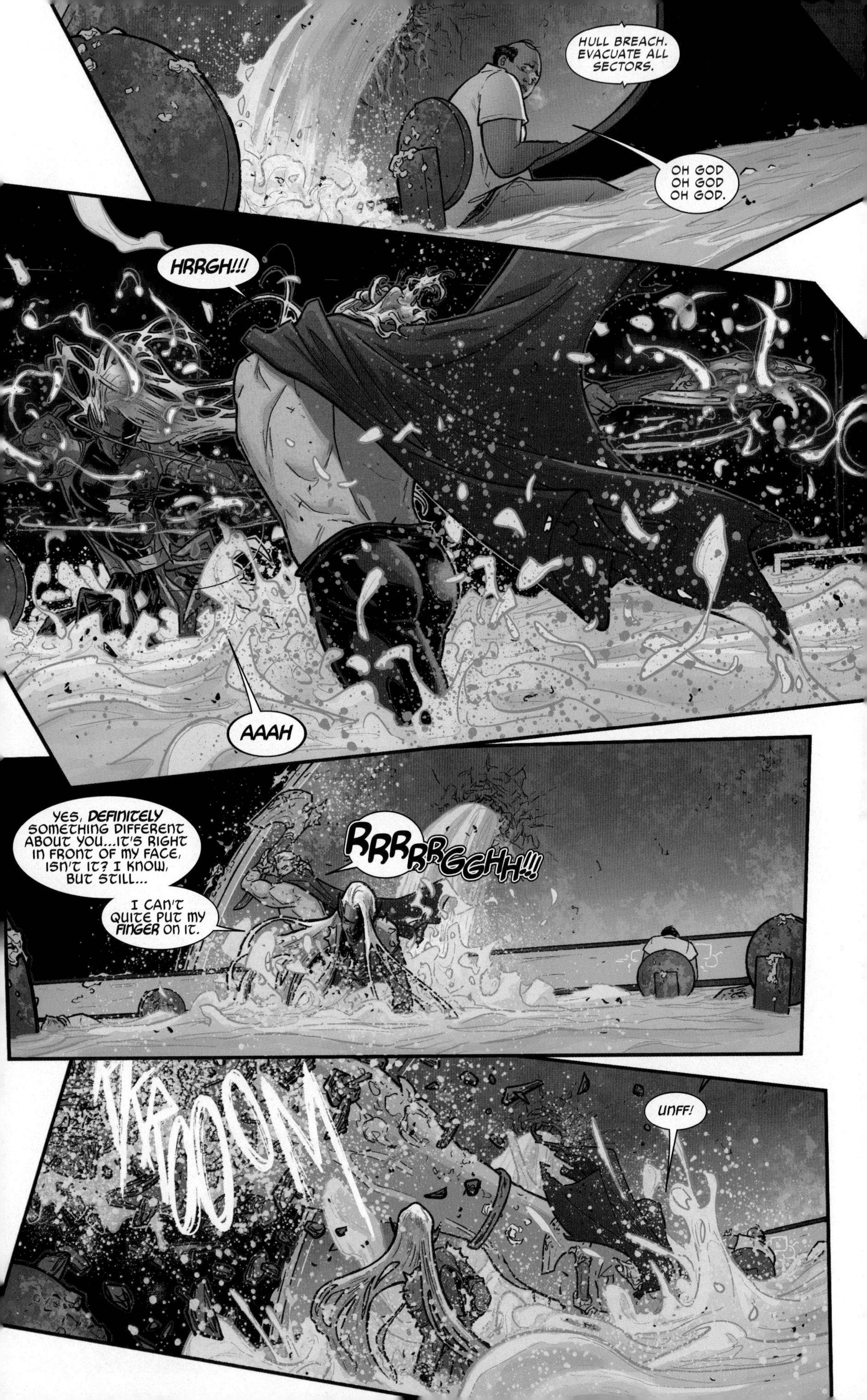
HULL BREACH. EVACUATE ALL SECTORS.
OH GOD OH GOD OH GOD.
HRRGH!!!
AAAH
YES, DEFINITELY SOMETHING DIFFERENT ABOUT YOU...IT'S RIGHT IN FRONT OF MY FACE, ISN'T IT? I KNOW, BUT STILL...
RRRRRGGHH!!!
I CAN'T QUITE PUT MY FINGER ON IT.
KRAOOOM
UNFF!

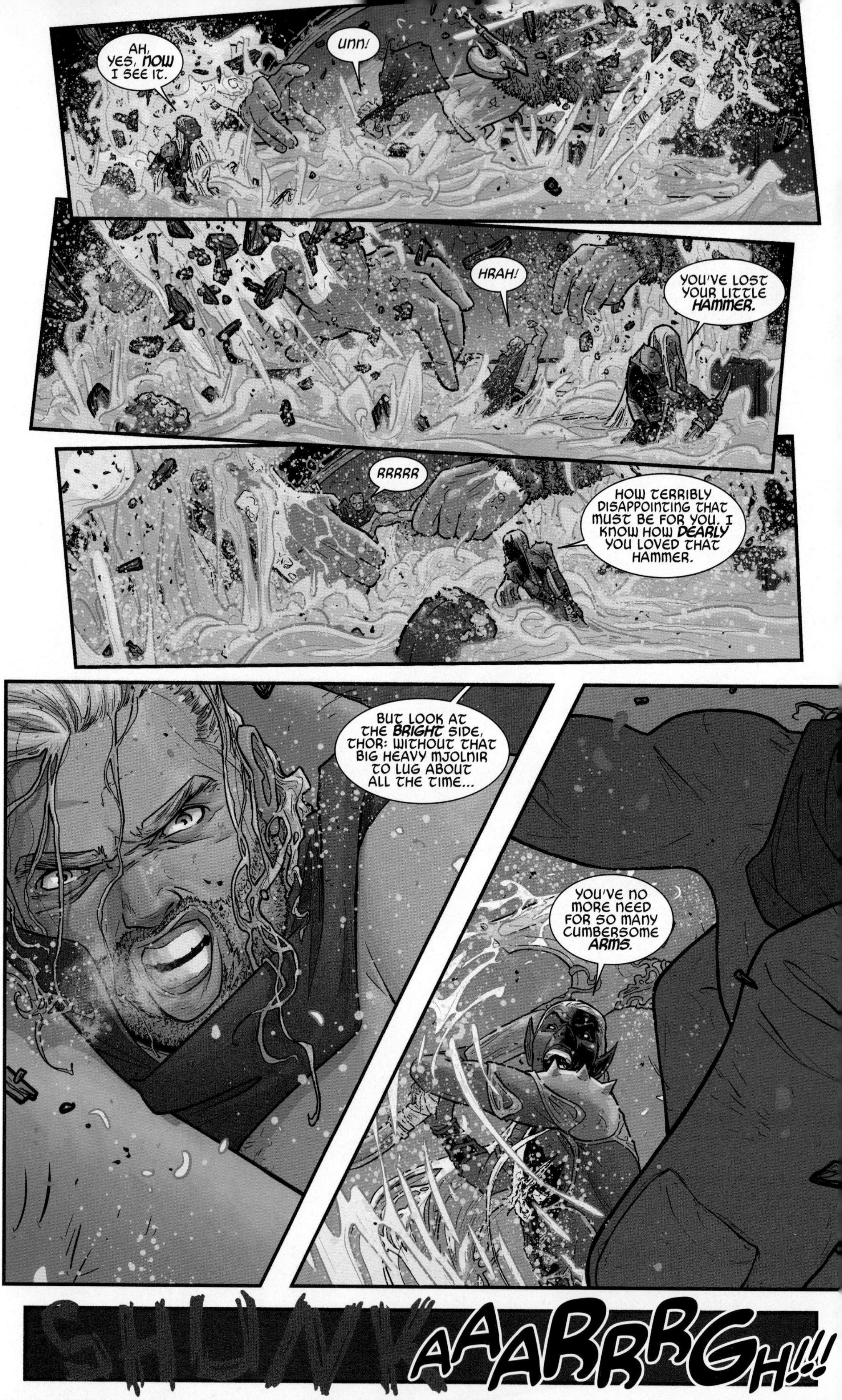
AH, YES, NOW I SEE IT.
UNN!
HRAH!
YOU'VE LOST YOUR LITTLE HAMMER.
RRRRR
HOW TERRIBLY DISAPPOINTING THAT MUST BE FOR YOU. I KNOW HOW DEARLY YOU LOVED THAT HAMMER.
BUT LOOK AT THE BRIGHT SIDE, THOR: WITHOUT THAT BIG HEAVY MJOLNIR TO LUG ABOUT ALL THE TIME...
YOU'VE NO MORE NEED FOR SO MANY CUMBERSOME ARMS.
AAAARRRGH!!!

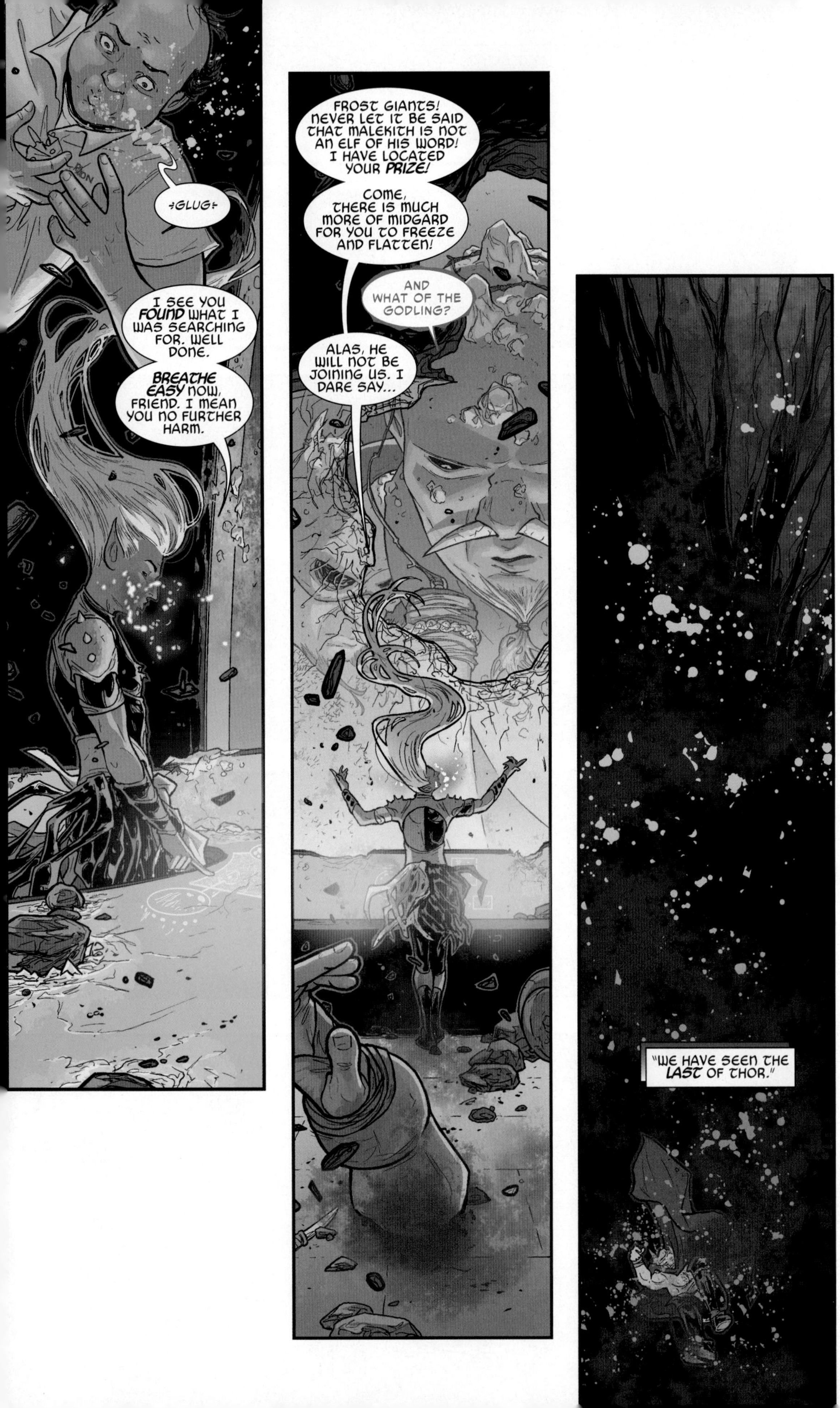

-GLUG-
I SEE YOU FOUND WHAT I WAS SEARCHING FOR. WELL DONE.
BREATHE EASY NOW, FRIEND. I MEAN YOU NO FURTHER HARM.
FROST GIANTS! NEVER LET IT BE SAID THAT MALEKITH IS NOT AN ELF OF HIS WORD! I HAVE LOCATED YOUR PRIZE!
COME, THERE IS MUCH MORE OF MIDGARD FOR YOU TO FREEZE AND FLATTEN!
AND WHAT OF THE GODLING?
ALAS, HE WILL NOT BE JOINING US. I DARE SAY...
"WE HAVE SEEN THE LAST OF THOR."

THERE MUST ALWAYS BE A THOR.

whosoever holds this hammer, if he be worthy, shall possess the power of... THOR

WHOSOEVER HOLDS THIS HAMMER, IF HE BE WORTHY, SHALL POSSESS THE

WHOSOEVER HOLDS THIS HAMMER, IF SHE BE WORTHY, SHALL POSSESS THE POWER OF... THOR

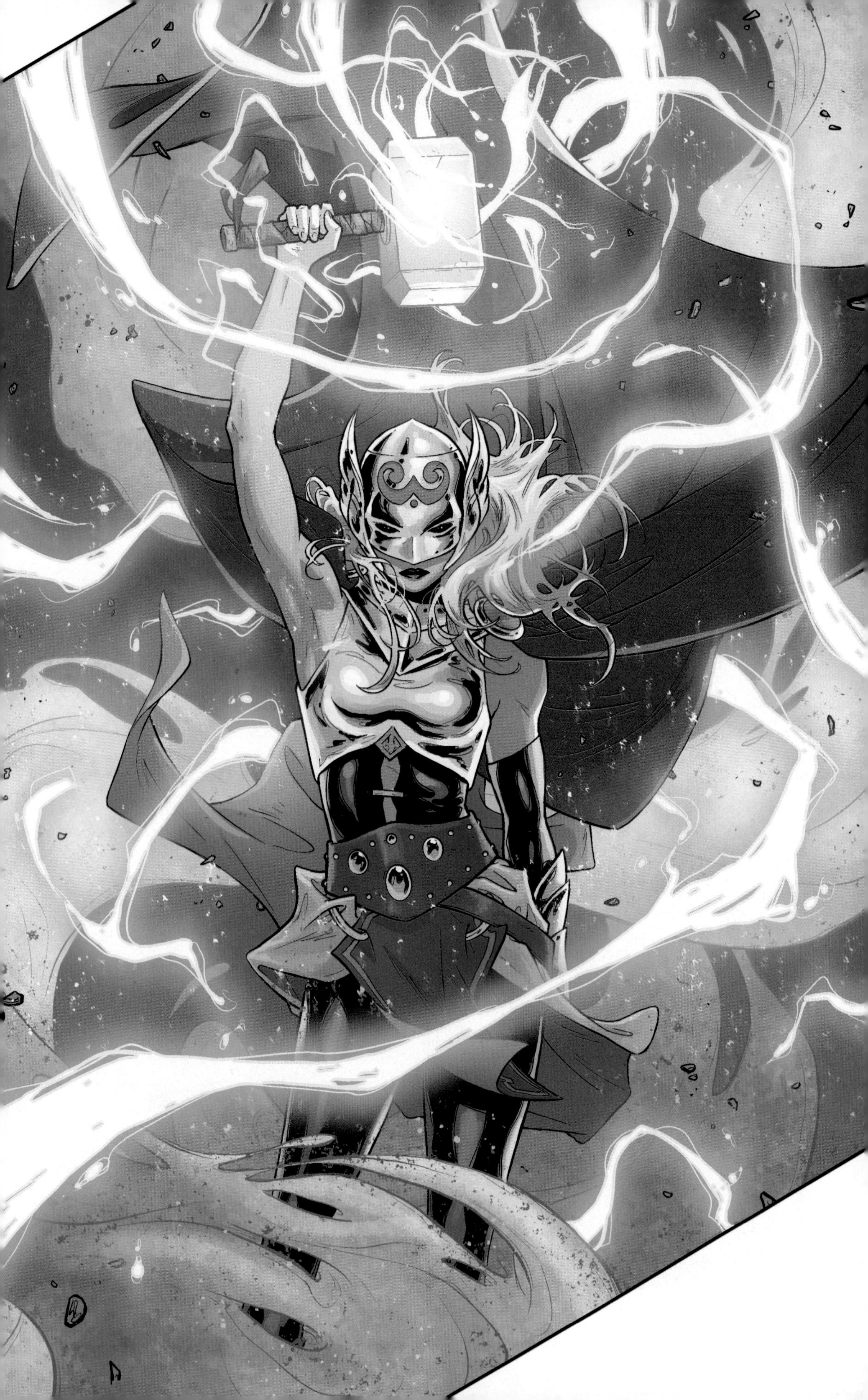

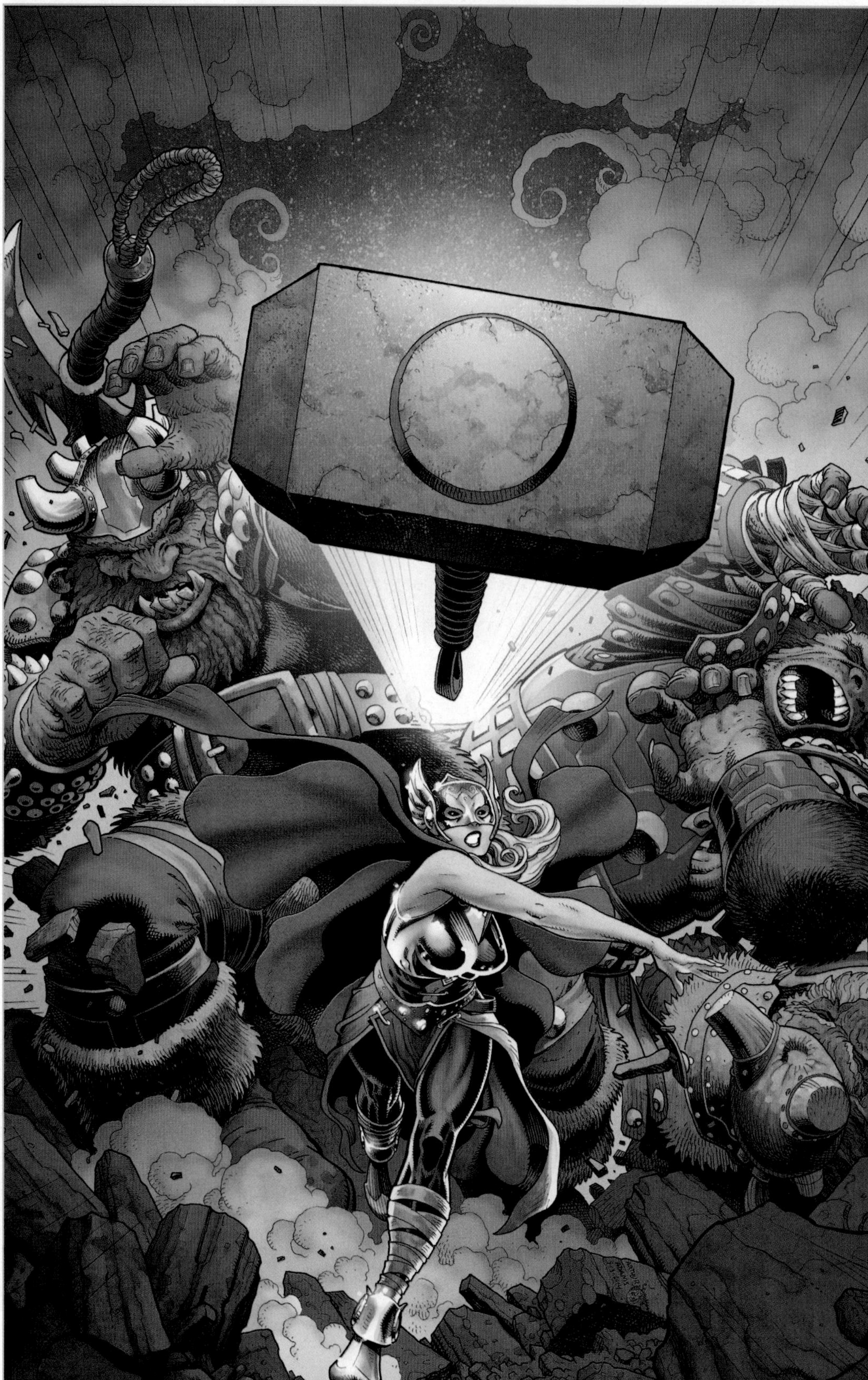

THOR # 1 VARIANT
BY **ARTHUR ADAMS & PETER STEIGERWALD**

2

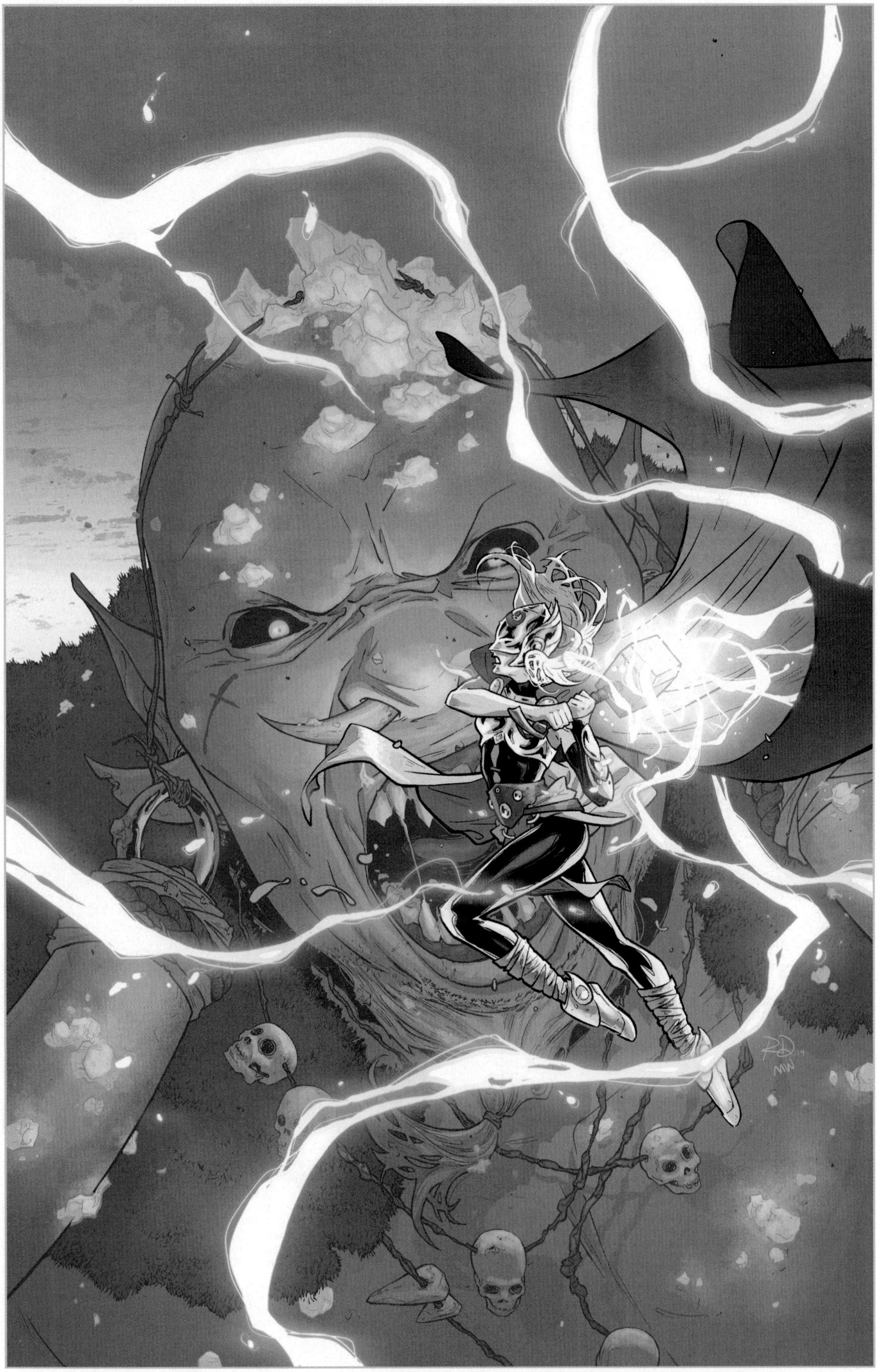

THE GODDESS OF THUNDER

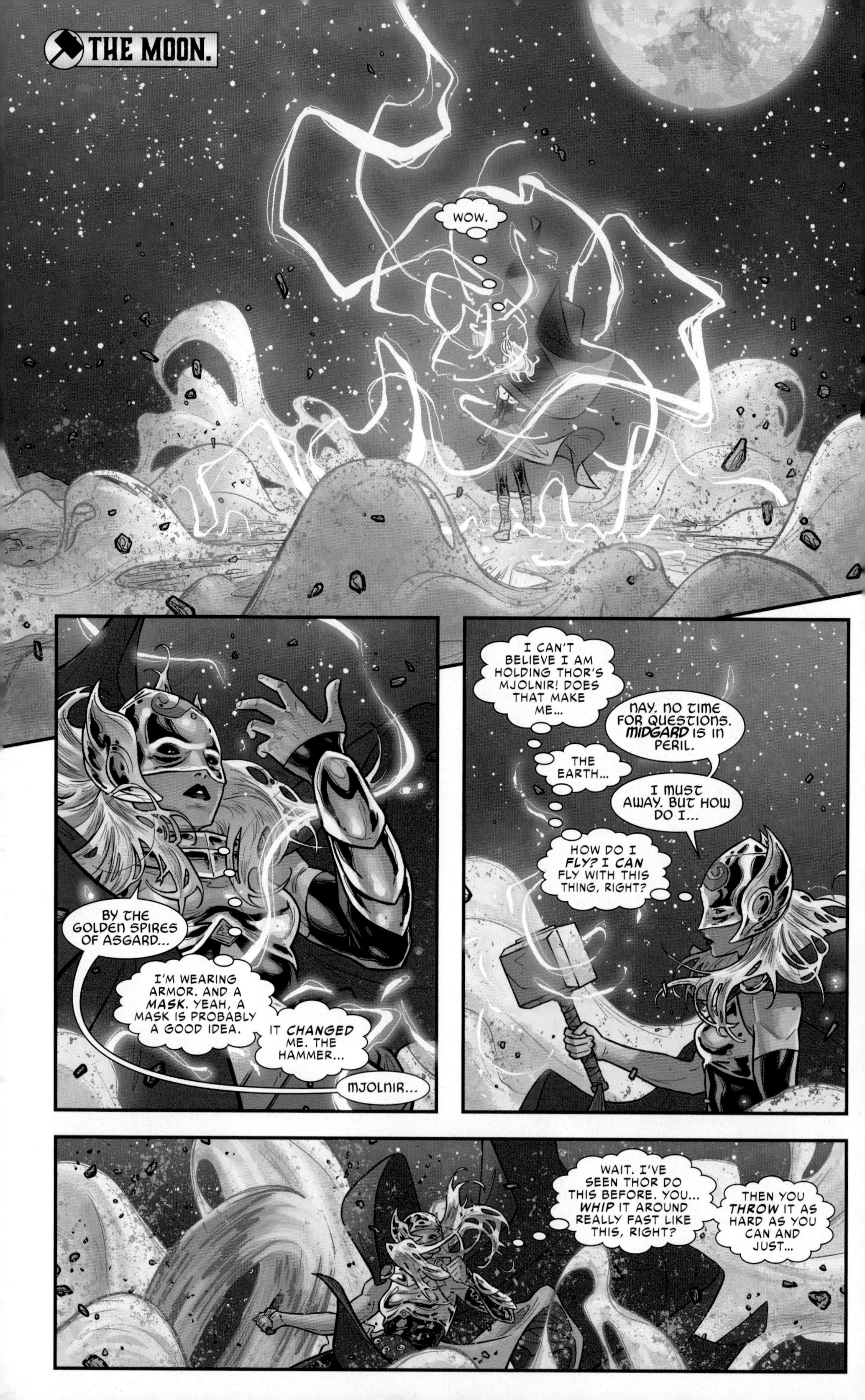
THE MOON.
WOW.
BY THE GOLDEN SPIRES OF ASGARD...
I'M WEARING ARMOR. AND A MASK. YEAH, A MASK IS PROBABLY A GOOD IDEA.
IT CHANGED ME. THE HAMMER...
MJOLNIR...
I CAN'T BELIEVE I AM HOLDING THOR'S MJOLNIR! DOES THAT MAKE ME...
THE EARTH...
NAY. NO TIME FOR QUESTIONS. MIDGARD IS IN PERIL.
I MUST AWAY. BUT HOW DO I...
HOW DO I FLY? I CAN FLY WITH THIS THING, RIGHT?
WAIT. I'VE SEEN THOR DO THIS BEFORE. YOU... WHIP IT AROUND REALLY FAST LIKE THIS, RIGHT?
THEN YOU THROW IT AS HARD AS YOU CAN AND JUST...

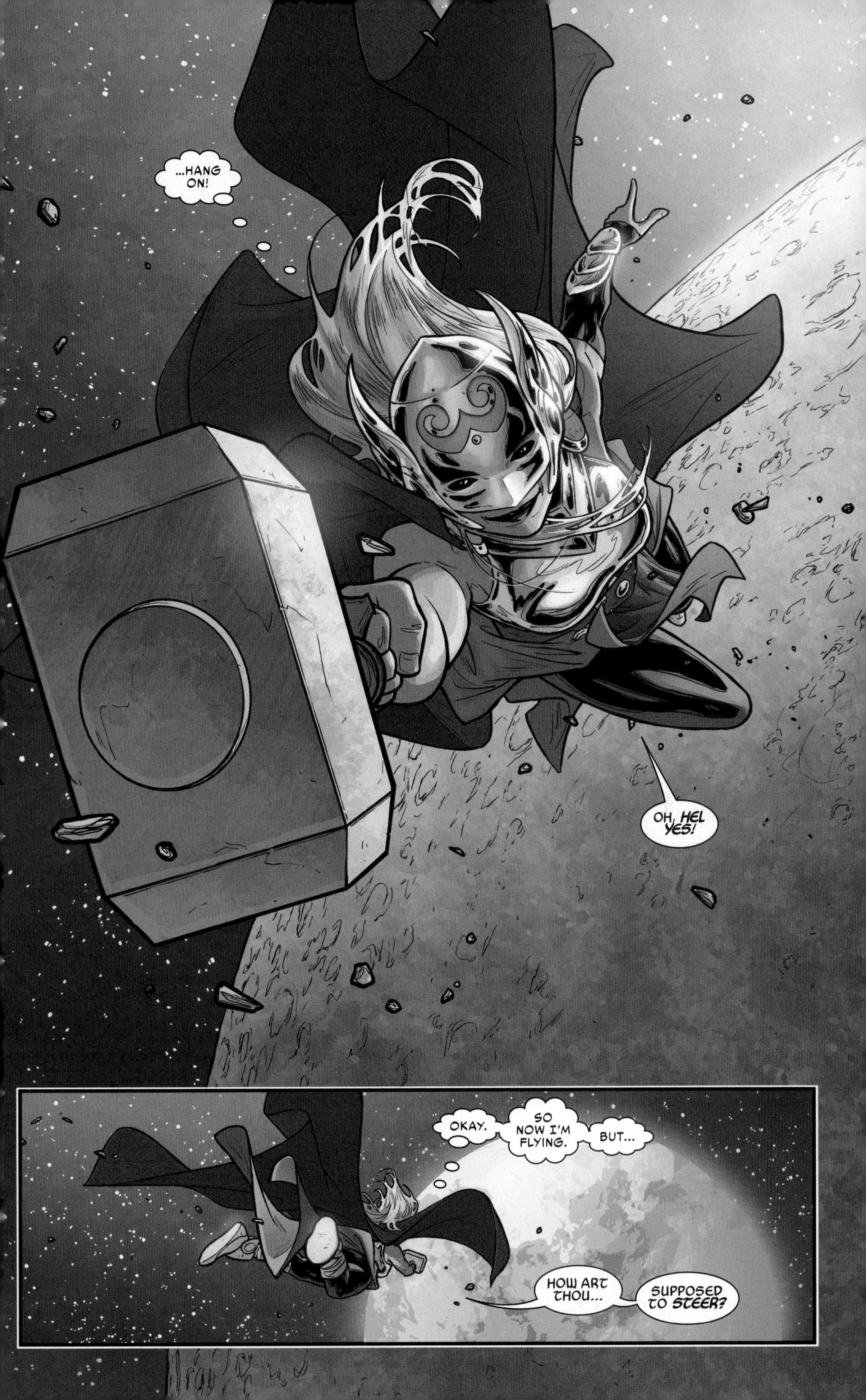
...HANG ON!
OH, HEL YES!
OKAY.
SO NOW I'M FLYING.
BUT...
HOW ART THOU...
SUPPOSED TO STEER?

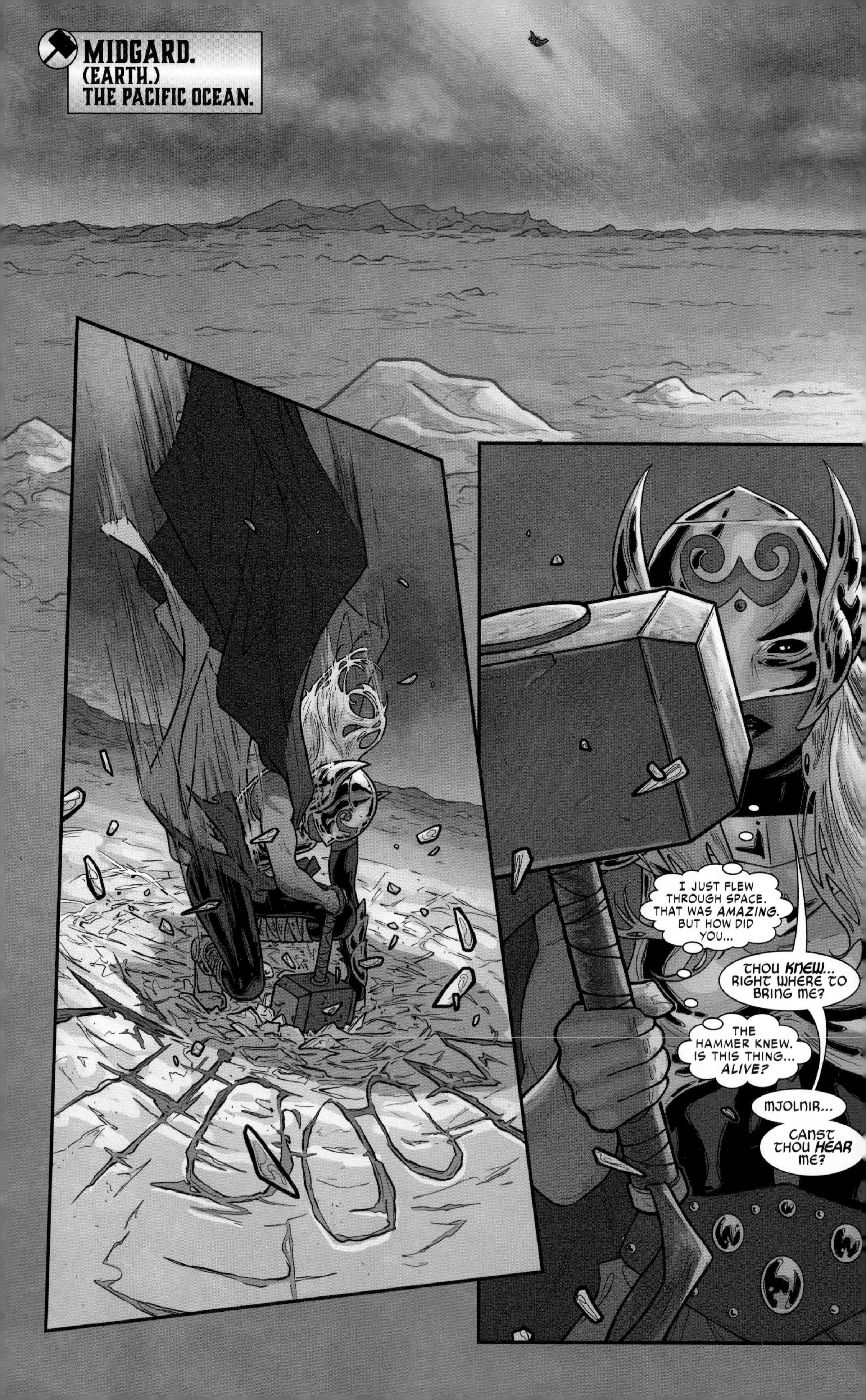
MIDGARD.
(EARTH.)
THE PACIFIC OCEAN.
I JUST FLEW THROUGH SPACE. THAT WAS AMAZING. BUT HOW DID YOU...
THOU KNEW... RIGHT WHERE TO BRING ME?
THE HAMMER KNEW. IS THIS THING... ALIVE?
MJOLNIR...
CANST THOU HEAR ME?

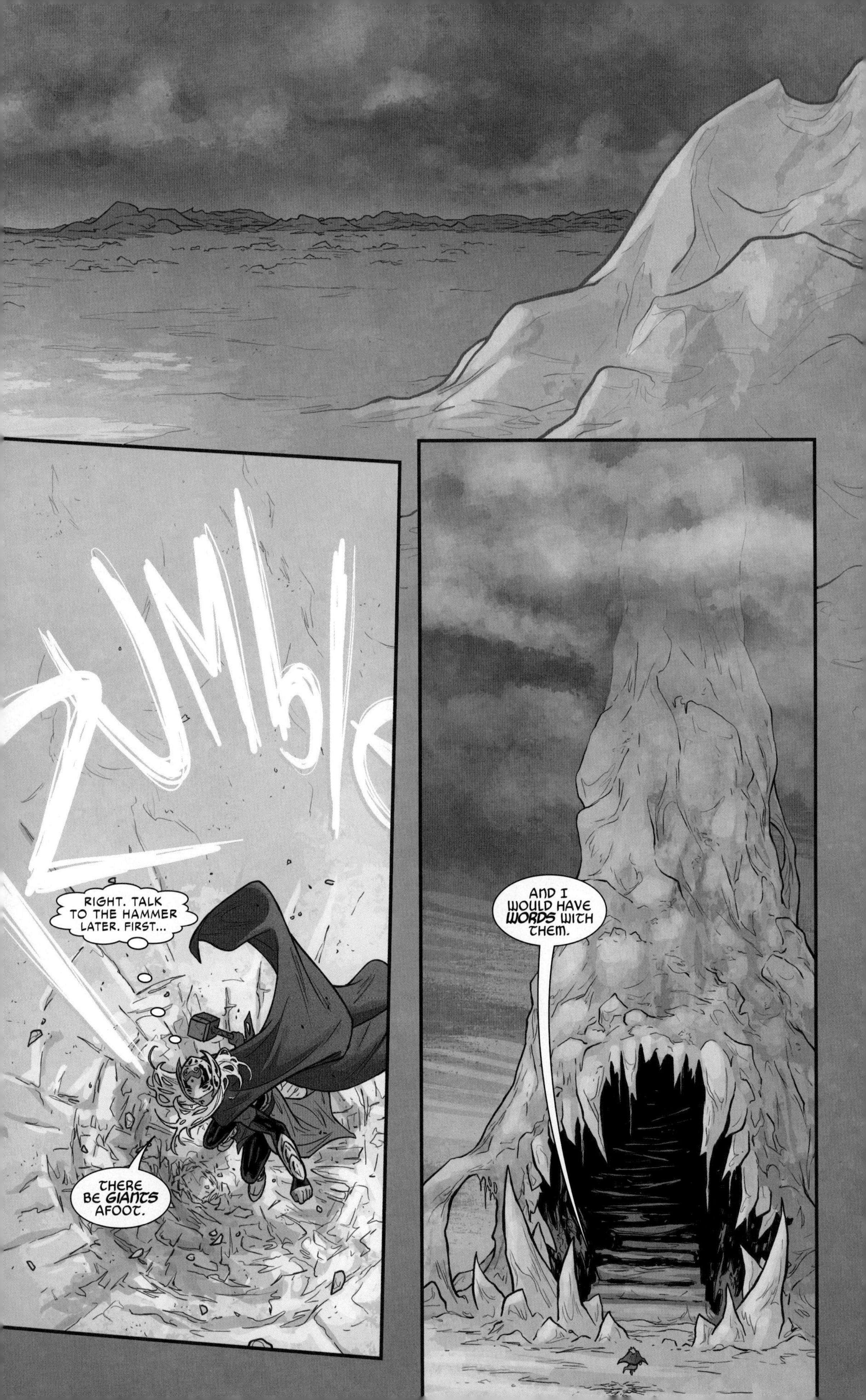
RUMBLE
RIGHT. TALK TO THE HAMMER LATER. FIRST...
THERE BE GIANTS AFOOT.
AND I WOULD HAVE WORDS WITH THEM.

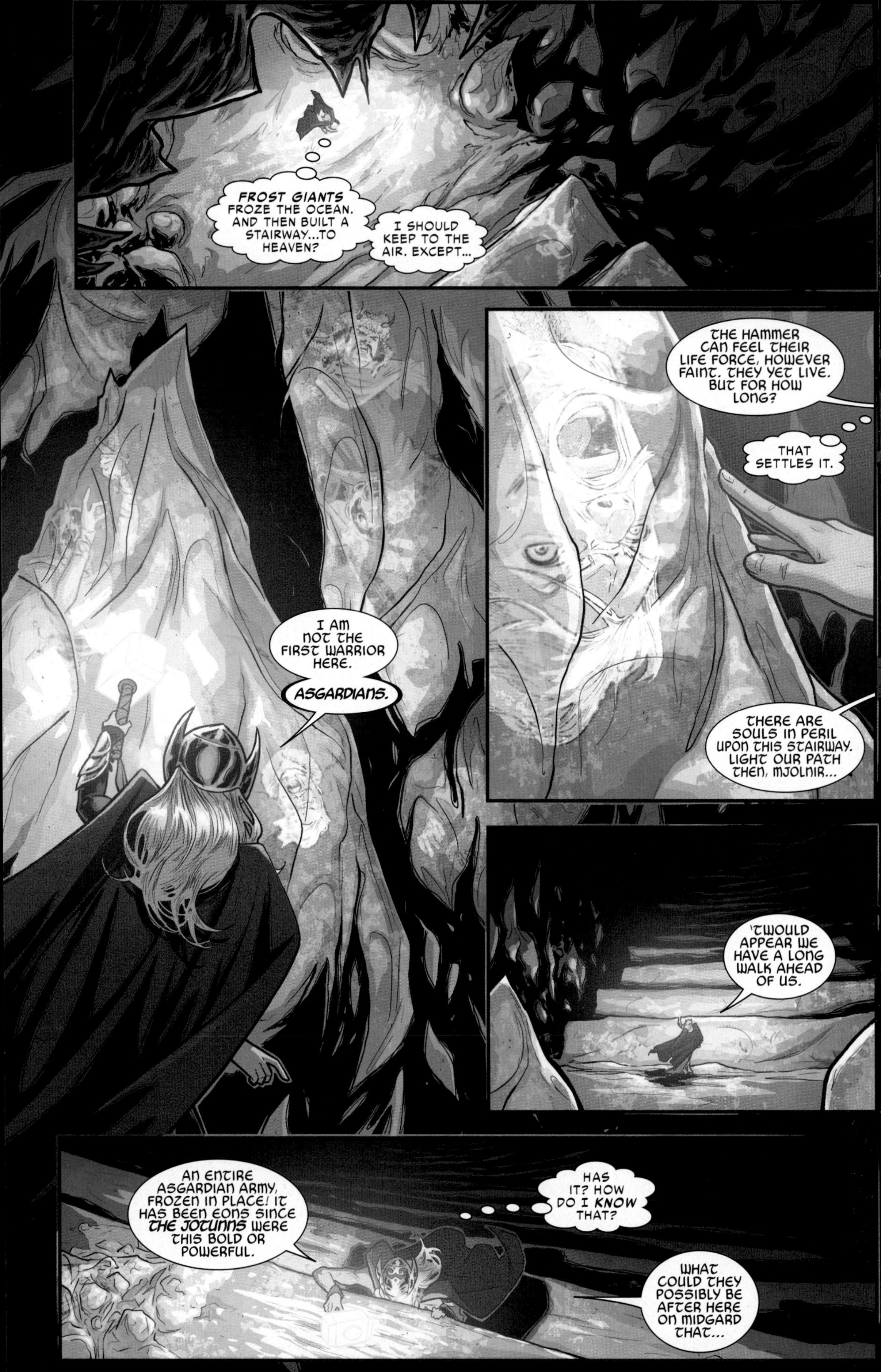
FROST GIANTS FROZE THE OCEAN. AND THEN BUILT A STAIRWAY...TO HEAVEN?
I SHOULD KEEP TO THE AIR. EXCEPT...
I AM NOT THE FIRST WARRIOR HERE.
ASGARDIANS.
THE HAMMER CAN FEEL THEIR LIFE FORCE, HOWEVER FAINT. THEY YET LIVE. BUT FOR HOW LONG?
THAT SETTLES IT.
THERE ARE SOULS IN PERIL UPON THIS STAIRWAY. LIGHT OUR PATH THEN, MJOLNIR...
'TWOULD APPEAR WE HAVE A LONG WALK AHEAD OF US.
AN ENTIRE ASGARDIAN ARMY, FROZEN IN PLACE! IT HAS BEEN EONS SINCE THE JOTUNNS WERE THIS BOLD OR POWERFUL.
HAS IT? HOW DO I KNOW THAT?
WHAT COULD THEY POSSIBLY BE AFTER HERE ON MIDGARD THAT...

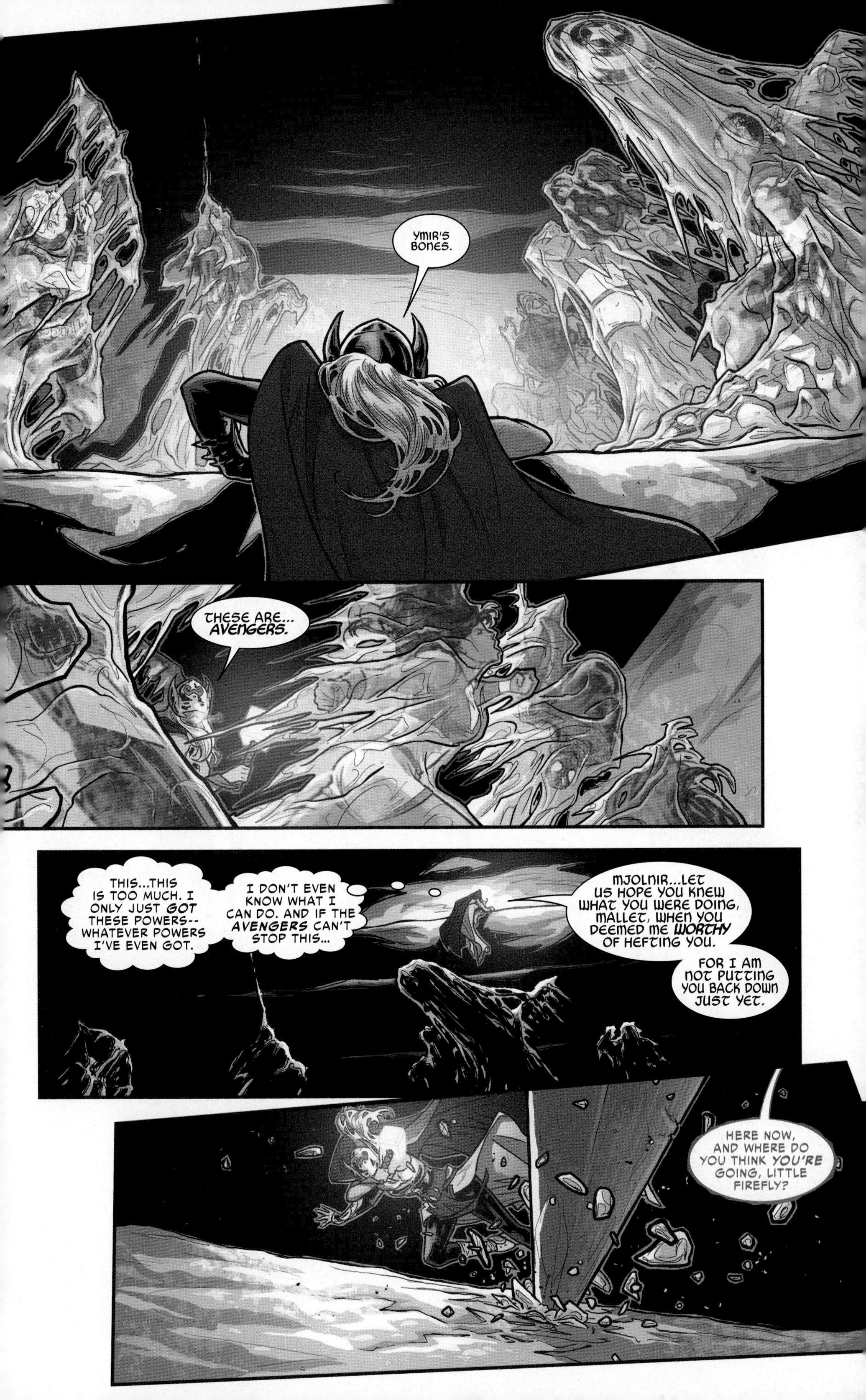
YMIR'S BONES.
THESE ARE... AVENGERS.
THIS...THIS IS TOO MUCH. I ONLY JUST GOT THESE POWERS-- WHATEVER POWERS I'VE EVEN GOT.
I DON'T EVEN KNOW WHAT I CAN DO. AND IF THE AVENGERS CAN'T STOP THIS...
MJOLNIR...LET US HOPE YOU KNEW WHAT YOU WERE DOING, MALLET, WHEN YOU DEEMED ME WORTHY OF HEFTING YOU.
FOR I AM NOT PUTTING YOU BACK DOWN JUST YET.
HERE NOW, AND WHERE DO YOU THINK YOU'RE GOING, LITTLE FIREFLY?

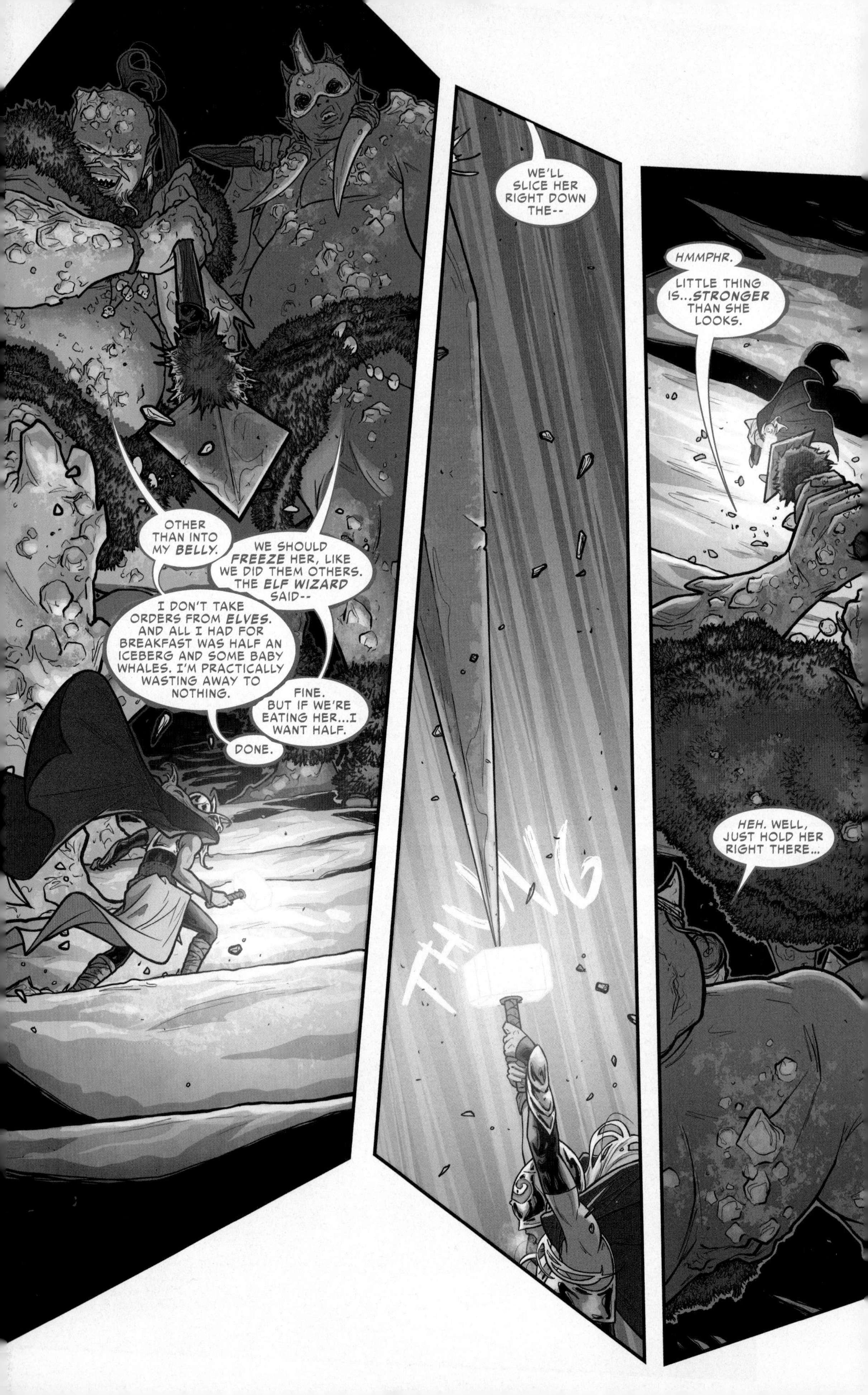
OTHER THAN INTO MY BELLY.
WE SHOULD FREEZE HER, LIKE WE DID THEM OTHERS. THE ELF WIZARD SAID--
I DON'T TAKE ORDERS FROM ELVES. AND ALL I HAD FOR BREAKFAST WAS HALF AN ICEBERG AND SOME BABY WHALES. I'M PRACTICALLY WASTING AWAY TO NOTHING.
FINE. BUT IF WE'RE EATING HER...I WANT HALF.
DONE.
WE'LL SLICE HER RIGHT DOWN THE--
THUNG
HMMPHR.
LITTLE THING IS...STRONGER THAN SHE LOOKS.
HEH. WELL, JUST HOLD HER RIGHT THERE...

I THINK THE *MUTTS* WANT A TASTE.

GGRRRRRRR

MJOLNIR... THIS TIME... LET *ME* STEER.

KRU

RRRROOOOORRR

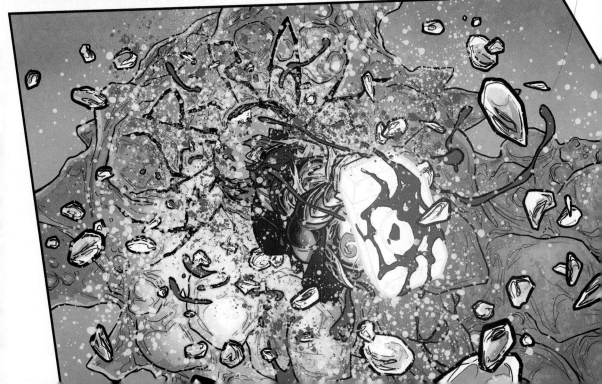

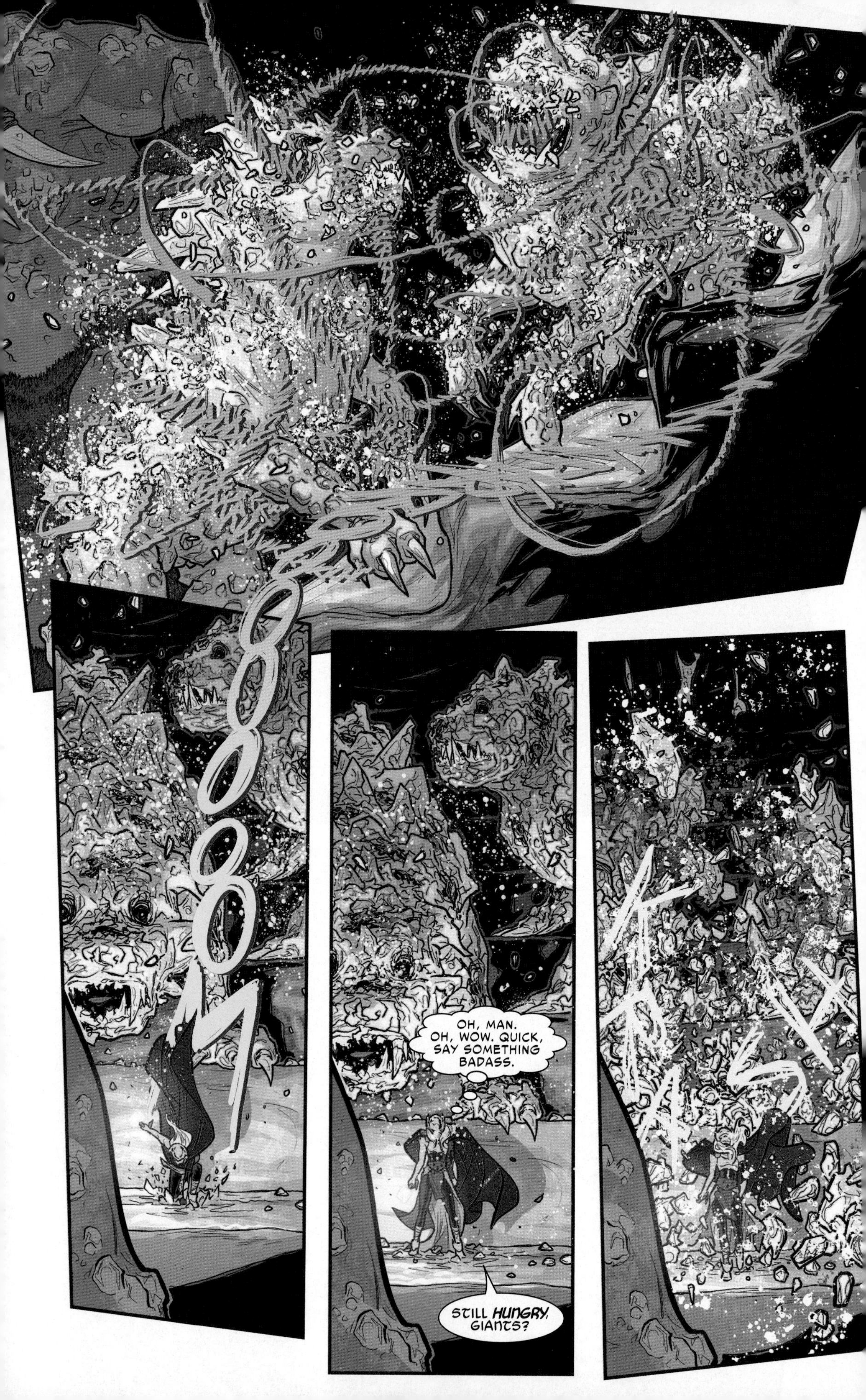
OH, MAN. OH, WOW. QUICK, SAY SOMETHING BADASS.
STILL *HUNGRY*, GIANTS?

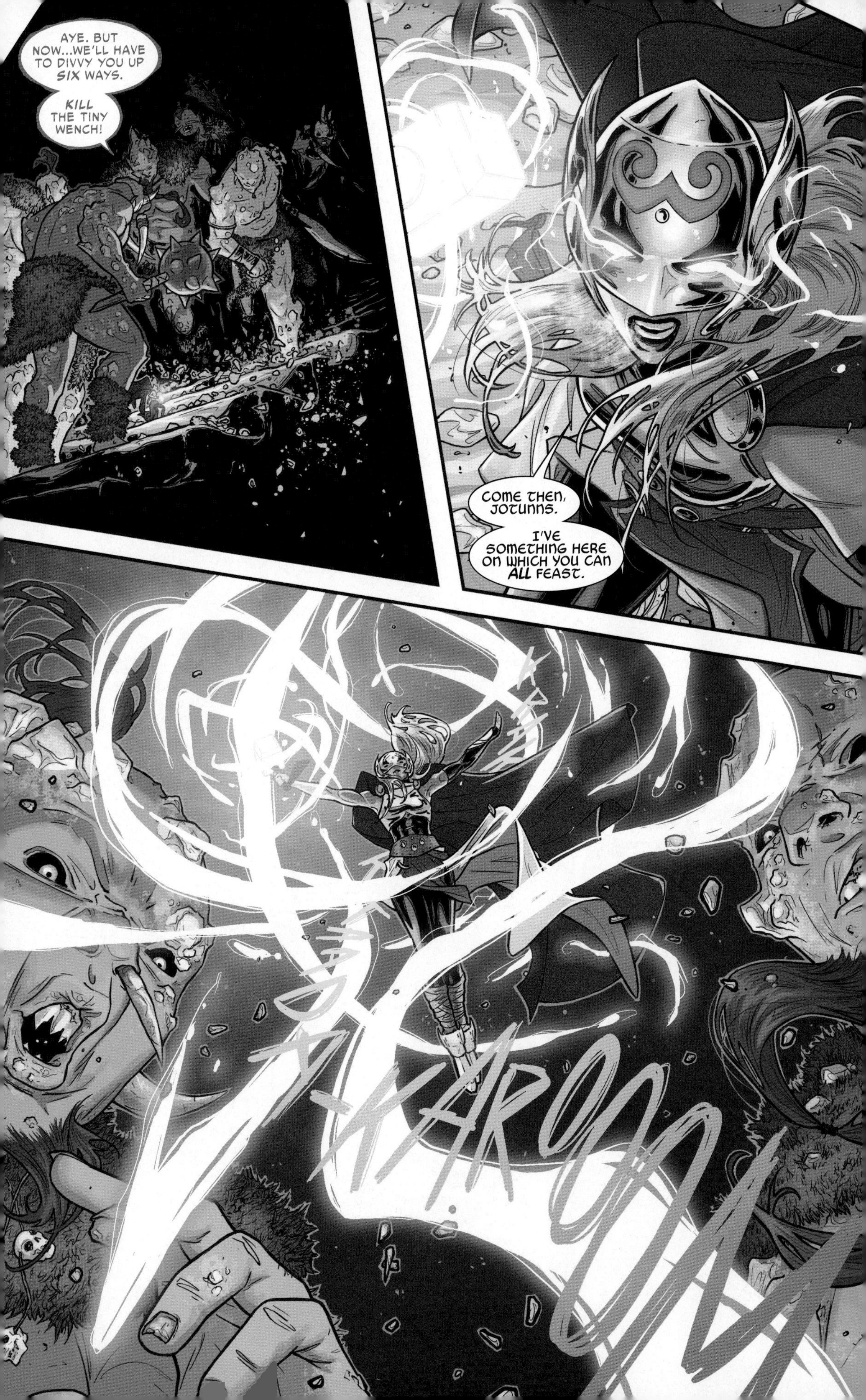
AYE. BUT NOW...WE'LL HAVE TO DIVVY YOU UP SIX WAYS.
KILL THE TINY WENCH!
COME THEN, JOTUNNS.
I'VE SOMETHING HERE ON WHICH YOU CAN ALL FEAST.

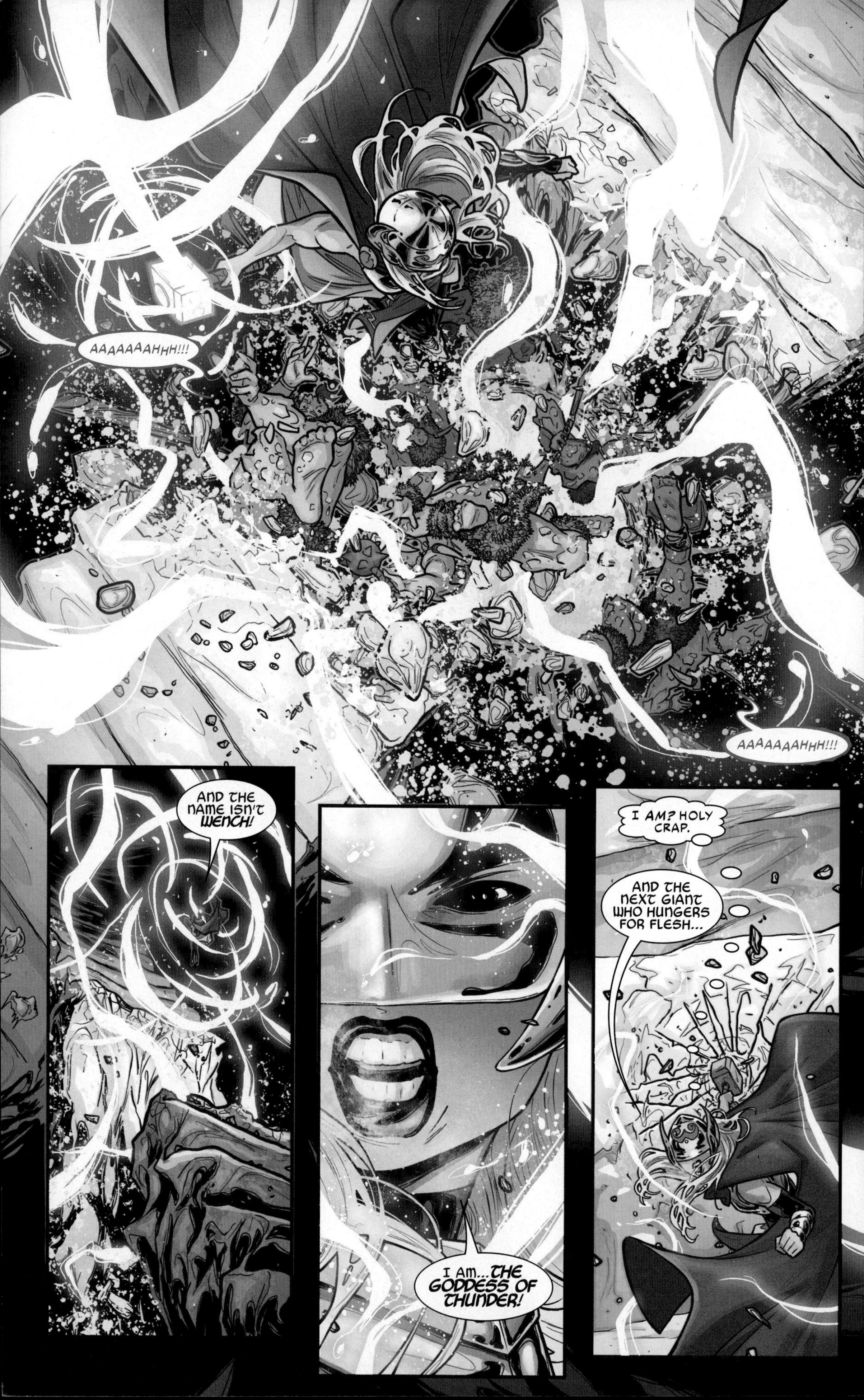
AAAAAAAHHH!!!
AAAAAAAHHH!!!
AND THE NAME ISN'T WENCH!
I AM...THE GODDESS OF THUNDER!
I AM? HOLY CRAP.
AND THE NEXT GIANT WHO HUNGERS FOR FLESH...

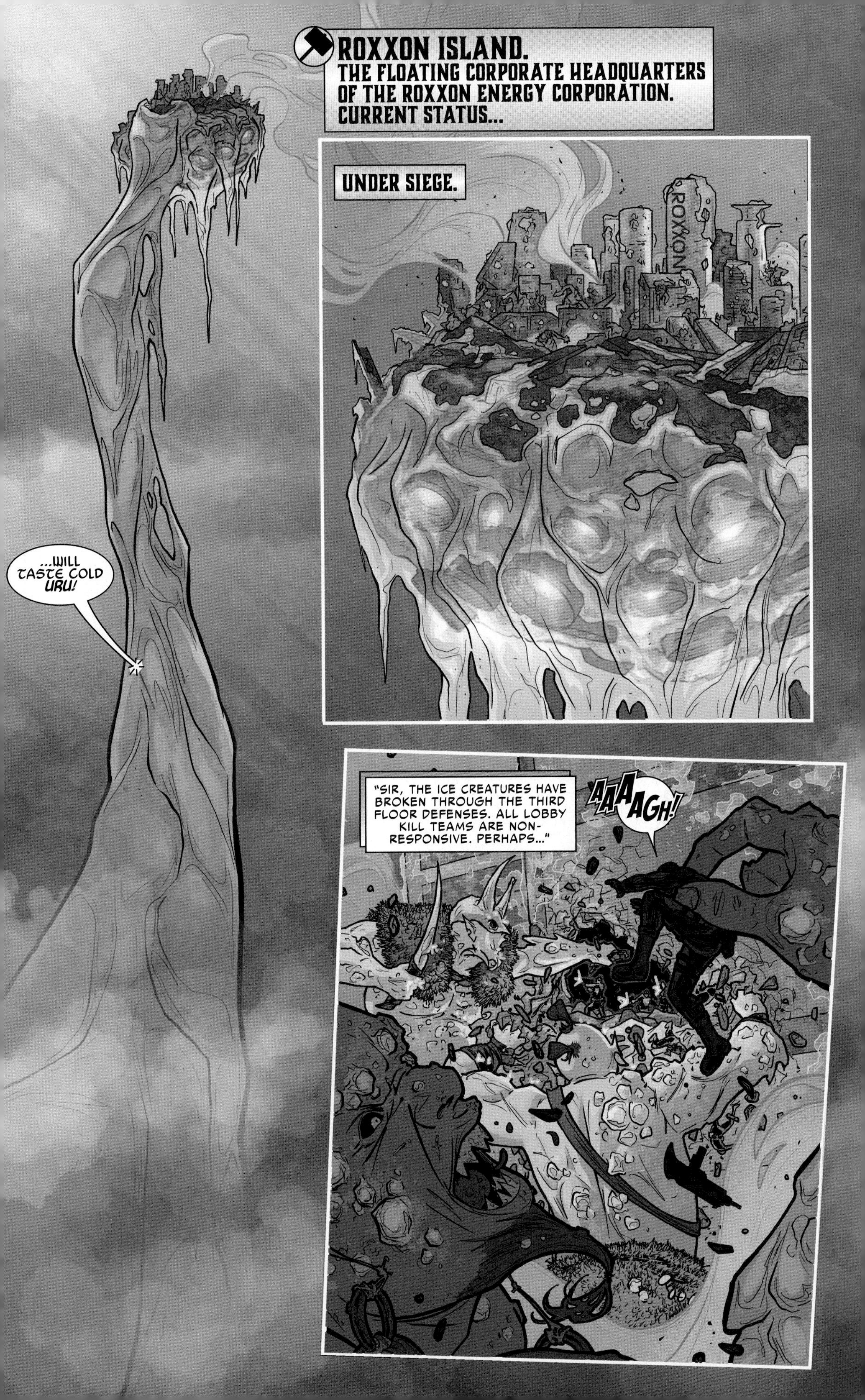
ROXXON ISLAND.
THE FLOATING CORPORATE HEADQUARTERS OF THE ROXXON ENERGY CORPORATION. CURRENT STATUS...
UNDER SIEGE.
ROXXON
...WILL TASTE COLD URU!
"SIR, THE ICE CREATURES HAVE BROKEN THROUGH THE THIRD FLOOR DEFENSES. ALL LOBBY KILL TEAMS ARE NON-RESPONSIVE. PERHAPS..."
AAAAGH!

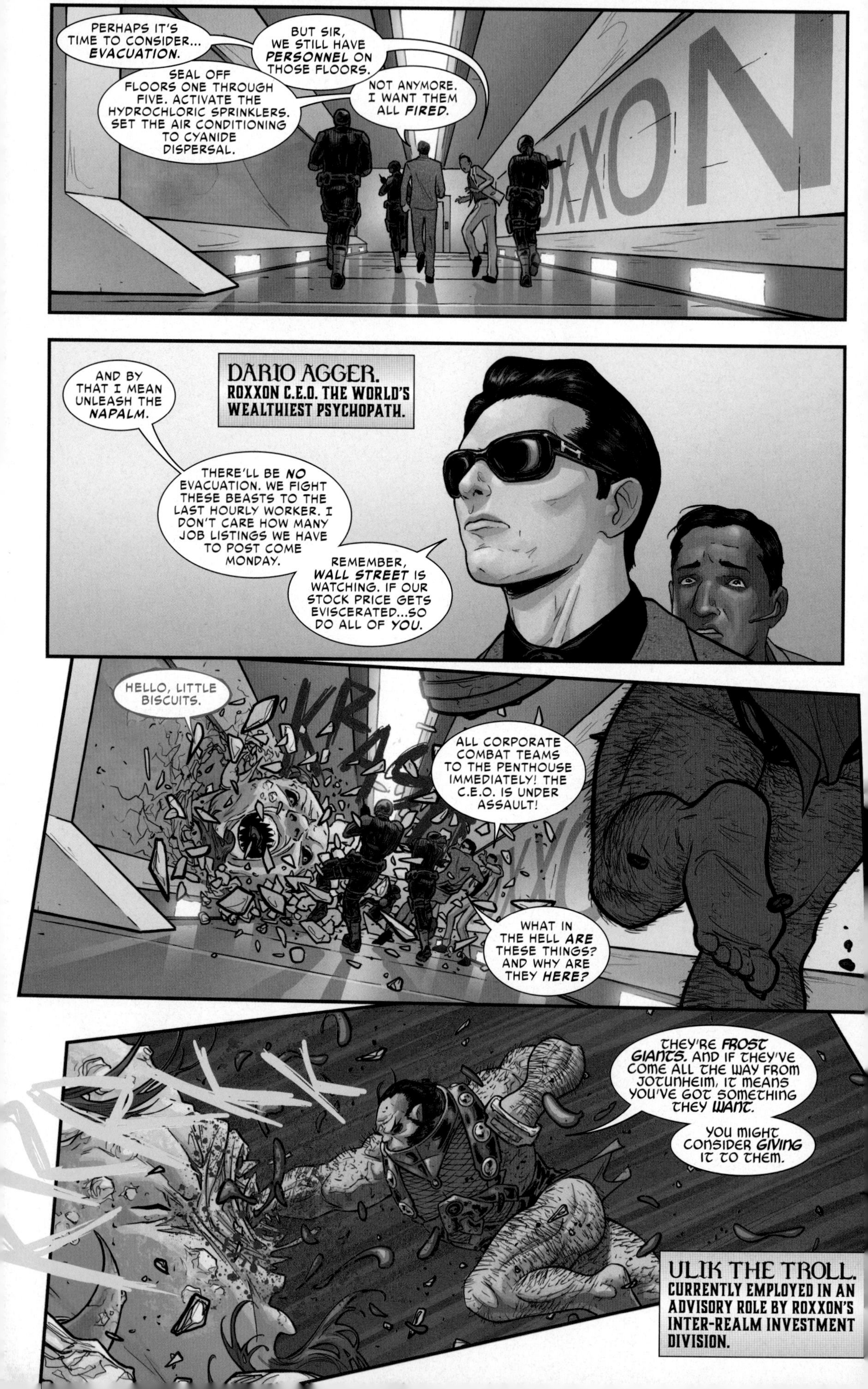
PERHAPS IT'S TIME TO CONSIDER... EVACUATION.
BUT SIR, WE STILL HAVE PERSONNEL ON THOSE FLOORS.
SEAL OFF FLOORS ONE THROUGH FIVE. ACTIVATE THE HYDROCHLORIC SPRINKLERS. SET THE AIR CONDITIONING TO CYANIDE DISPERSAL.
NOT ANYMORE. I WANT THEM ALL FIRED.
ROXXON
AND BY THAT I MEAN UNLEASH THE NAPALM.
DARIO AGGER. ROXXON C.E.O. THE WORLD'S WEALTHIEST PSYCHOPATH.
THERE'LL BE NO EVACUATION. WE FIGHT THESE BEASTS TO THE LAST HOURLY WORKER. I DON'T CARE HOW MANY JOB LISTINGS WE HAVE TO POST COME MONDAY.
REMEMBER, WALL STREET IS WATCHING. IF OUR STOCK PRICE GETS EVISCERATED...SO DO ALL OF YOU.
HELLO, LITTLE BISCUITS.
KRASH
ALL CORPORATE COMBAT TEAMS TO THE PENTHOUSE IMMEDIATELY! THE C.E.O. IS UNDER ASSAULT!
WHAT IN THE HELL ARE THESE THINGS? AND WHY ARE THEY HERE?
THEY'RE FROST GIANTS. AND IF THEY'VE COME ALL THE WAY FROM JOTUNHEIM, IT MEANS YOU'VE GOT SOMETHING THEY WANT.
YOU MIGHT CONSIDER GIVING IT TO THEM.
ULIK THE TROLL. CURRENTLY EMPLOYED IN AN ADVISORY ROLE BY ROXXON'S INTER-REALM INVESTMENT DIVISION.

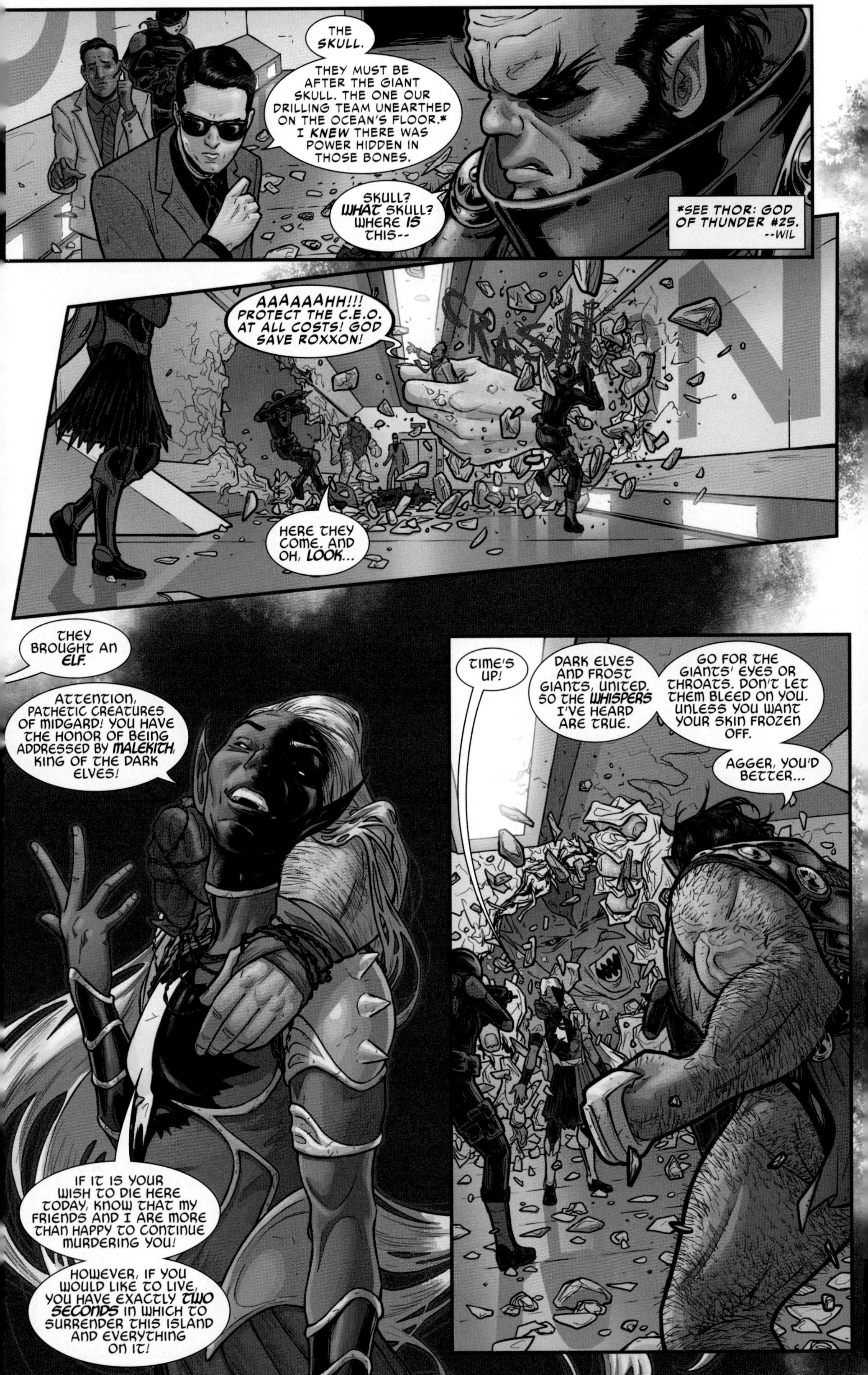
THE SKULL.
THEY MUST BE AFTER THE GIANT SKULL. THE ONE OUR DRILLING TEAM UNEARTHED ON THE OCEAN'S FLOOR.* I KNEW THERE WAS POWER HIDDEN IN THOSE BONES.
SKULL? WHAT SKULL? WHERE IS THIS--
*SEE THOR: GOD OF THUNDER #25. --WIL
AAAAAAHH!!! PROTECT THE C.E.O. AT ALL COSTS! GOD SAVE ROXXON!
CRASH
HERE THEY COME. AND OH, LOOK...
THEY BROUGHT AN ELF.
ATTENTION, PATHETIC CREATURES OF MIDGARD! YOU HAVE THE HONOR OF BEING ADDRESSED BY MALEKITH, KING OF THE DARK ELVES!
IF IT IS YOUR WISH TO DIE HERE TODAY, KNOW THAT MY FRIENDS AND I ARE MORE THAN HAPPY TO CONTINUE MURDERING YOU!
HOWEVER, IF YOU WOULD LIKE TO LIVE, YOU HAVE EXACTLY TWO SECONDS IN WHICH TO SURRENDER THIS ISLAND AND EVERYTHING ON IT!
TIME'S UP!
DARK ELVES AND FROST GIANTS, UNITED. SO THE WHISPERS I'VE HEARD ARE TRUE.
GO FOR THE GIANTS' EYES OR THROATS. DON'T LET THEM BLEED ON YOU. UNLESS YOU WANT YOUR SKIN FROZEN OFF.
AGGER, YOU'D BETTER...

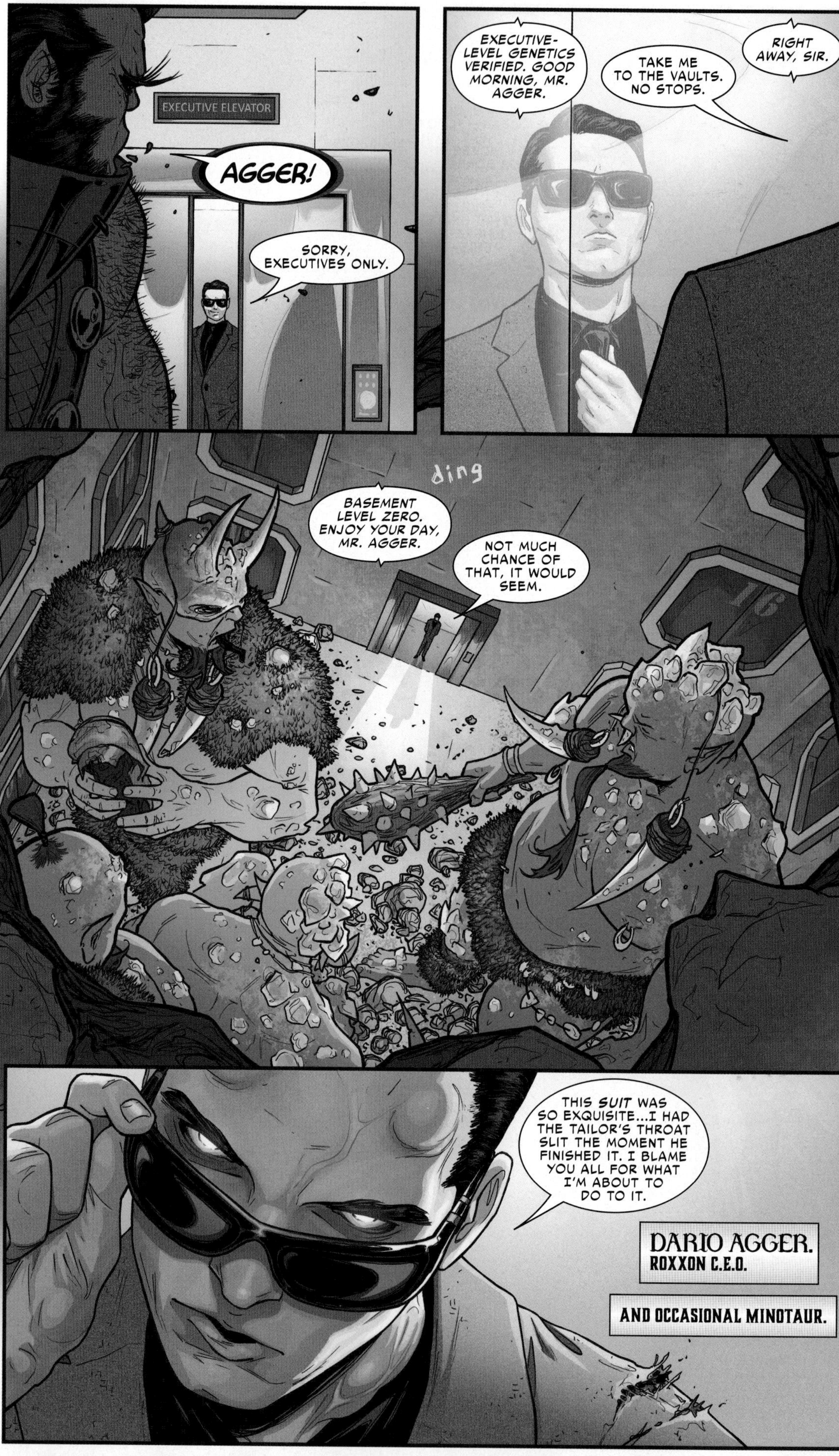

EXECUTIVE ELEVATOR
AGGER!
SORRY, EXECUTIVES ONLY.
EXECUTIVE-LEVEL GENETICS VERIFIED. GOOD MORNING, MR. AGGER.
TAKE ME TO THE VAULTS. NO STOPS.
RIGHT AWAY, SIR.
ding
BASEMENT LEVEL ZERO. ENJOY YOUR DAY, MR. AGGER.
NOT MUCH CHANCE OF THAT, IT WOULD SEEM.
16
THIS SUIT WAS SO EXQUISITE...I HAD THE TAILOR'S THROAT SLIT THE MOMENT HE FINISHED IT. I BLAME YOU ALL FOR WHAT I'M ABOUT TO DO TO IT.
DARIO AGGER. ROXXON C.E.O.
AND OCCASIONAL MINOTAUR.

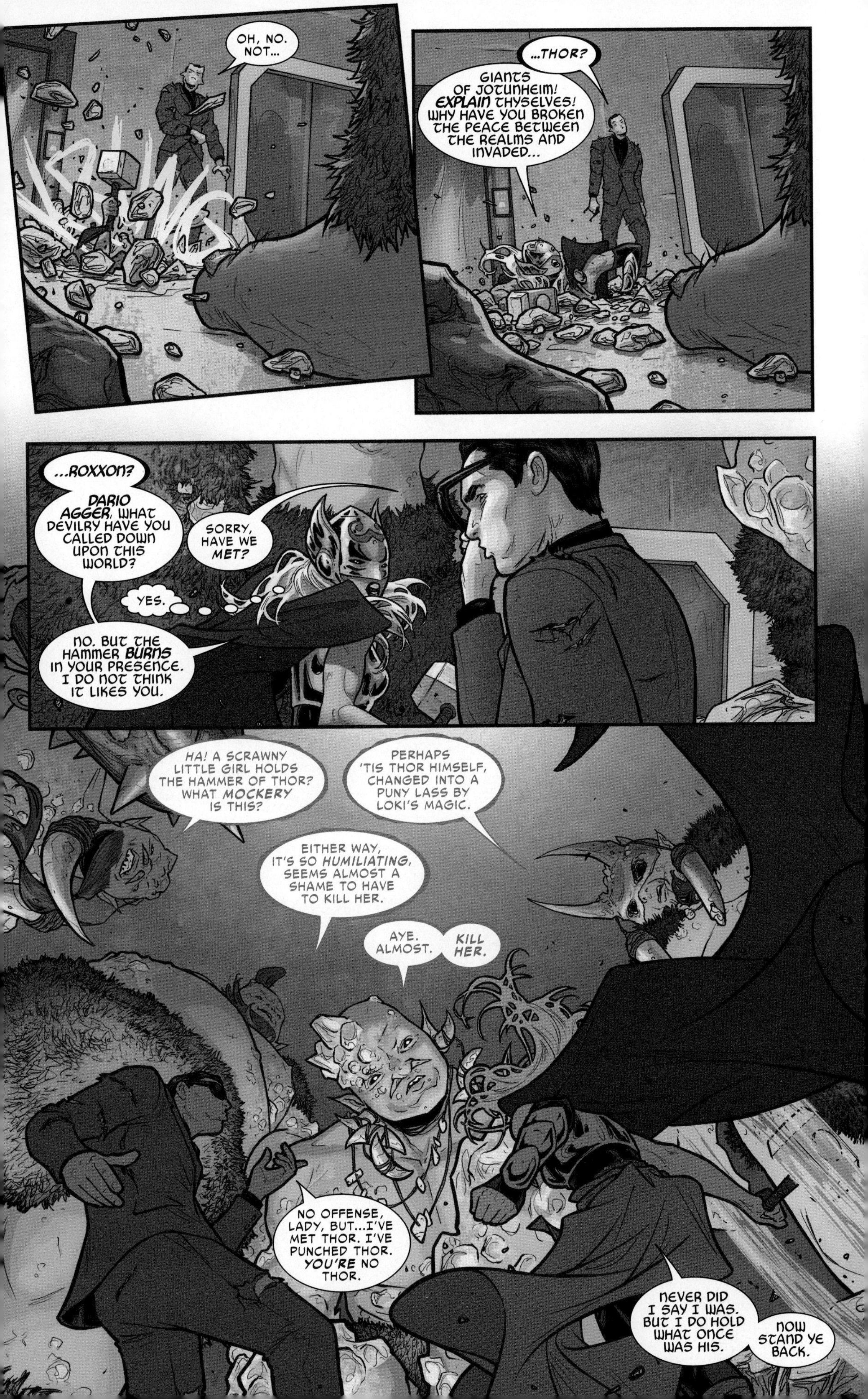
OH, NO. NOT...
...THOR?
GIANTS OF JOTUNHEIM! EXPLAIN THYSELVES! WHY HAVE YOU BROKEN THE PEACE BETWEEN THE REALMS AND INVADED...
...ROXXON?
DARIO AGGER, WHAT DEVILRY HAVE YOU CALLED DOWN UPON THIS WORLD?
SORRY, HAVE WE MET?
YES.
NO. BUT THE HAMMER BURNS IN YOUR PRESENCE. I DO NOT THINK IT LIKES YOU.
HA! A SCRAWNY LITTLE GIRL HOLDS THE HAMMER OF THOR? WHAT MOCKERY IS THIS?
PERHAPS 'TIS THOR HIMSELF, CHANGED INTO A PUNY LASS BY LOKI'S MAGIC.
EITHER WAY, IT'S SO HUMILIATING, SEEMS ALMOST A SHAME TO HAVE TO KILL HER.
AYE. ALMOST.
KILL HER.
NO OFFENSE, LADY, BUT...I'VE MET THOR. I'VE PUNCHED THOR. YOU'RE NO THOR.
NEVER DID I SAY I WAS. BUT I DO HOLD WHAT ONCE WAS HIS.
NOW STAND YE BACK.

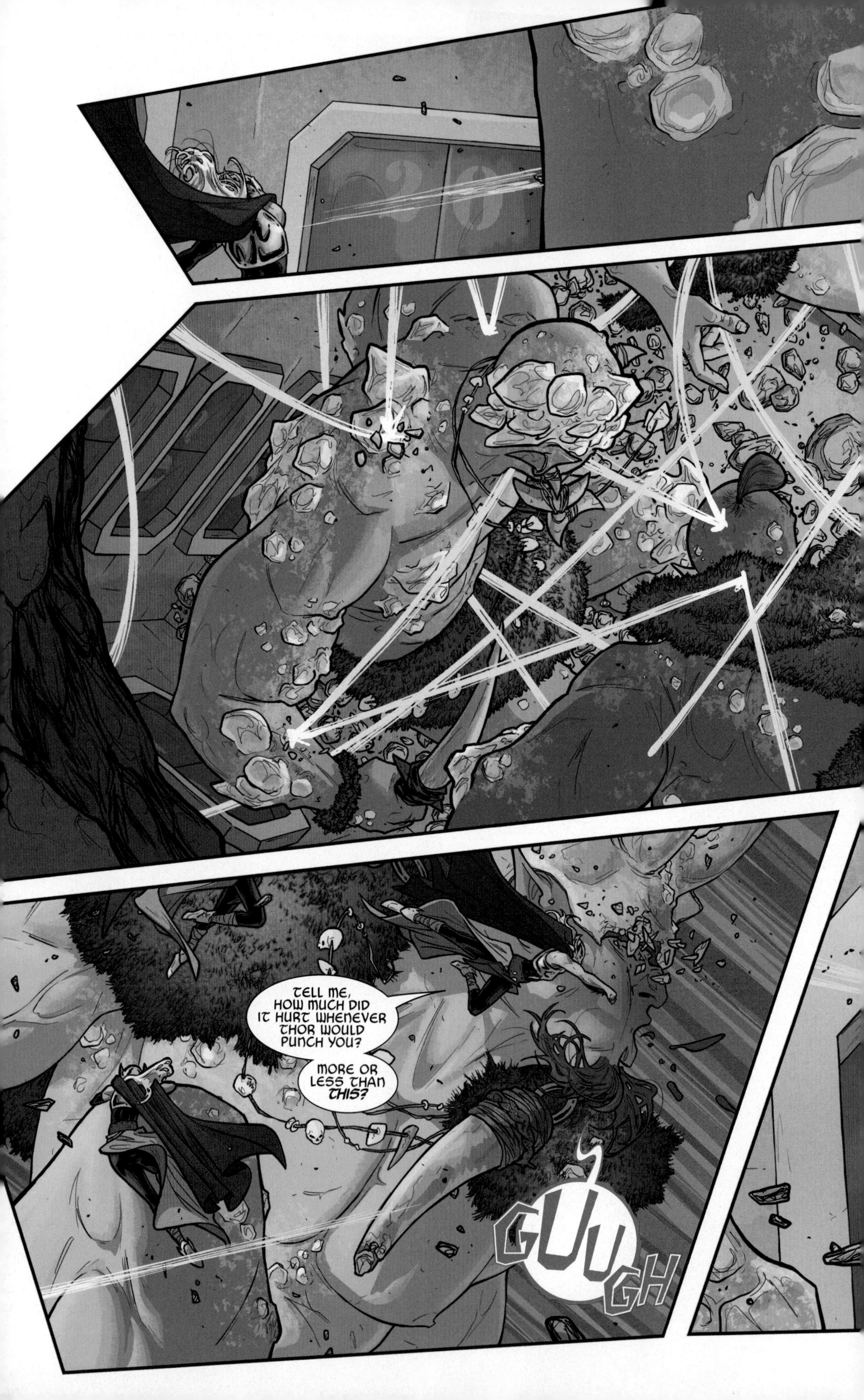
TELL ME, HOW MUCH DID IT HURT WHENEVER THOR WOULD PUNCH YOU?
MORE OR LESS THAN *THIS?*
GUUGH

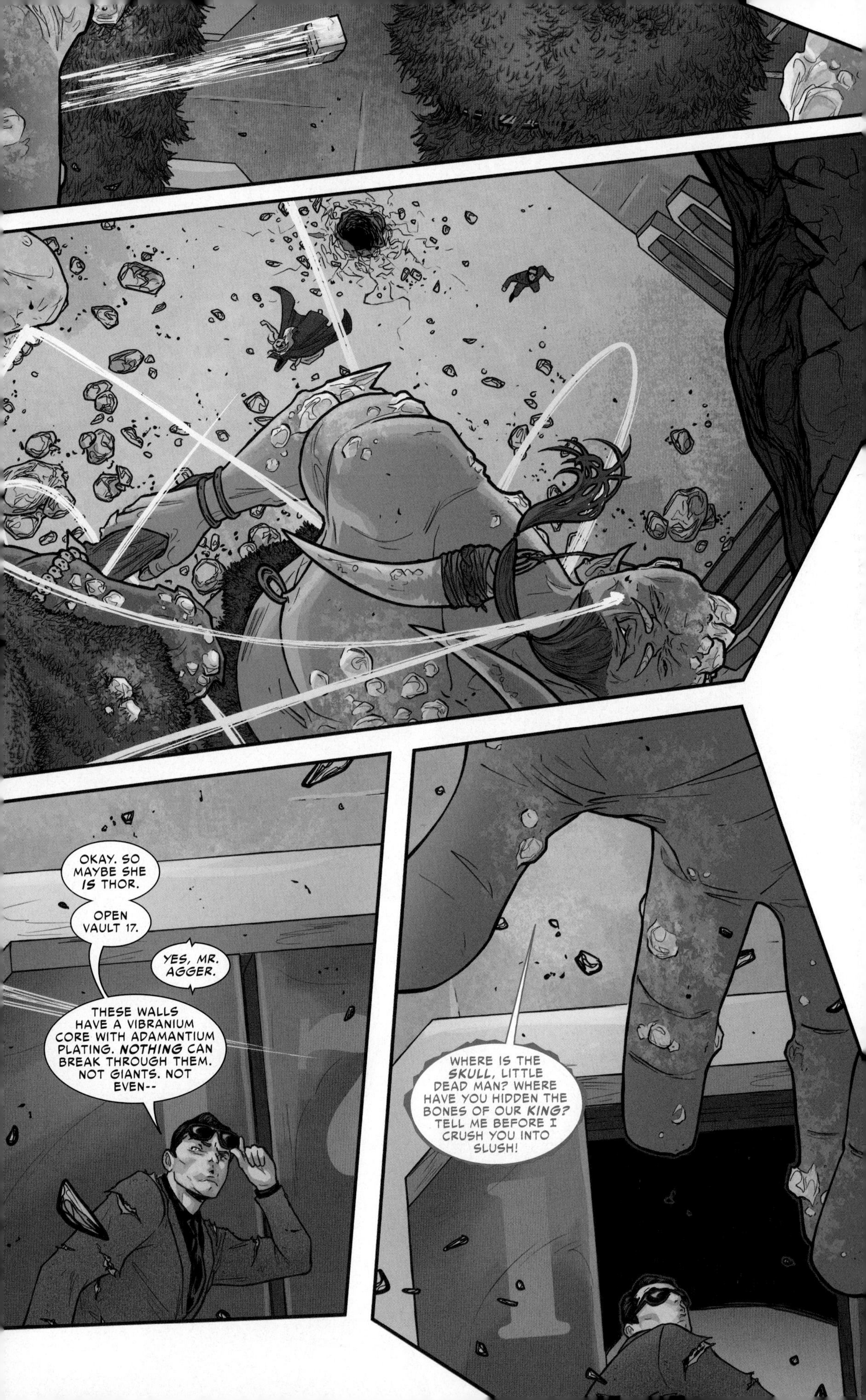
OKAY. SO MAYBE SHE *IS* THOR.
OPEN VAULT 17.
YES, MR. AGGER.
THESE WALLS HAVE A VIBRANIUM CORE WITH ADAMANTIUM PLATING. *NOTHING* CAN BREAK THROUGH THEM. NOT GIANTS. NOT EVEN--
WHERE IS THE *SKULL*, LITTLE DEAD MAN? WHERE HAVE YOU HIDDEN THE BONES OF OUR *KING?* TELL ME BEFORE I CRUSH YOU INTO SLUSH!

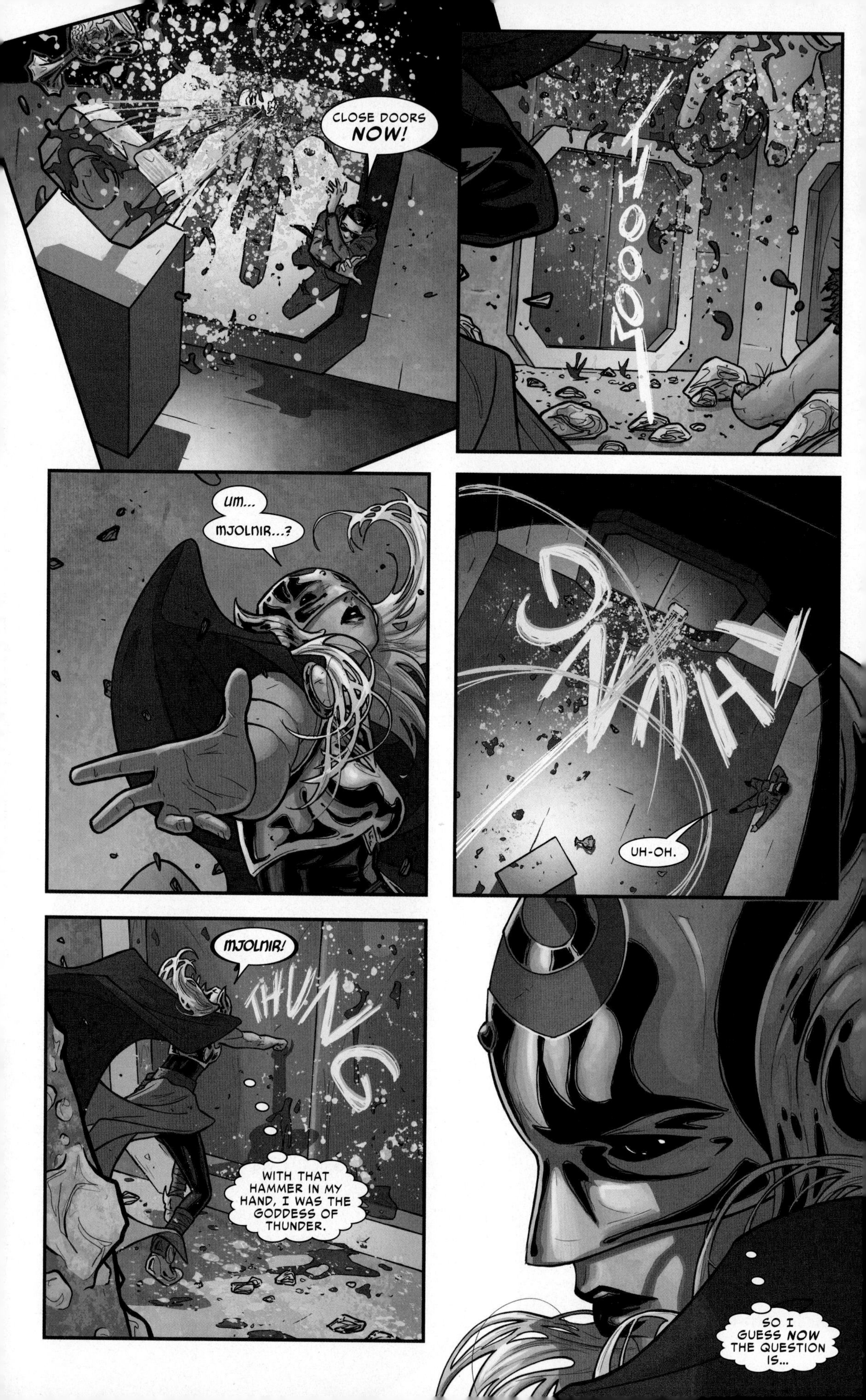
CLOSE DOORS NOW!
THOOOOM
UM... MJOLNIR...?
DWAH!
UH-OH.
MJOLNIR!
THUNG
WITH THAT HAMMER IN MY HAND, I WAS THE GODDESS OF THUNDER.
SO I GUESS NOW THE QUESTION IS...

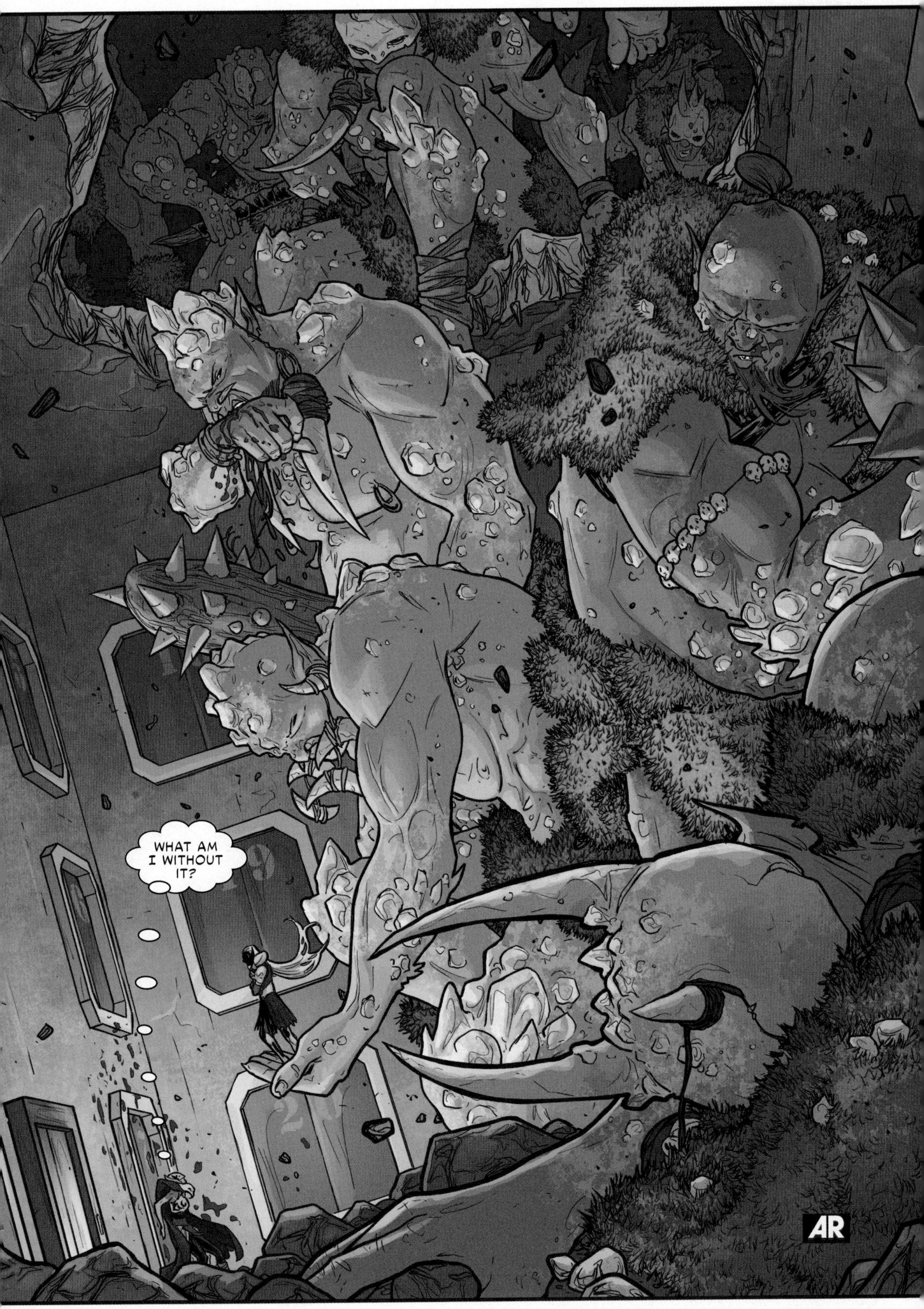
WHAT AM I WITHOUT IT?

3

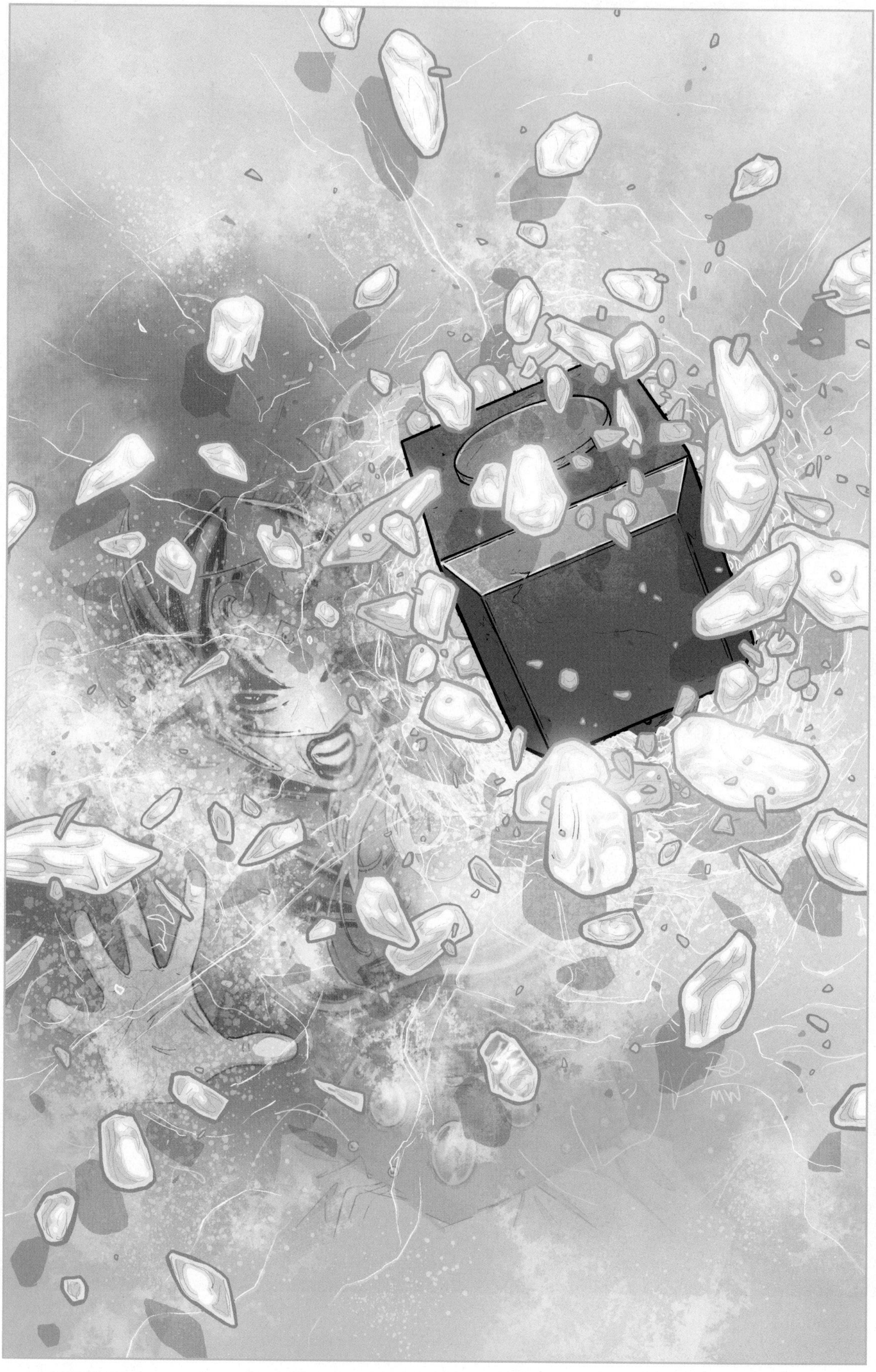

WHEN THE ICE LORDS MAKE WAR

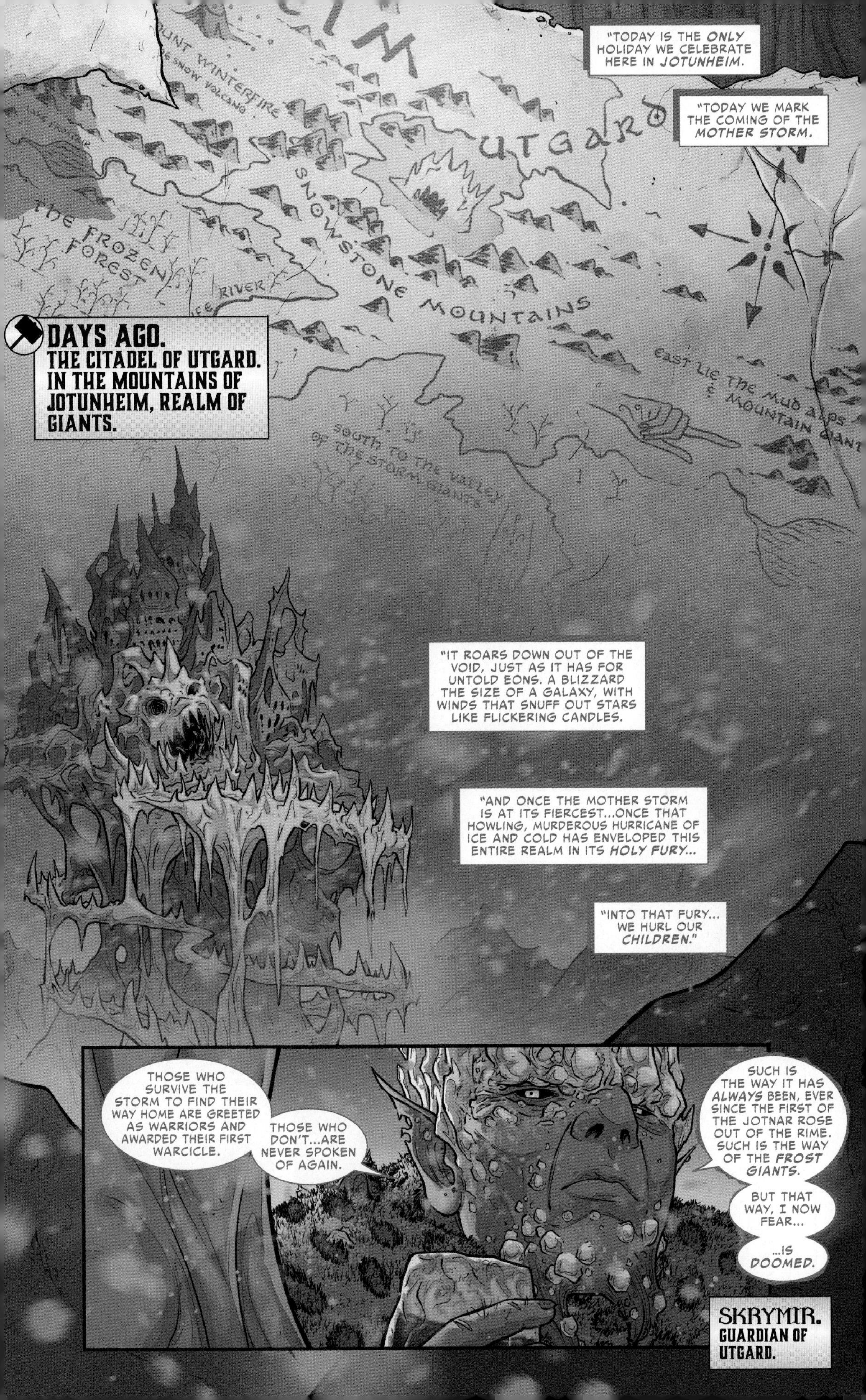

"TODAY IS THE ONLY HOLIDAY WE CELEBRATE HERE IN JOTUNHEIM.
"TODAY WE MARK THE COMING OF THE MOTHER STORM.
UTGARD
SNOWSTONE MOUNTAINS
THE FROZEN FOREST
RIVER
LAKE FROSTRIR
EAST LIE THE MUD ALPS & MOUNTAIN GIANT
SOUTH TO THE VALLEY OF THE STORM GIANTS
DAYS AGO. THE CITADEL OF UTGARD. IN THE MOUNTAINS OF JOTUNHEIM, REALM OF GIANTS.
"IT ROARS DOWN OUT OF THE VOID, JUST AS IT HAS FOR UNTOLD EONS. A BLIZZARD THE SIZE OF A GALAXY, WITH WINDS THAT SNUFF OUT STARS LIKE FLICKERING CANDLES.
"AND ONCE THE MOTHER STORM IS AT ITS FIERCEST...ONCE THAT HOWLING, MURDEROUS HURRICANE OF ICE AND COLD HAS ENVELOPED THIS ENTIRE REALM IN ITS HOLY FURY...
"INTO THAT FURY... WE HURL OUR CHILDREN."
THOSE WHO SURVIVE THE STORM TO FIND THEIR WAY HOME ARE GREETED AS WARRIORS AND AWARDED THEIR FIRST WARCICLE.
THOSE WHO DON'T...ARE NEVER SPOKEN OF AGAIN.
SUCH IS THE WAY IT HAS ALWAYS BEEN, EVER SINCE THE FIRST OF THE JOTNAR ROSE OUT OF THE RIME. SUCH IS THE WAY OF THE FROST GIANTS.
BUT THAT WAY, I NOW FEAR...
...IS DOOMED.
SKRYMIR. GUARDIAN OF UTGARD.

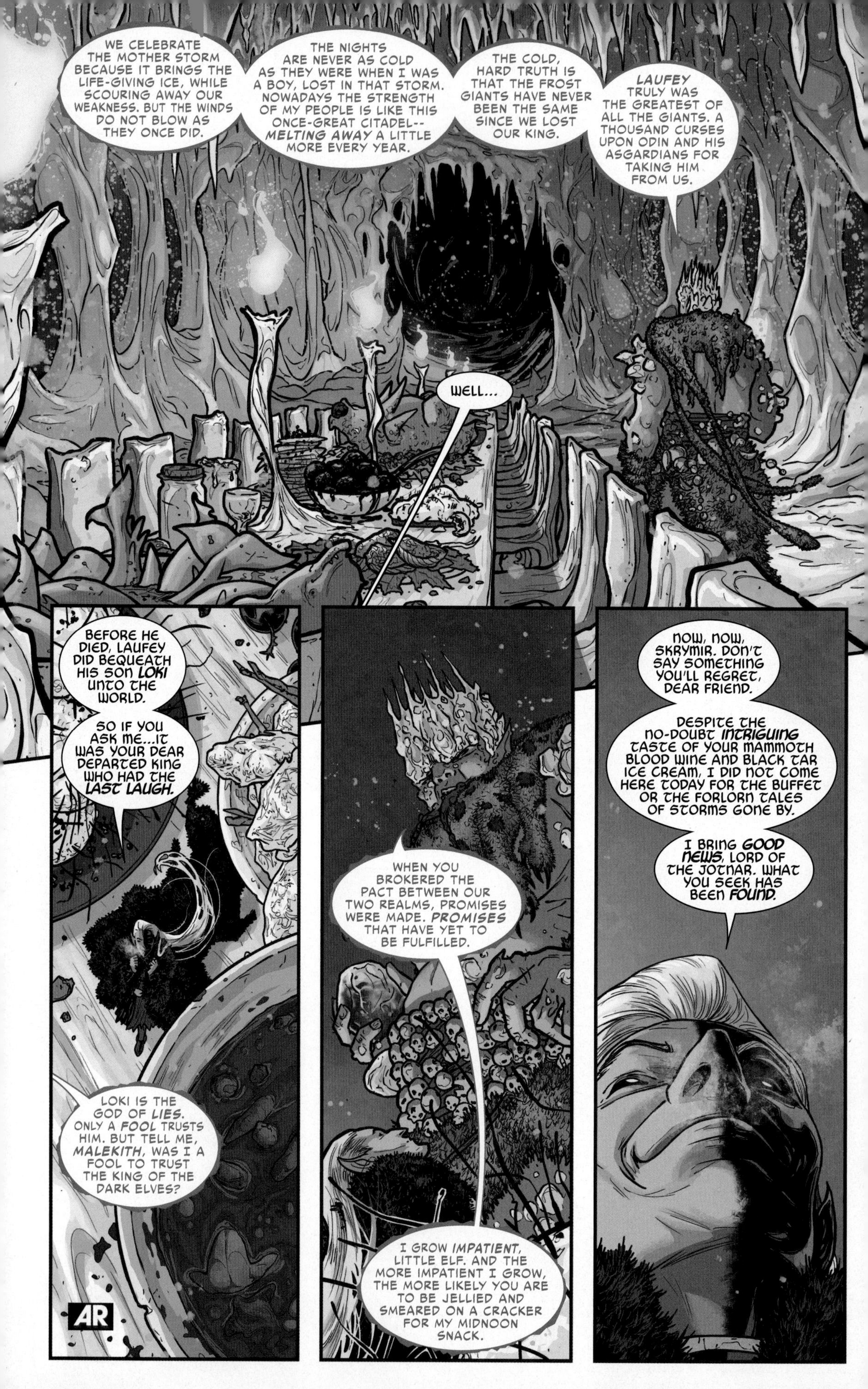
WE CELEBRATE THE MOTHER STORM BECAUSE IT BRINGS THE LIFE-GIVING ICE, WHILE SCOURING AWAY OUR WEAKNESS. BUT THE WINDS DO NOT BLOW AS THEY ONCE DID.
THE NIGHTS ARE NEVER AS COLD AS THEY WERE WHEN I WAS A BOY, LOST IN THAT STORM. NOWADAYS THE STRENGTH OF MY PEOPLE IS LIKE THIS ONCE-GREAT CITADEL-- MELTING AWAY A LITTLE MORE EVERY YEAR.
THE COLD, HARD TRUTH IS THAT THE FROST GIANTS HAVE NEVER BEEN THE SAME SINCE WE LOST OUR KING.
LAUFEY TRULY WAS THE GREATEST OF ALL THE GIANTS. A THOUSAND CURSES UPON ODIN AND HIS ASGARDIANS FOR TAKING HIM FROM US.
WELL...
BEFORE HE DIED, LAUFEY DID BEQUEATH HIS SON LOKI UNTO THE WORLD.
SO IF YOU ASK ME...IT WAS YOUR DEAR DEPARTED KING WHO HAD THE LAST LAUGH.
LOKI IS THE GOD OF LIES. ONLY A FOOL TRUSTS HIM. BUT TELL ME, MALEKITH, WAS I A FOOL TO TRUST THE KING OF THE DARK ELVES?
WHEN YOU BROKERED THE PACT BETWEEN OUR TWO REALMS, PROMISES WERE MADE. PROMISES THAT HAVE YET TO BE FULFILLED.
I GROW IMPATIENT, LITTLE ELF. AND THE MORE IMPATIENT I GROW, THE MORE LIKELY YOU ARE TO BE JELLIED AND SMEARED ON A CRACKER FOR MY MIDNOON SNACK.
NOW, NOW, SKRYMIR. DON'T SAY SOMETHING YOU'LL REGRET, DEAR FRIEND.
DESPITE THE NO-DOUBT INTRIGUING TASTE OF YOUR MAMMOTH BLOOD WINE AND BLACK TAR ICE CREAM, I DID NOT COME HERE TODAY FOR THE BUFFET OR THE FORLORN TALES OF STORMS GONE BY.
I BRING GOOD NEWS, LORD OF THE JOTNAR. WHAT YOU SEEK HAS BEEN FOUND.
AR

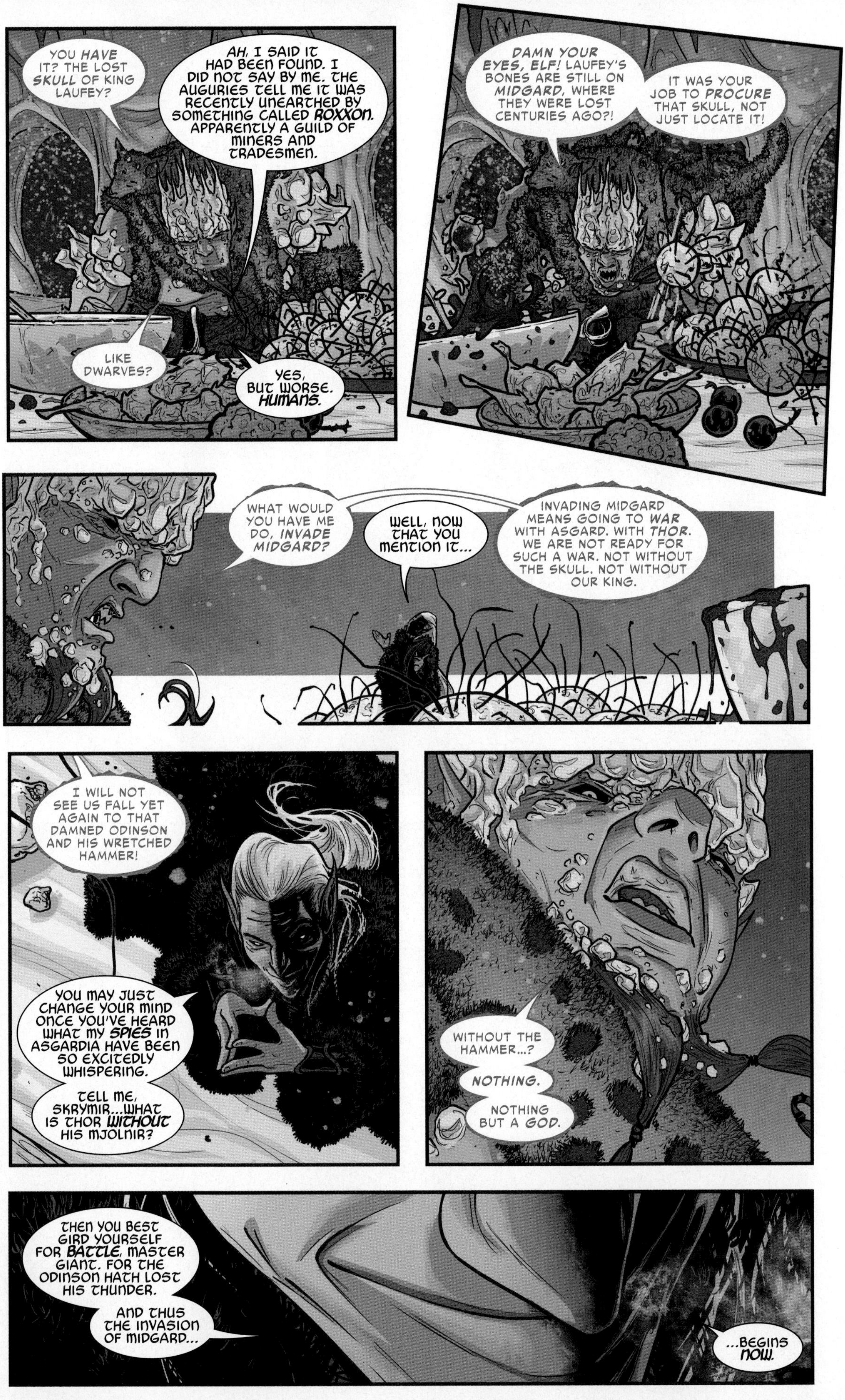
YOU HAVE IT? THE LOST SKULL OF KING LAUFEY?
AH, I SAID IT HAD BEEN FOUND. I DID NOT SAY BY ME. THE AUGURIES TELL ME IT WAS RECENTLY UNEARTHED BY SOMETHING CALLED ROXXON. APPARENTLY A GUILD OF MINERS AND TRADESMEN.
LIKE DWARVES?
YES, BUT WORSE. HUMANS.
DAMN YOUR EYES, ELF! LAUFEY'S BONES ARE STILL ON MIDGARD, WHERE THEY WERE LOST CENTURIES AGO?!
IT WAS YOUR JOB TO PROCURE THAT SKULL, NOT JUST LOCATE IT!
WHAT WOULD YOU HAVE ME DO, INVADE MIDGARD?
WELL, NOW THAT YOU MENTION IT...
INVADING MIDGARD MEANS GOING TO WAR WITH ASGARD. WITH THOR. WE ARE NOT READY FOR SUCH A WAR. NOT WITHOUT THE SKULL. NOT WITHOUT OUR KING.
I WILL NOT SEE US FALL YET AGAIN TO THAT DAMNED ODINSON AND HIS WRETCHED HAMMER!
YOU MAY JUST CHANGE YOUR MIND ONCE YOU'VE HEARD WHAT MY SPIES IN ASGARDIA HAVE BEEN SO EXCITEDLY WHISPERING.
TELL ME, SKRYMIR...WHAT IS THOR WITHOUT HIS MJOLNIR?
WITHOUT THE HAMMER...?
NOTHING.
NOTHING BUT A GOD.
THEN YOU BEST GIRD YOURSELF FOR BATTLE, MASTER GIANT. FOR THE ODINSON HATH LOST HIS THUNDER.
AND THUS THE INVASION OF MIDGARD...
...BEGINS NOW.

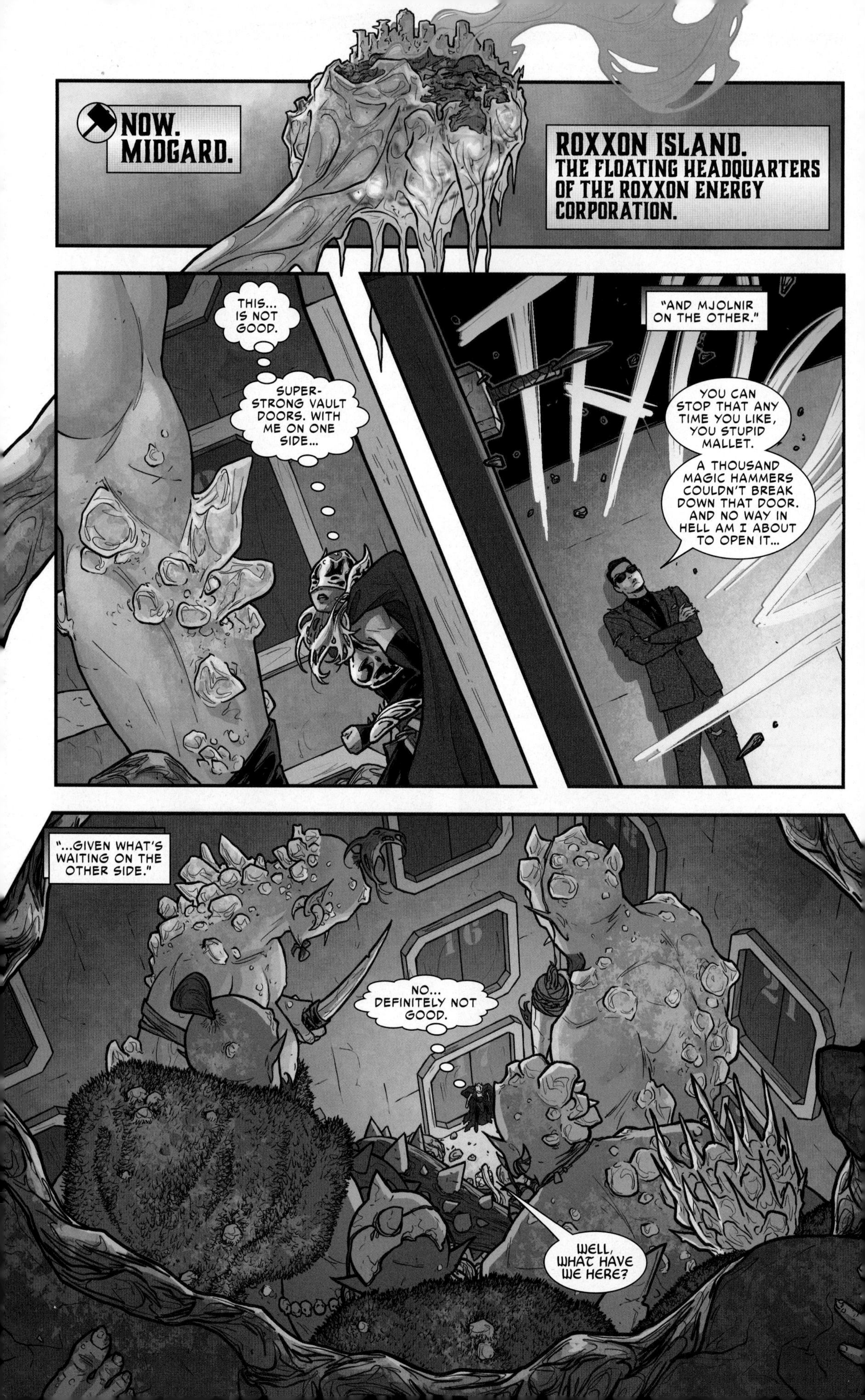
NOW. MIDGARD.
ROXXON ISLAND. THE FLOATING HEADQUARTERS OF THE ROXXON ENERGY CORPORATION.
THIS... IS NOT GOOD.
SUPER-STRONG VAULT DOORS. WITH ME ON ONE SIDE...
"AND MJOLNIR ON THE OTHER."
YOU CAN STOP THAT ANY TIME YOU LIKE, YOU STUPID MALLET.
A THOUSAND MAGIC HAMMERS COULDN'T BREAK DOWN THAT DOOR. AND NO WAY IN HELL AM I ABOUT TO OPEN IT...
"...GIVEN WHAT'S WAITING ON THE OTHER SIDE."
NO... DEFINITELY NOT GOOD.
WELL, WHAT HAVE WE HERE?

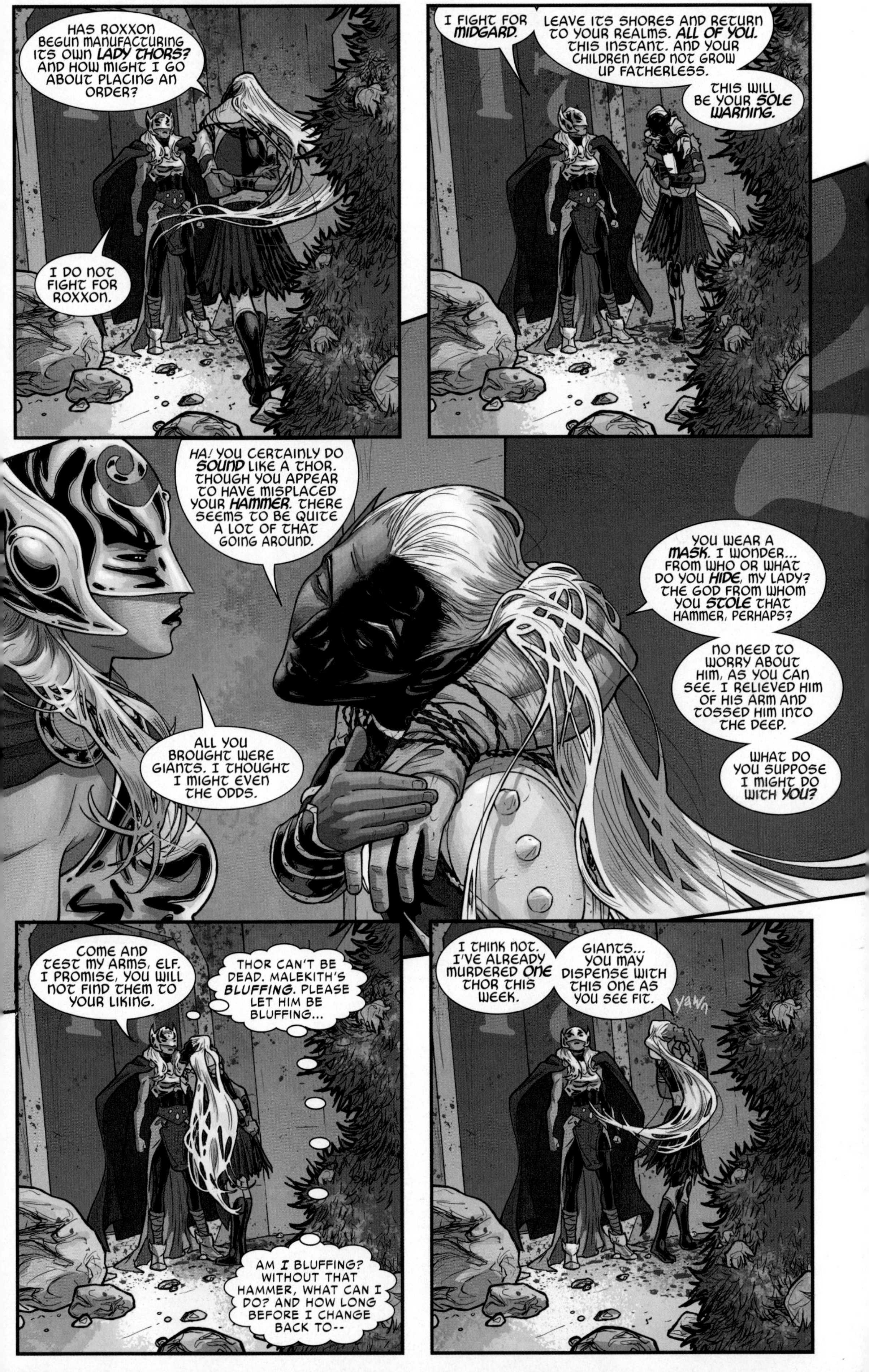
HAS ROXXON BEGUN MANUFACTURING ITS OWN LADY THORS? AND HOW MIGHT I GO ABOUT PLACING AN ORDER?
I DO NOT FIGHT FOR ROXXON.
I FIGHT FOR MIDGARD.
LEAVE ITS SHORES AND RETURN TO YOUR REALMS. ALL OF YOU. THIS INSTANT. AND YOUR CHILDREN NEED NOT GROW UP FATHERLESS.
THIS WILL BE YOUR SOLE WARNING.
HA! YOU CERTAINLY DO SOUND LIKE A THOR. THOUGH YOU APPEAR TO HAVE MISPLACED YOUR HAMMER. THERE SEEMS TO BE QUITE A LOT OF THAT GOING AROUND.
ALL YOU BROUGHT WERE GIANTS. I THOUGHT I MIGHT EVEN THE ODDS.
YOU WEAR A MASK. I WONDER... FROM WHO OR WHAT DO YOU HIDE, MY LADY? THE GOD FROM WHOM YOU STOLE THAT HAMMER, PERHAPS?
NO NEED TO WORRY ABOUT HIM, AS YOU CAN SEE. I RELIEVED HIM OF HIS ARM AND TOSSED HIM INTO THE DEEP.
WHAT DO YOU SUPPOSE I MIGHT DO WITH YOU?
COME AND TEST MY ARMS, ELF. I PROMISE, YOU WILL NOT FIND THEM TO YOUR LIKING.
THOR CAN'T BE DEAD. MALEKITH'S BLUFFING. PLEASE LET HIM BE BLUFFING...
AM I BLUFFING? WITHOUT THAT HAMMER, WHAT CAN I DO? AND HOW LONG BEFORE I CHANGE BACK TO--
I THINK NOT. I'VE ALREADY MURDERED ONE THOR THIS WEEK.
GIANTS... YOU MAY DISPENSE WITH THIS ONE AS YOU SEE FIT.
YAWN

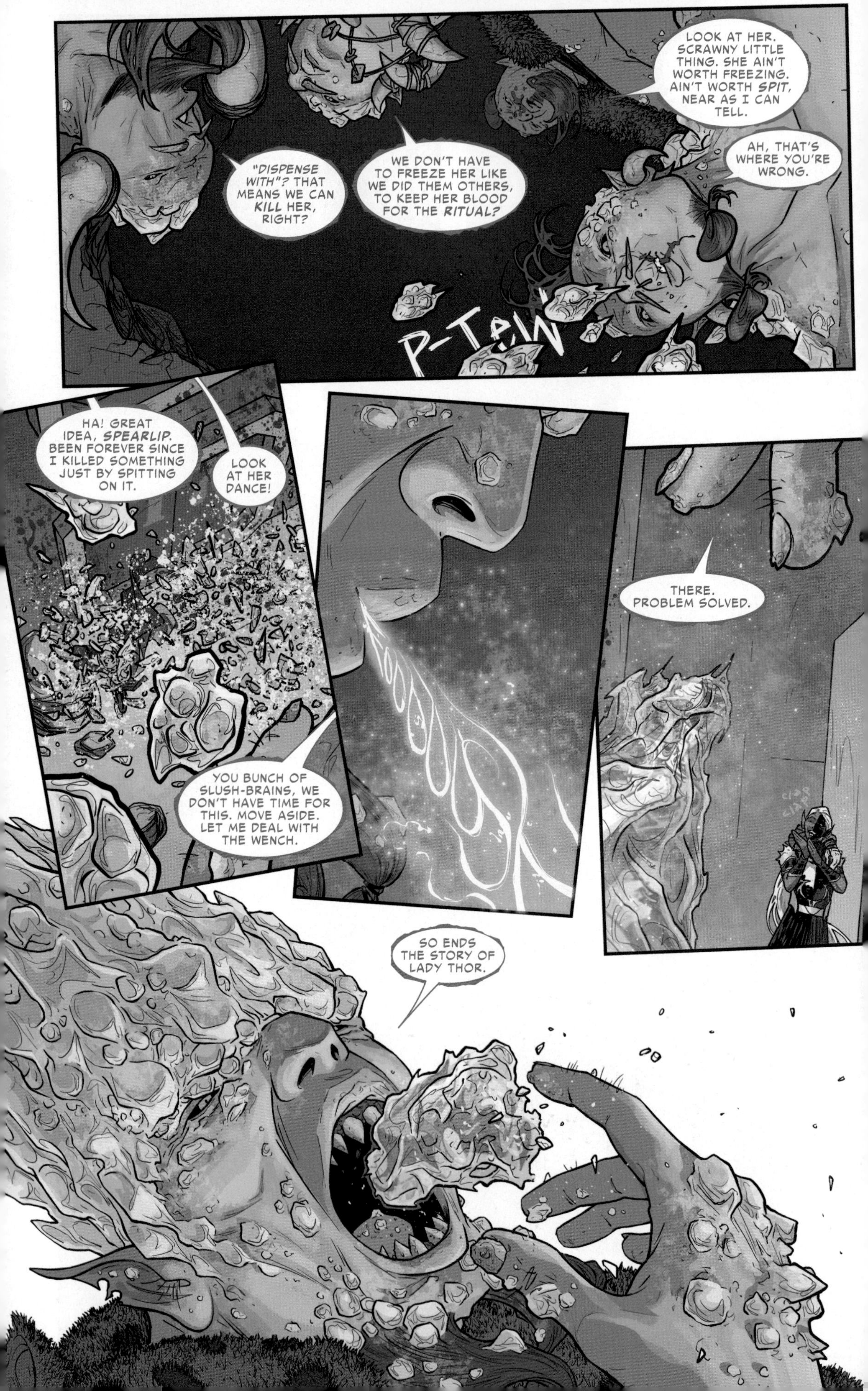
LOOK AT HER. SCRAWNY LITTLE THING. SHE AIN'T WORTH FREEZING. AIN'T WORTH *SPIT*, NEAR AS I CAN TELL.
AH, THAT'S WHERE YOU'RE WRONG.
"DISPENSE WITH"? THAT MEANS WE CAN *KILL* HER, RIGHT?
WE DON'T HAVE TO FREEZE HER LIKE WE DID THEM OTHERS, TO KEEP HER BLOOD FOR THE *RITUAL?*
HA! GREAT IDEA, *SPEARLIP*. BEEN FOREVER SINCE I KILLED SOMETHING JUST BY SPITTING ON IT.
LOOK AT HER DANCE!
YOU BUNCH OF SLUSH-BRAINS, WE DON'T HAVE TIME FOR THIS. MOVE ASIDE. LET ME DEAL WITH THE WENCH.
THERE. PROBLEM SOLVED.
clap clap
SO ENDS THE STORY OF LADY THOR.

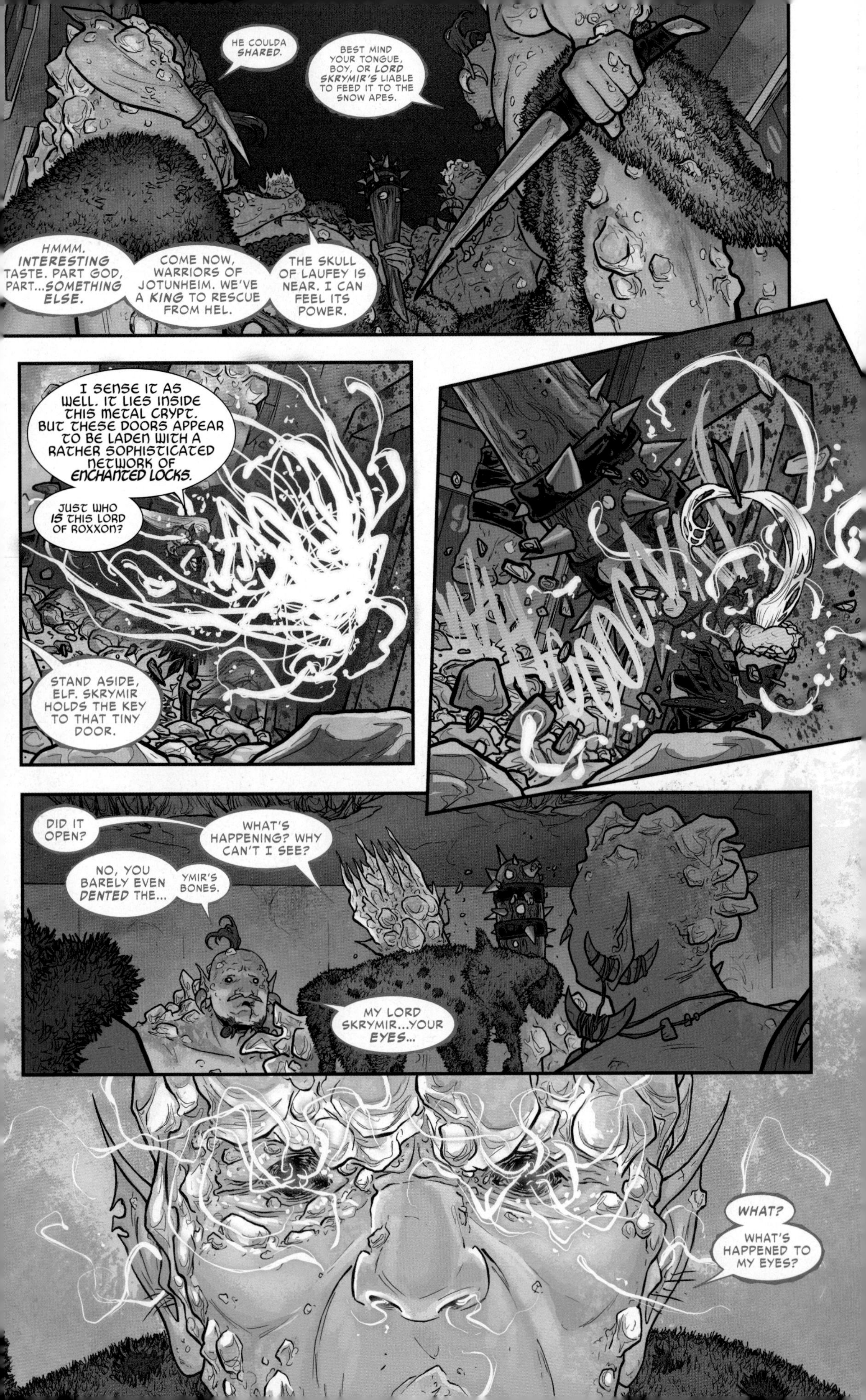
HE COULDA SHARED.
BEST MIND YOUR TONGUE, BOY, OR LORD SKRYMIR'S LIABLE TO FEED IT TO THE SNOW APES.
HMMM. INTERESTING TASTE. PART GOD, PART...SOMETHING ELSE.
COME NOW, WARRIORS OF JOTUNHEIM. WE'VE A KING TO RESCUE FROM HEL.
THE SKULL OF LAUFEY IS NEAR. I CAN FEEL ITS POWER.
I SENSE IT AS WELL. IT LIES INSIDE THIS METAL CRYPT. BUT THESE DOORS APPEAR TO BE LADEN WITH A RATHER SOPHISTICATED NETWORK OF ENCHANTED LOCKS.
JUST WHO IS THIS LORD OF ROXXON?
STAND ASIDE, ELF. SKRYMIR HOLDS THE KEY TO THAT TINY DOOR.
WHHOOOM
DID IT OPEN?
WHAT'S HAPPENING? WHY CAN'T I SEE?
NO, YOU BARELY EVEN DENTED THE...
YMIR'S BONES.
MY LORD SKRYMIR...YOUR EYES...
WHAT?
WHAT'S HAPPENED TO MY EYES?

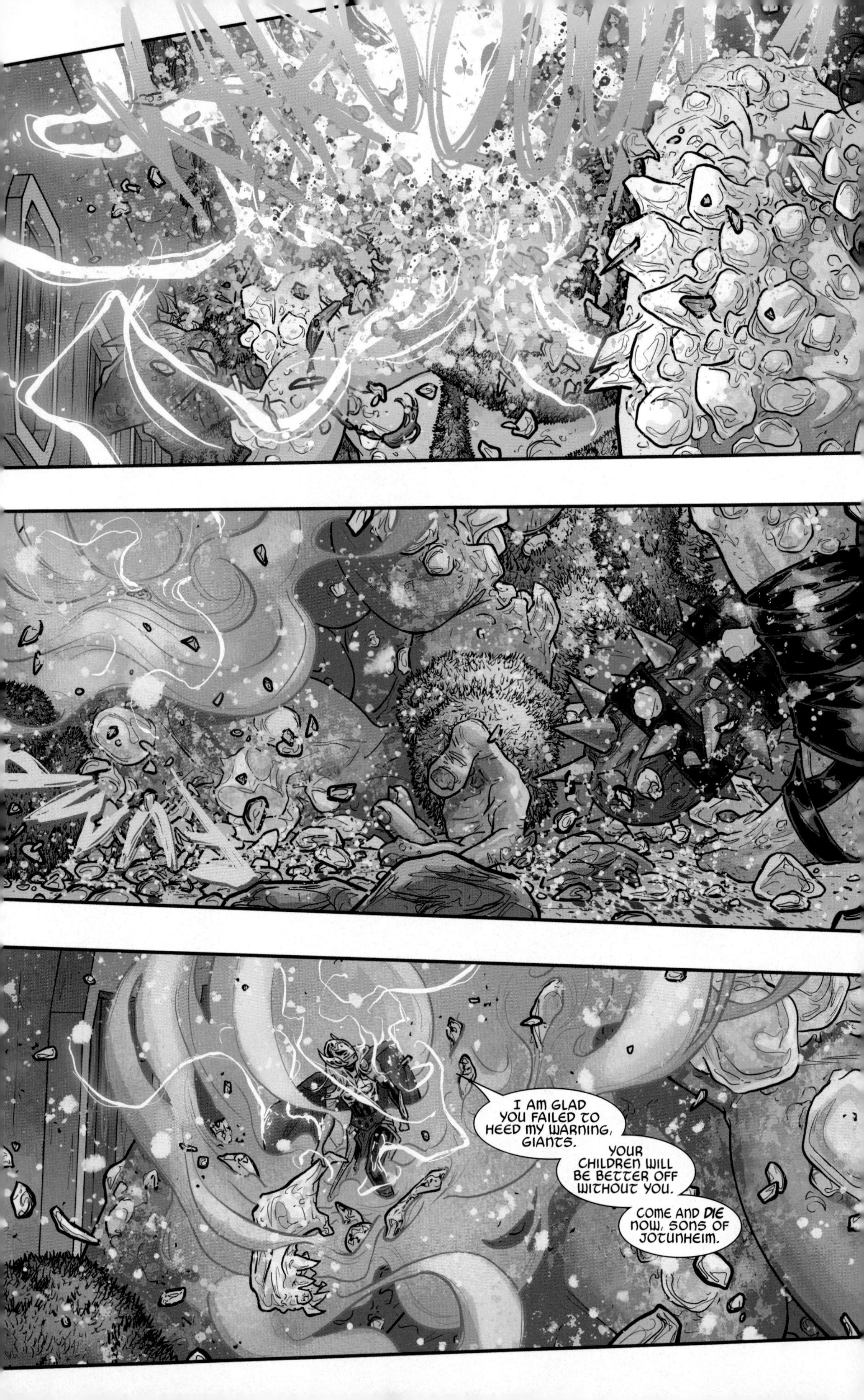
I AM GLAD YOU FAILED TO HEED MY WARNING, GIANTS.
YOUR CHILDREN WILL BE BETTER OFF WITHOUT YOU.
COME AND DIE NOW, SONS OF JOTUNHEIM.

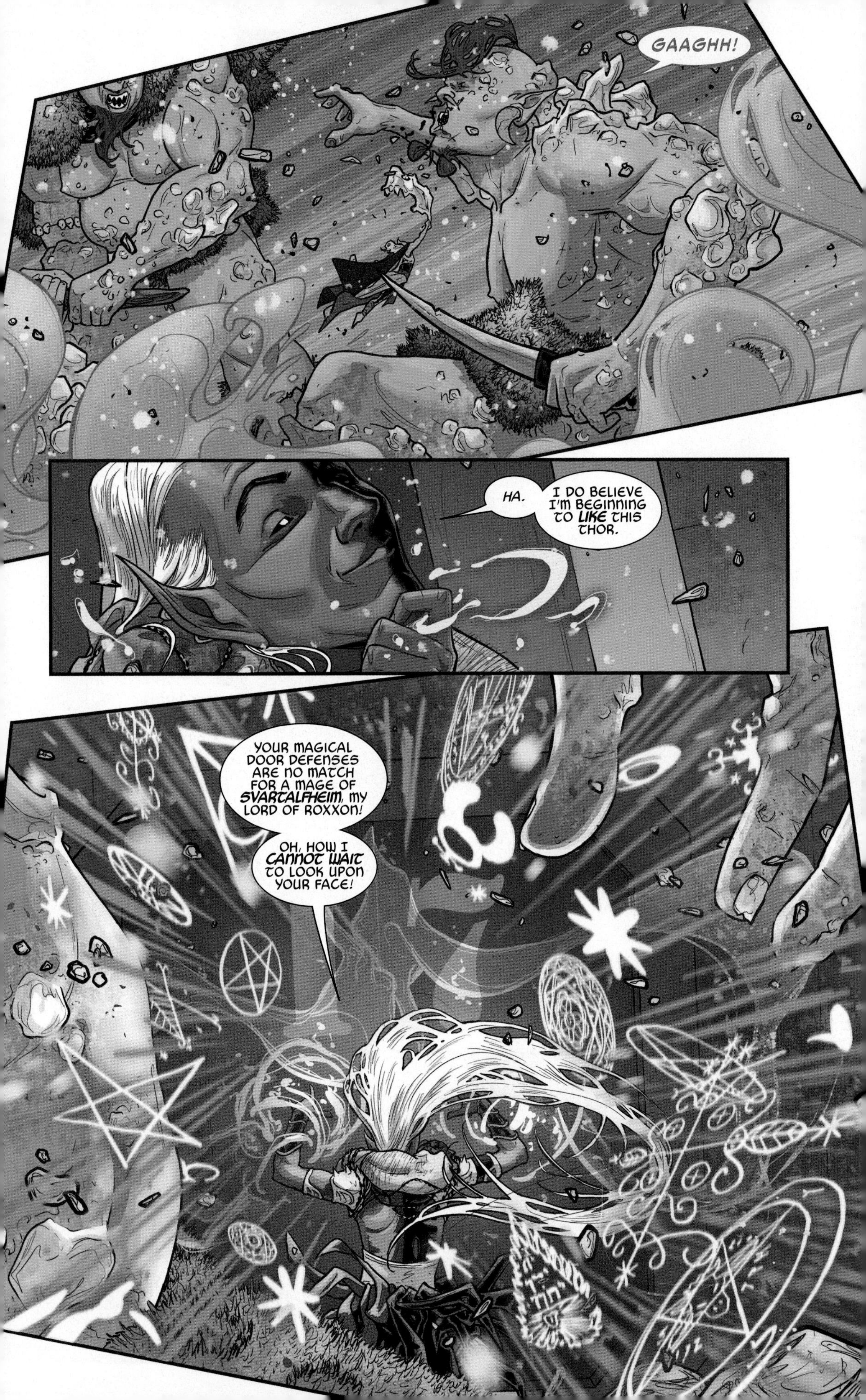
GAAGHH!
HA.
I DO BELIEVE I'M BEGINNING TO LIKE THIS THOR.
YOUR MAGICAL DOOR DEFENSES ARE NO MATCH FOR A MAGE OF SVARTALFHEIM, MY LORD OF ROXXON!
OH, HOW I CANNOT WAIT TO LOOK UPON YOUR FACE!

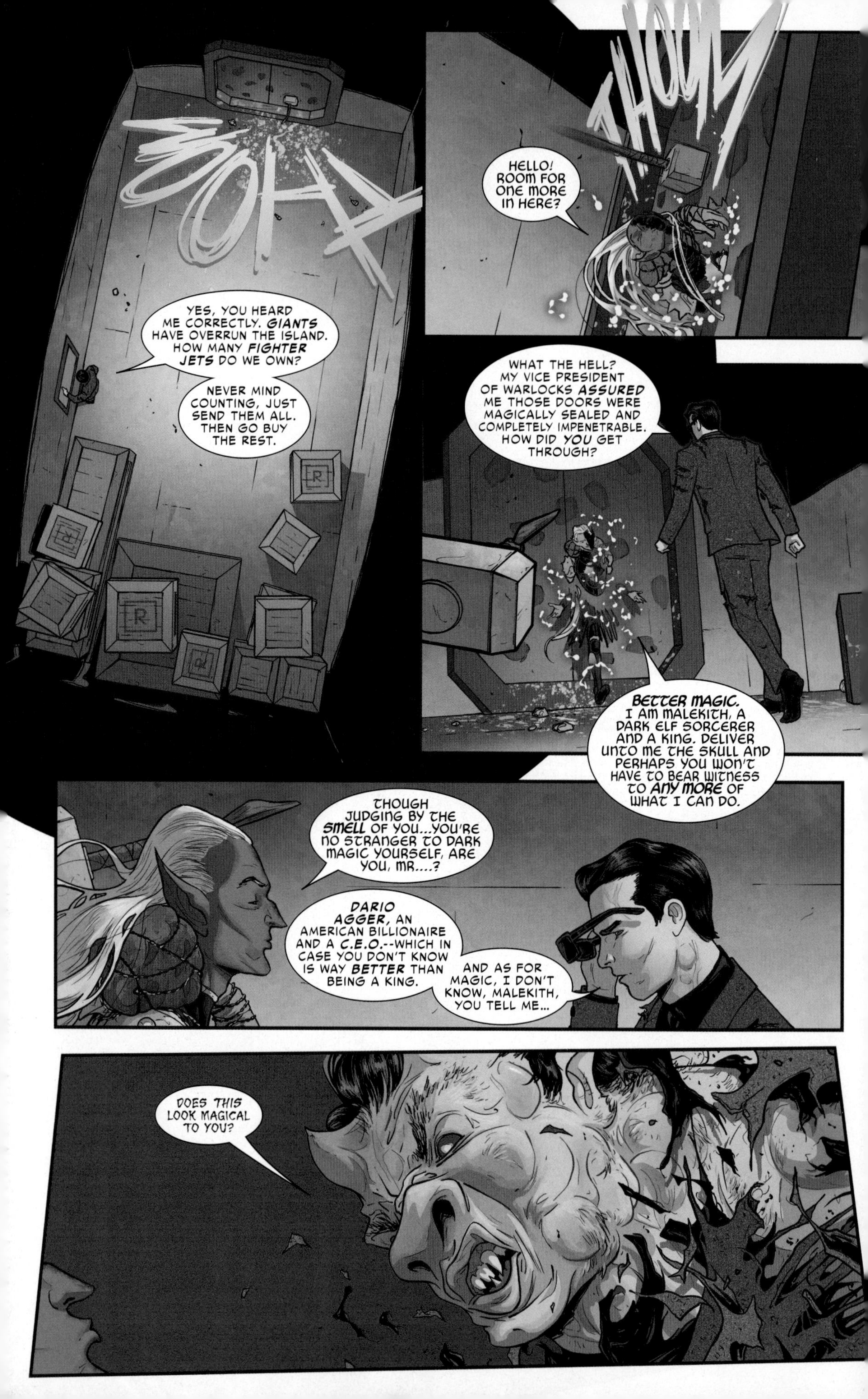
WOOSH
YES, YOU HEARD ME CORRECTLY. GIANTS HAVE OVERRUN THE ISLAND. HOW MANY FIGHTER JETS DO WE OWN?
NEVER MIND COUNTING, JUST SEND THEM ALL. THEN GO BUY THE REST.
THOOM
HELLO! ROOM FOR ONE MORE IN HERE?
WHAT THE HELL? MY VICE PRESIDENT OF WARLOCKS ASSURED ME THOSE DOORS WERE MAGICALLY SEALED AND COMPLETELY IMPENETRABLE. HOW DID YOU GET THROUGH?
BETTER MAGIC. I AM MALEKITH, A DARK ELF SORCERER AND A KING. DELIVER UNTO ME THE SKULL AND PERHAPS YOU WON'T HAVE TO BEAR WITNESS TO ANY MORE OF WHAT I CAN DO.
THOUGH JUDGING BY THE SMELL OF YOU...YOU'RE NO STRANGER TO DARK MAGIC YOURSELF, ARE YOU, MR....?
DARIO AGGER, AN AMERICAN BILLIONAIRE AND A C.E.O.--WHICH IN CASE YOU DON'T KNOW IS WAY BETTER THAN BEING A KING.
AND AS FOR MAGIC, I DON'T KNOW, MALEKITH, YOU TELL ME...
DOES THIS LOOK MAGICAL TO YOU?

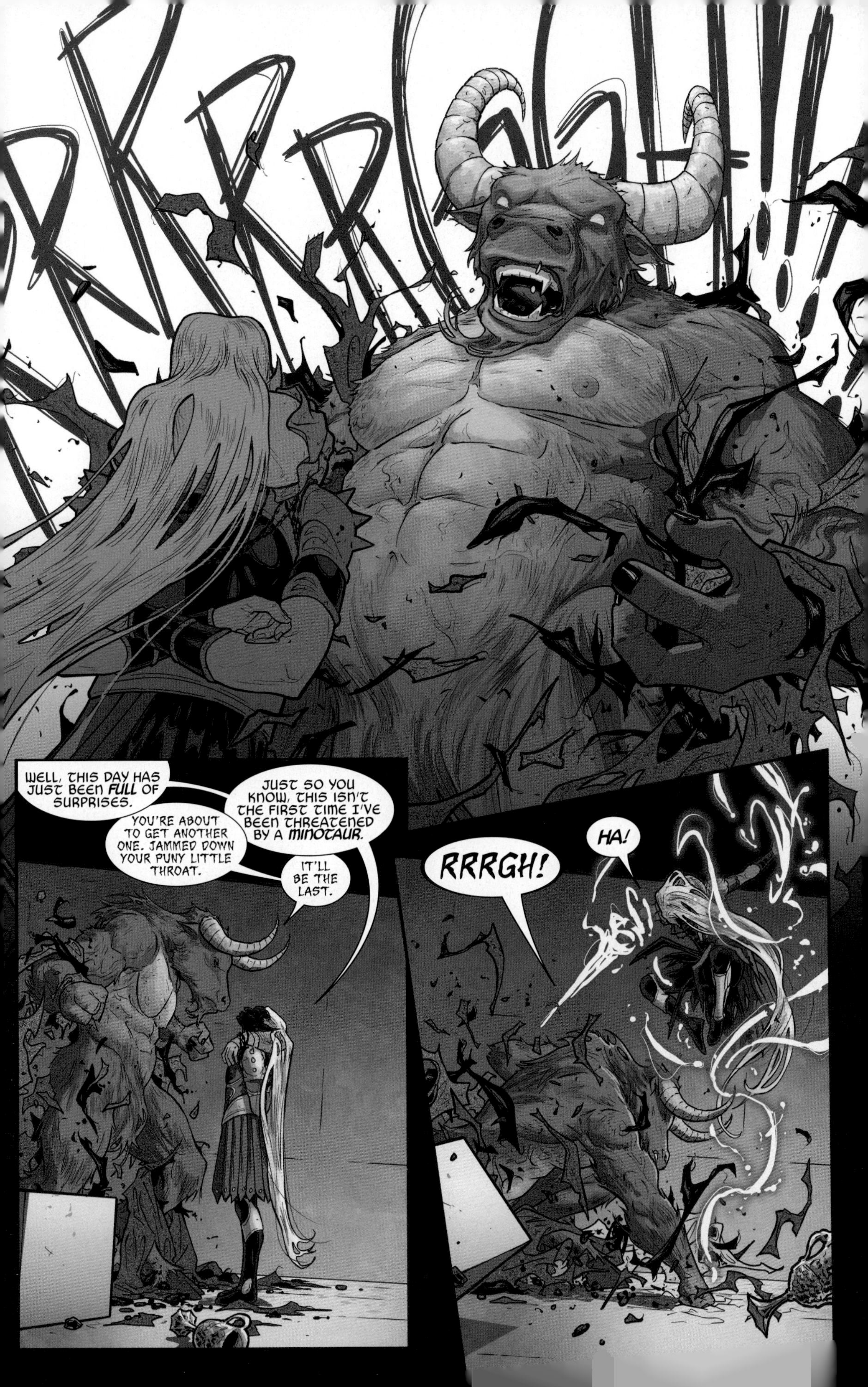
WELL, THIS DAY HAS JUST BEEN FULL OF SURPRISES.
YOU'RE ABOUT TO GET ANOTHER ONE. JAMMED DOWN YOUR PUNY LITTLE THROAT.
JUST SO YOU KNOW, THIS ISN'T THE FIRST TIME I'VE BEEN THREATENED BY A MINOTAUR.
IT'LL BE THE LAST.
RRRGH!
HA!

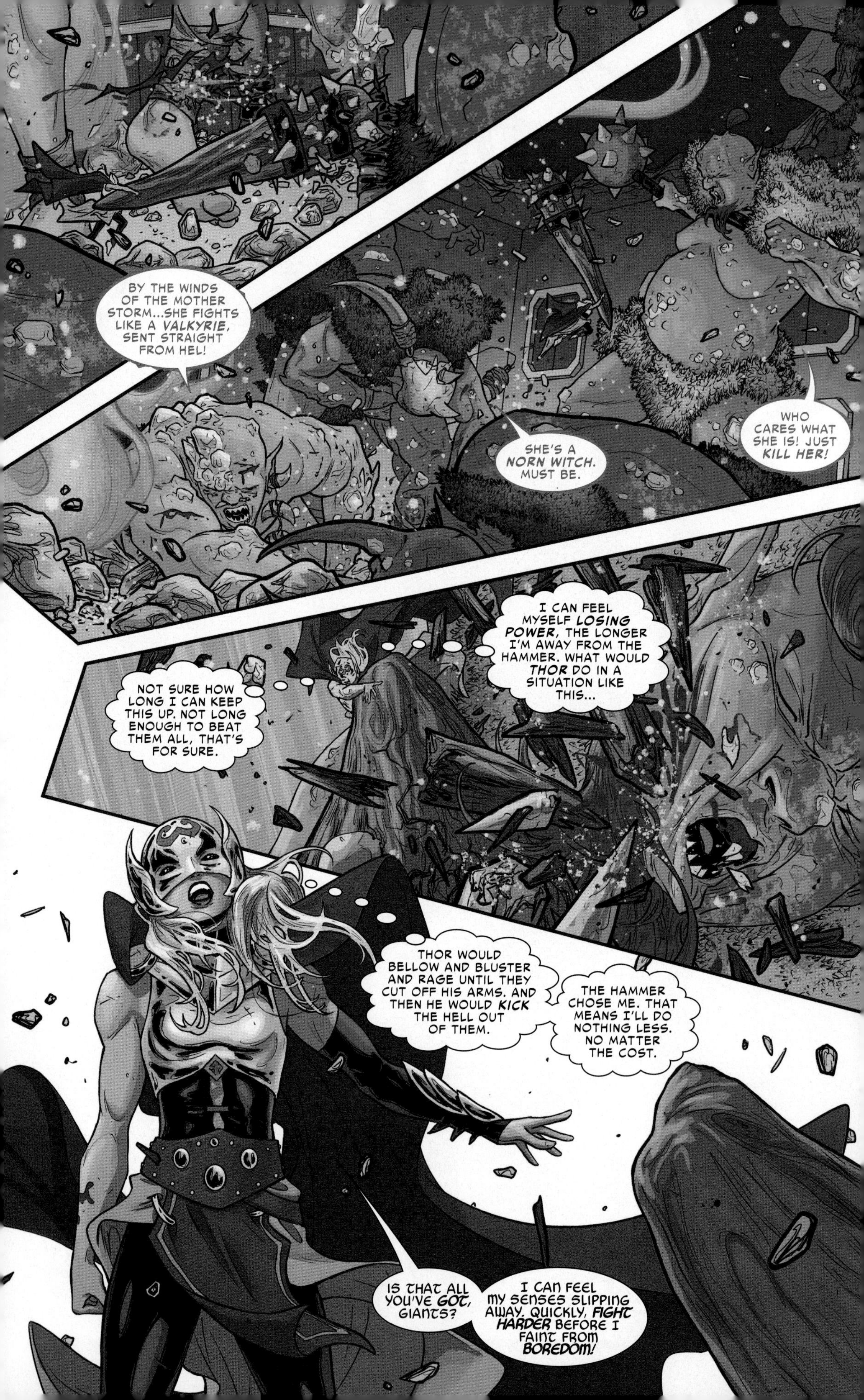

BY THE WINDS OF THE MOTHER STORM...SHE FIGHTS LIKE A *VALKYRIE*, SENT STRAIGHT FROM HEL!
SHE'S A *NORN WITCH*. MUST BE.
WHO CARES WHAT SHE IS! JUST *KILL HER!*
NOT SURE HOW LONG I CAN KEEP THIS UP. NOT LONG ENOUGH TO BEAT THEM ALL, THAT'S FOR SURE.
I CAN FEEL MYSELF *LOSING POWER*, THE LONGER I'M AWAY FROM THE HAMMER. WHAT WOULD *THOR* DO IN A SITUATION LIKE THIS...
THOR WOULD BELLOW AND BLUSTER AND RAGE UNTIL THEY CUT OFF HIS ARMS. AND THEN HE WOULD *KICK* THE HELL OUT OF THEM.
THE HAMMER CHOSE ME. THAT MEANS I'LL DO NOTHING LESS. NO MATTER THE COST.
IS THAT ALL YOU'VE *GOT*, GIANTS?
I CAN FEEL MY SENSES SLIPPING AWAY. QUICKLY, *FIGHT HARDER* BEFORE I FAINT FROM *BOREDOM!*

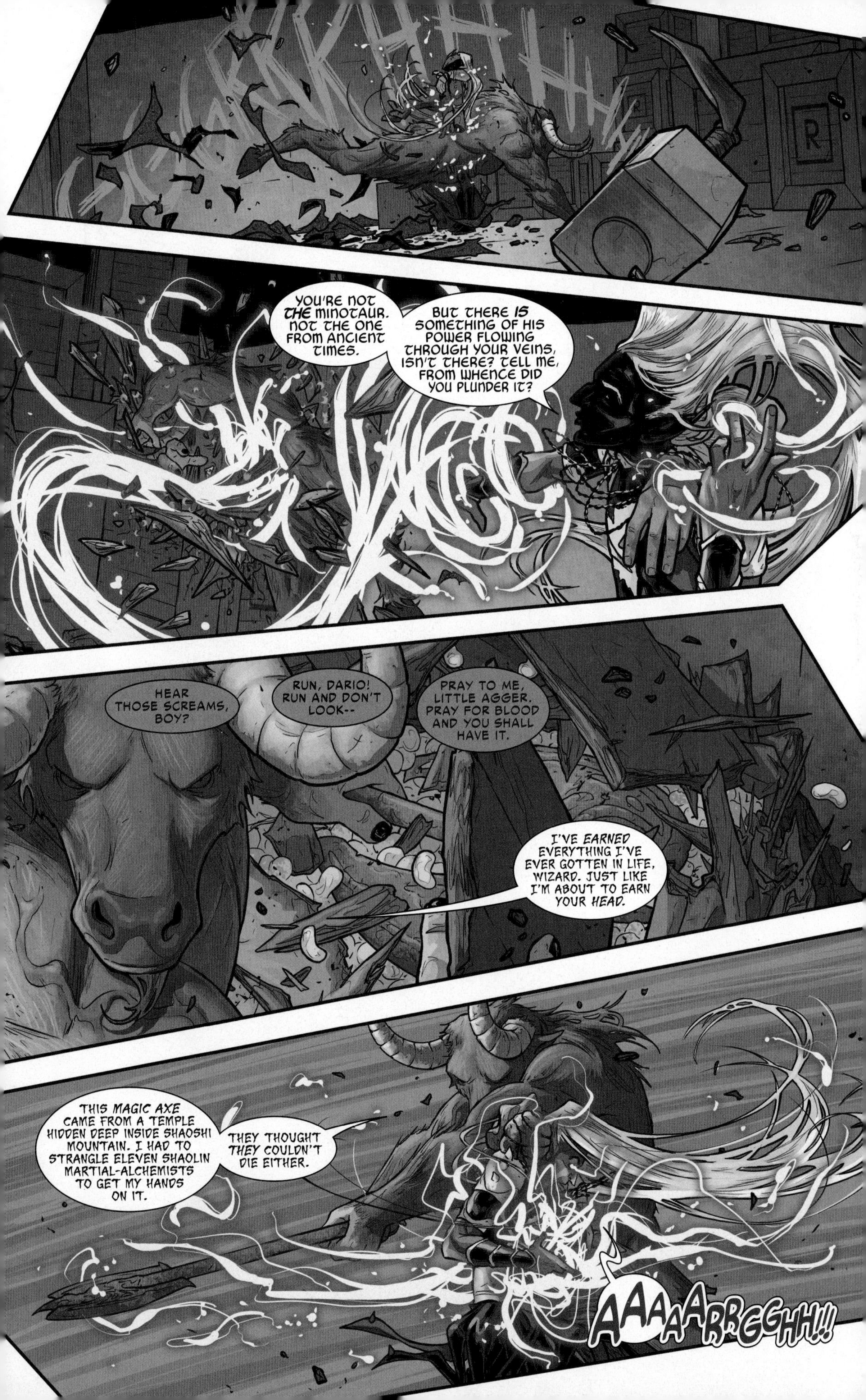
YOU'RE NOT THE MINOTAUR. NOT THE ONE FROM ANCIENT TIMES.
BUT THERE IS SOMETHING OF HIS POWER FLOWING THROUGH YOUR VEINS, ISN'T THERE? TELL ME, FROM WHENCE DID YOU PLUNDER IT?
HEAR THOSE SCREAMS, BOY?
RUN, DARIO! RUN AND DON'T LOOK--
PRAY TO ME, LITTLE AGGER. PRAY FOR BLOOD AND YOU SHALL HAVE IT.
I'VE EARNED EVERYTHING I'VE EVER GOTTEN IN LIFE, WIZARD. JUST LIKE I'M ABOUT TO EARN YOUR HEAD.
THIS MAGIC AXE CAME FROM A TEMPLE HIDDEN DEEP INSIDE SHAOSHI MOUNTAIN. I HAD TO STRANGLE ELEVEN SHAOLIN MARTIAL-ALCHEMISTS TO GET MY HANDS ON IT.
THEY THOUGHT THEY COULDN'T DIE EITHER.
AAAAARRGGHH!!!

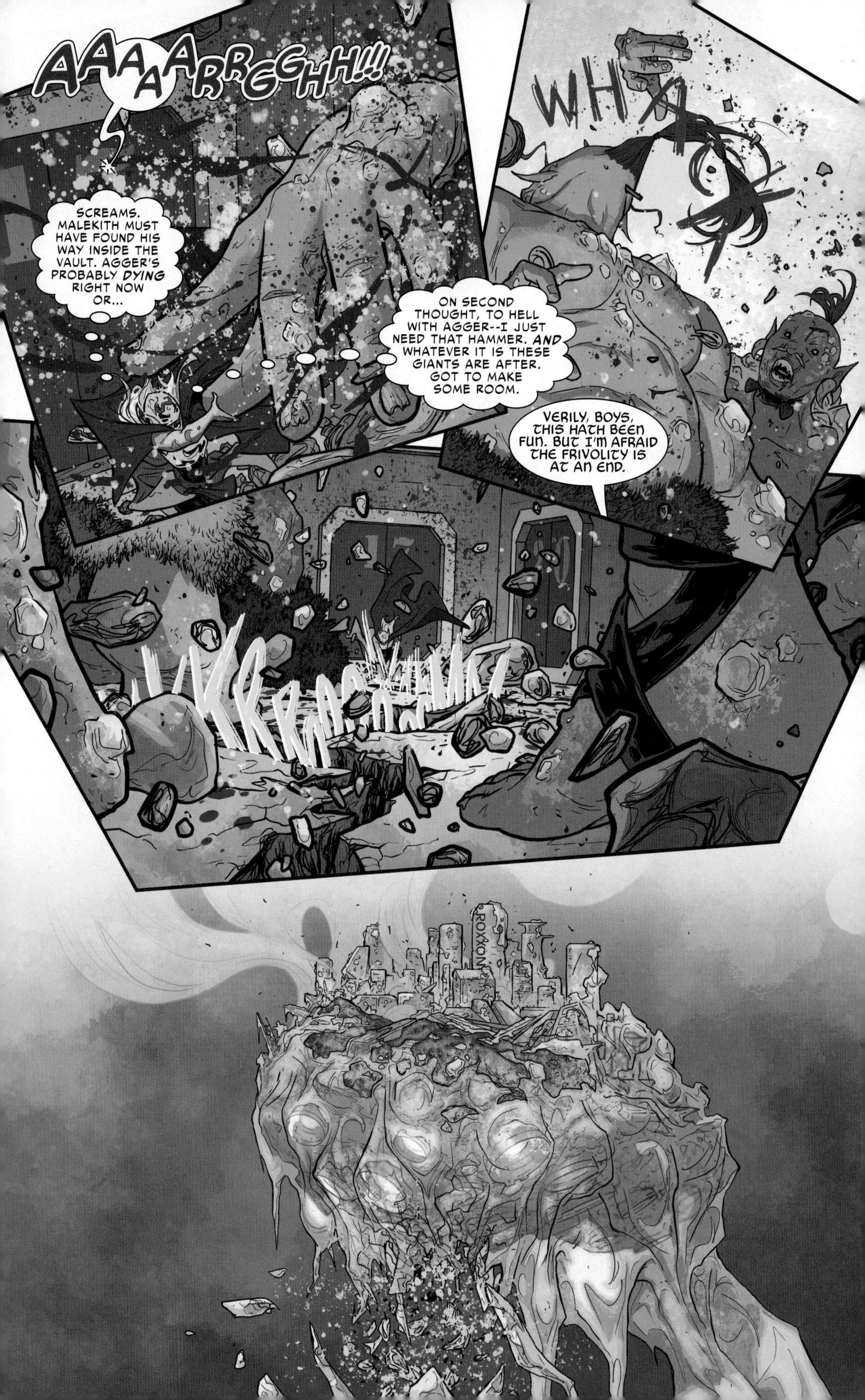
AAAAARRGGHH!!!
SCREAMS. MALEKITH MUST HAVE FOUND HIS WAY INSIDE THE VAULT. AGGER'S PROBABLY DYING RIGHT NOW OR...
ON SECOND THOUGHT, TO HELL WITH AGGER--I JUST NEED THAT HAMMER. AND WHATEVER IT IS THESE GIANTS ARE AFTER. GOT TO MAKE SOME ROOM.
WHA
VERILY, BOYS, THIS HATH BEEN FUN. BUT I'M AFRAID THE FRIVOLITY IS AT AN END.
KRAKOOM
ROXXON

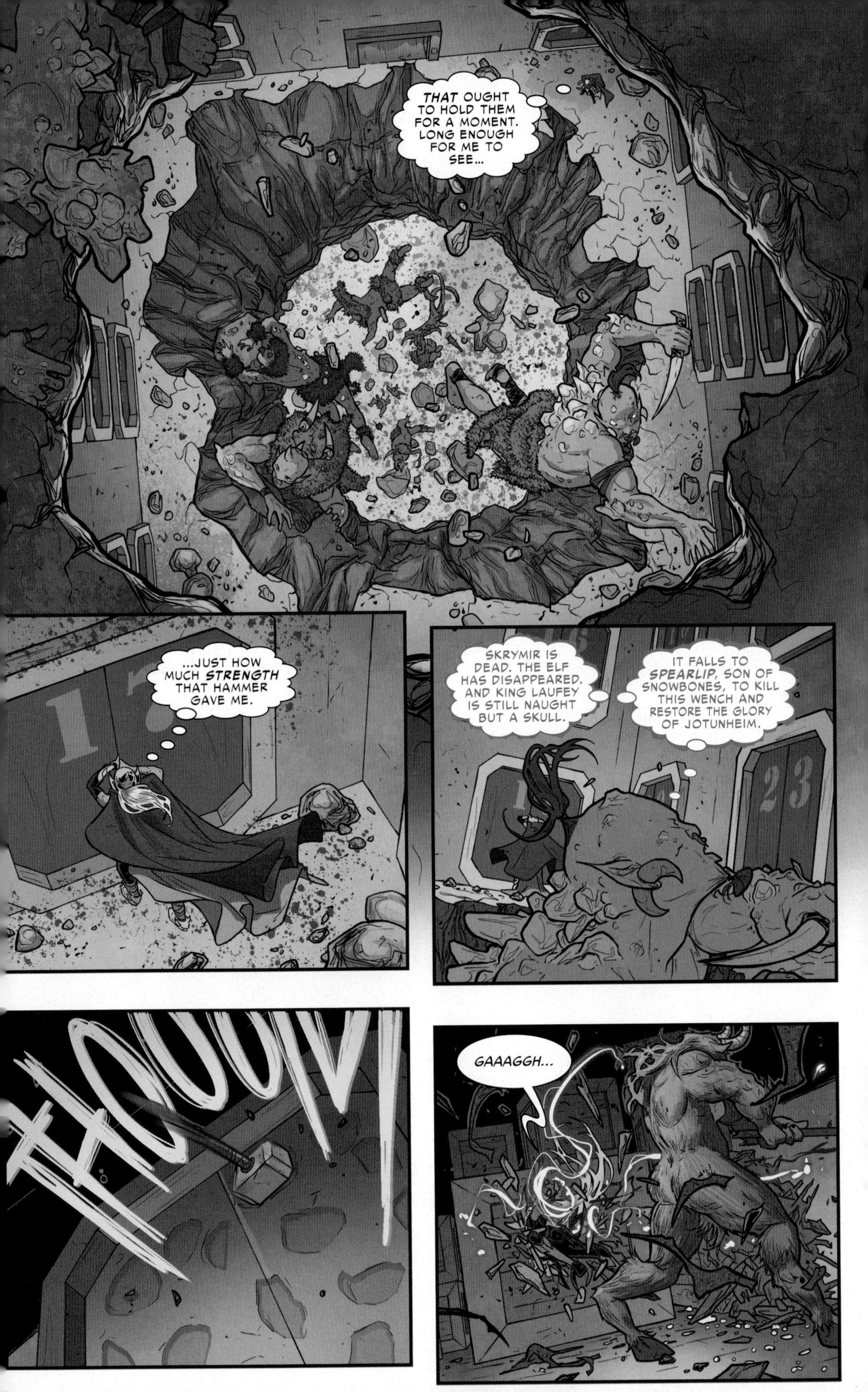
THAT OUGHT TO HOLD THEM FOR A MOMENT. LONG ENOUGH FOR ME TO SEE...
...JUST HOW MUCH STRENGTH THAT HAMMER GAVE ME.
SKRYMIR IS DEAD. THE ELF HAS DISAPPEARED. AND KING LAUFEY IS STILL NAUGHT BUT A SKULL.
IT FALLS TO SPEARLIP, SON OF SNOWBONES, TO KILL THIS WENCH AND RESTORE THE GLORY OF JOTUNHEIM.
THOOOM
GAAAGGH...

I WILL ROAST YOU ON A SPIT, YOU JUMPED-UP BOVINE. HOW *DARE* YOU LAY HANDS ON...ON...

OH, MY.

HHRRRRGHH

HEH. GOOD THING I BROUGHT MY *BACKSTABBING* KNIFE.

NNNNGGH

STARTING TO CHANGE... NO, PLEASE... NOT YET...

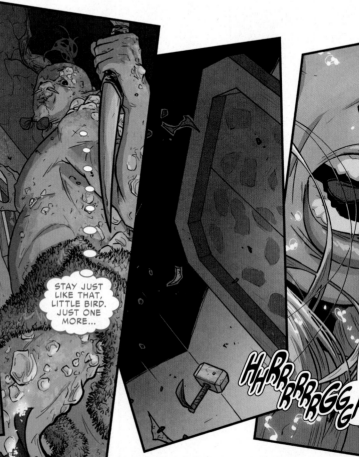

STAY JUST LIKE THAT, LITTLE BIRD. JUST ONE MORE...

HHRRRRRRGGGHH!

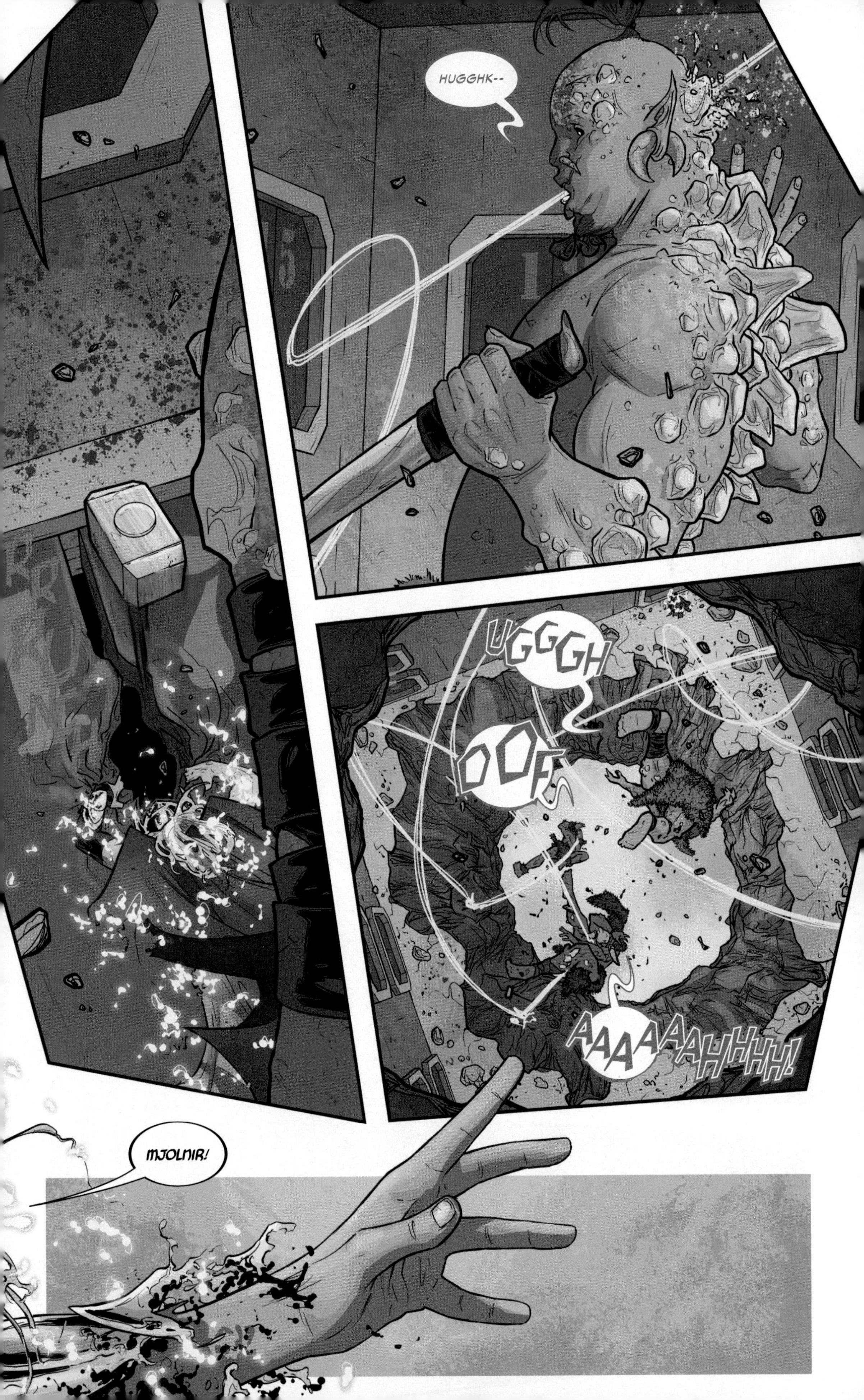
HUGGHK--
UGGGH
OOF
AAAAAAHHHHH!
MJOLNIR!

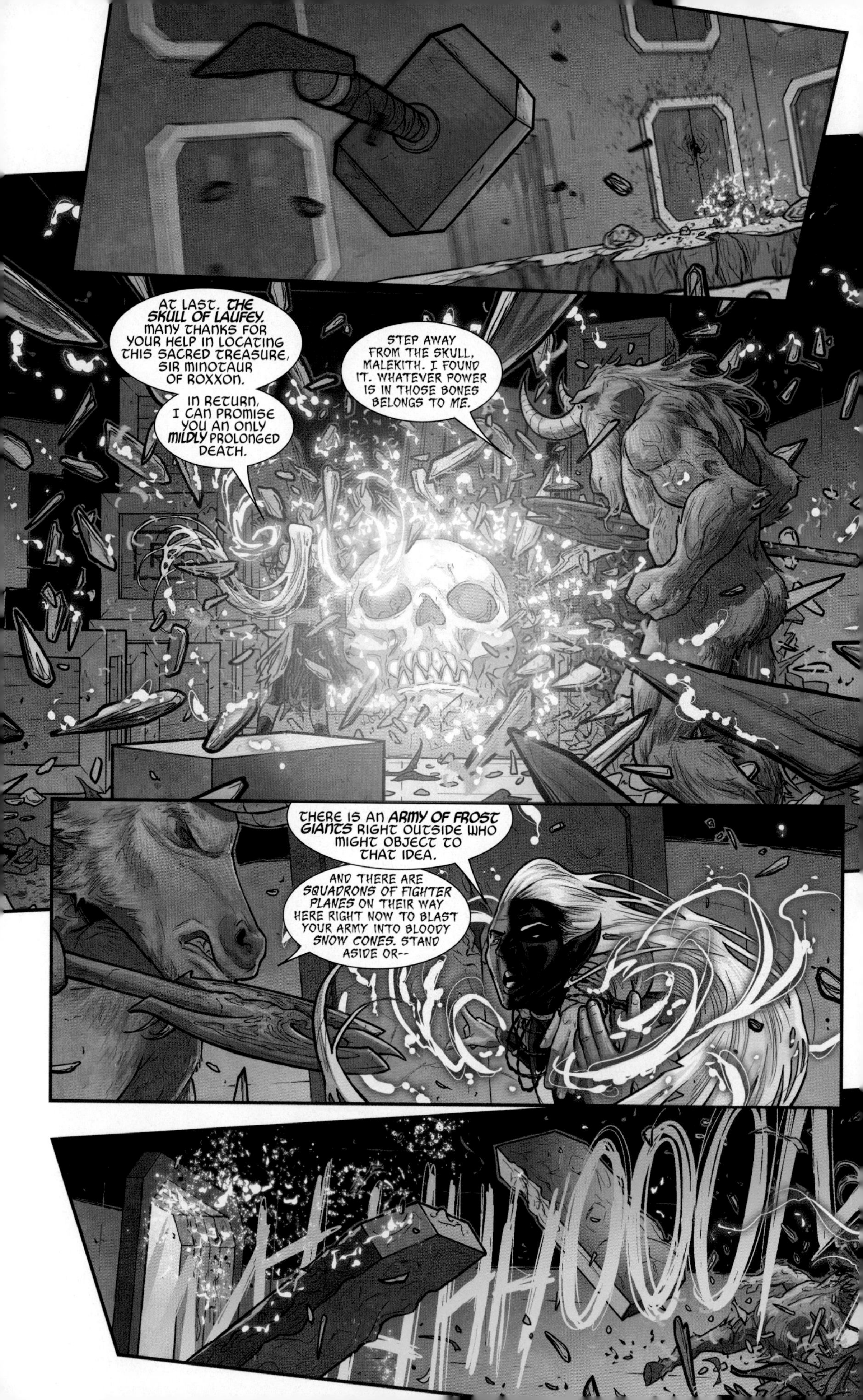
AT LAST. THE SKULL OF LAUFEY. MANY THANKS FOR YOUR HELP IN LOCATING THIS SACRED TREASURE, SIR MINOTAUR OF ROXXON.
IN RETURN, I CAN PROMISE YOU AN ONLY MILDLY PROLONGED DEATH.
STEP AWAY FROM THE SKULL, MALEKITH. I FOUND IT. WHATEVER POWER IS IN THOSE BONES BELONGS TO ME.
THERE IS AN ARMY OF FROST GIANTS RIGHT OUTSIDE WHO MIGHT OBJECT TO THAT IDEA.
AND THERE ARE SQUADRONS OF FIGHTER PLANES ON THEIR WAY HERE RIGHT NOW TO BLAST YOUR ARMY INTO BLOODY SNOW CONES. STAND ASIDE OR--

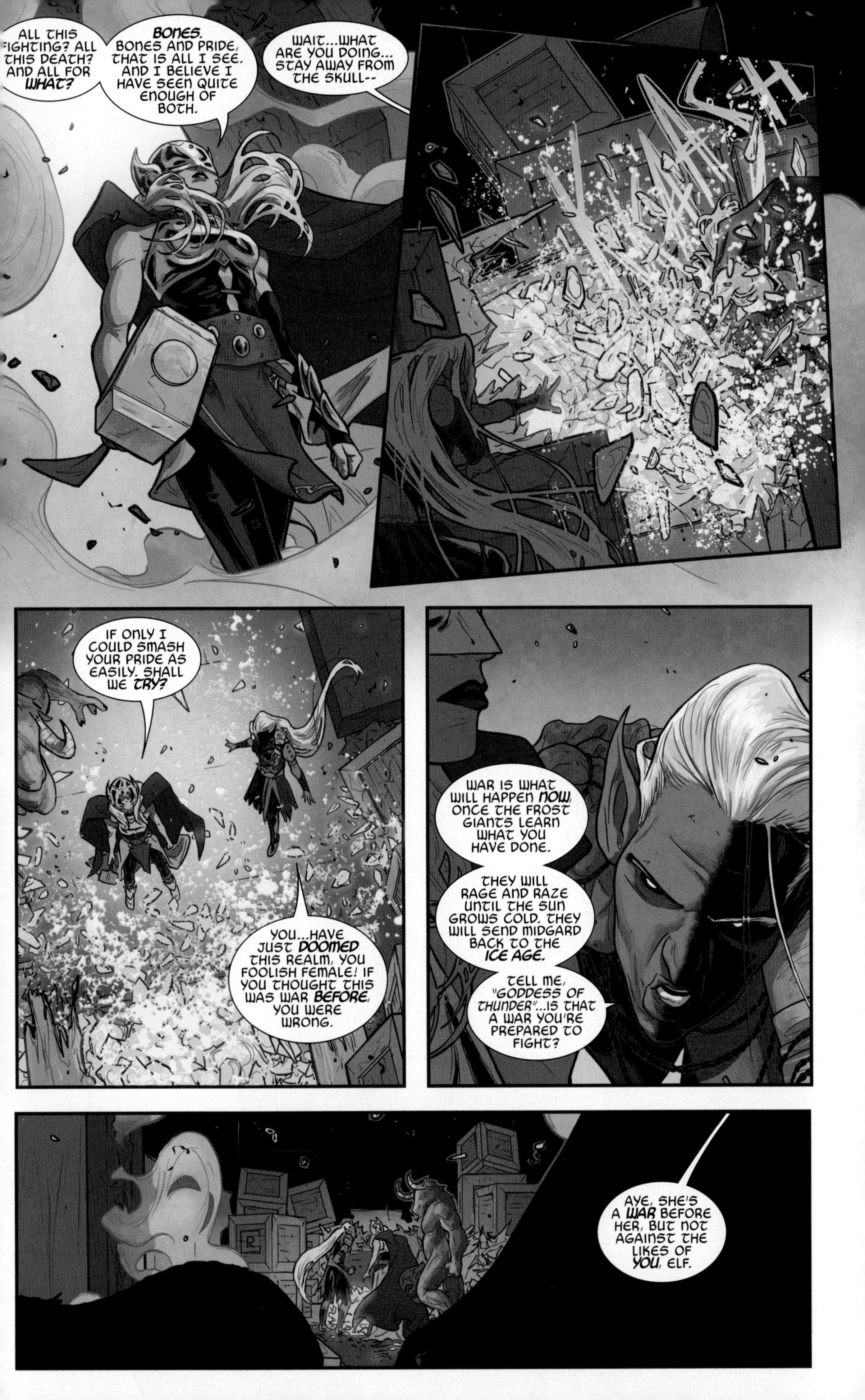
ALL THIS FIGHTING? ALL THIS DEATH? AND ALL FOR WHAT?
BONES. BONES AND PRIDE, THAT IS ALL I SEE. AND I BELIEVE I HAVE SEEN QUITE ENOUGH OF BOTH.
WAIT...WHAT ARE YOU DOING... STAY AWAY FROM THE SKULL--
IF ONLY I COULD SMASH YOUR PRIDE AS EASILY. SHALL WE TRY?
YOU...HAVE JUST DOOMED THIS REALM, YOU FOOLISH FEMALE! IF YOU THOUGHT THIS WAS WAR BEFORE, YOU WERE WRONG.
WAR IS WHAT WILL HAPPEN NOW, ONCE THE FROST GIANTS LEARN WHAT YOU HAVE DONE.
THEY WILL RAGE AND RAZE UNTIL THE SUN GROWS COLD. THEY WILL SEND MIDGARD BACK TO THE ICE AGE.
TELL ME, "GODDESS OF THUNDER"...IS THAT A WAR YOU'RE PREPARED TO FIGHT?
AYE, SHE'S A WAR BEFORE HER, BUT NOT AGAINST THE LIKES OF YOU, ELF.

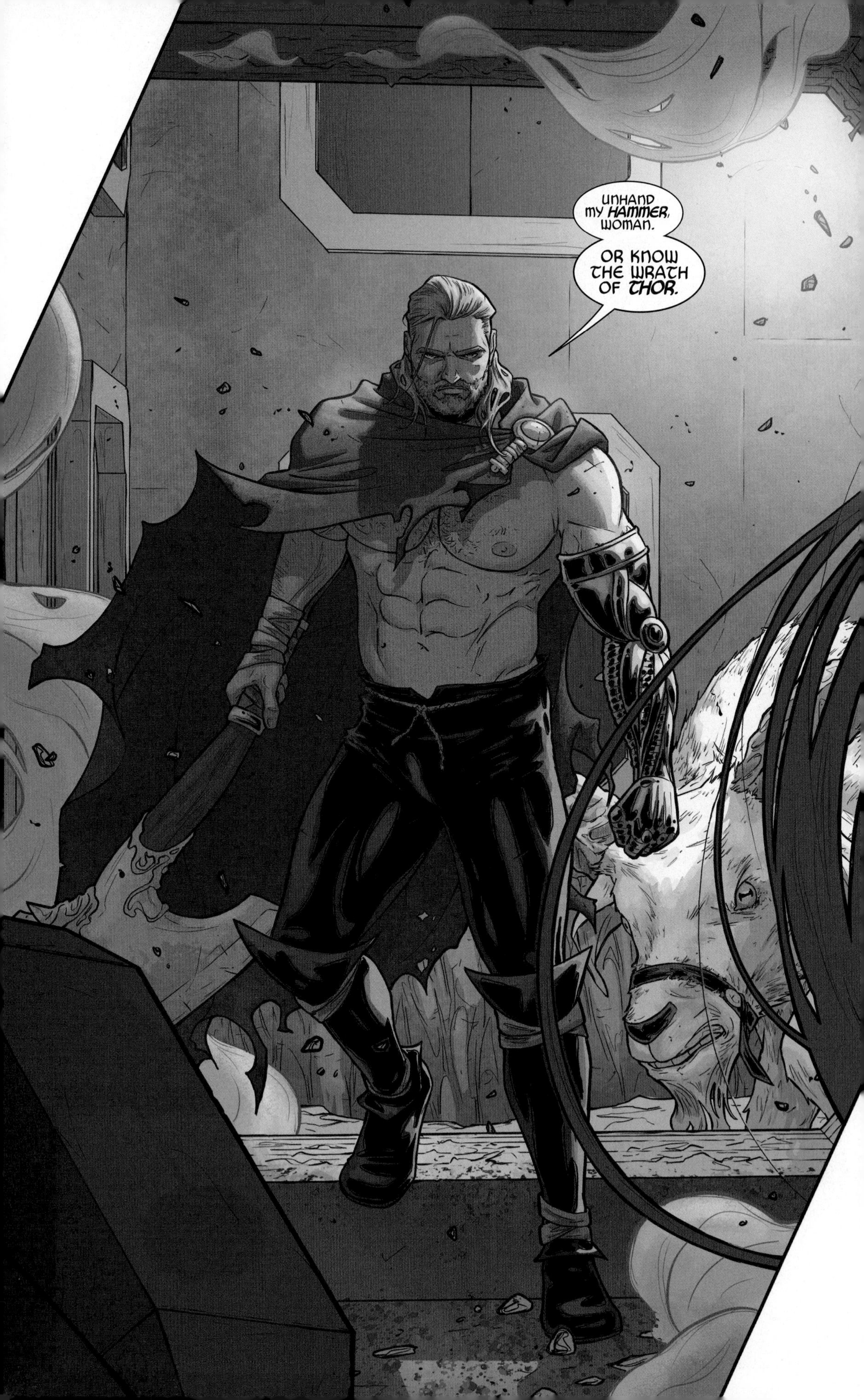
UNHAND MY HAMMER, WOMAN.
OR KNOW THE WRATH OF THOR.

4

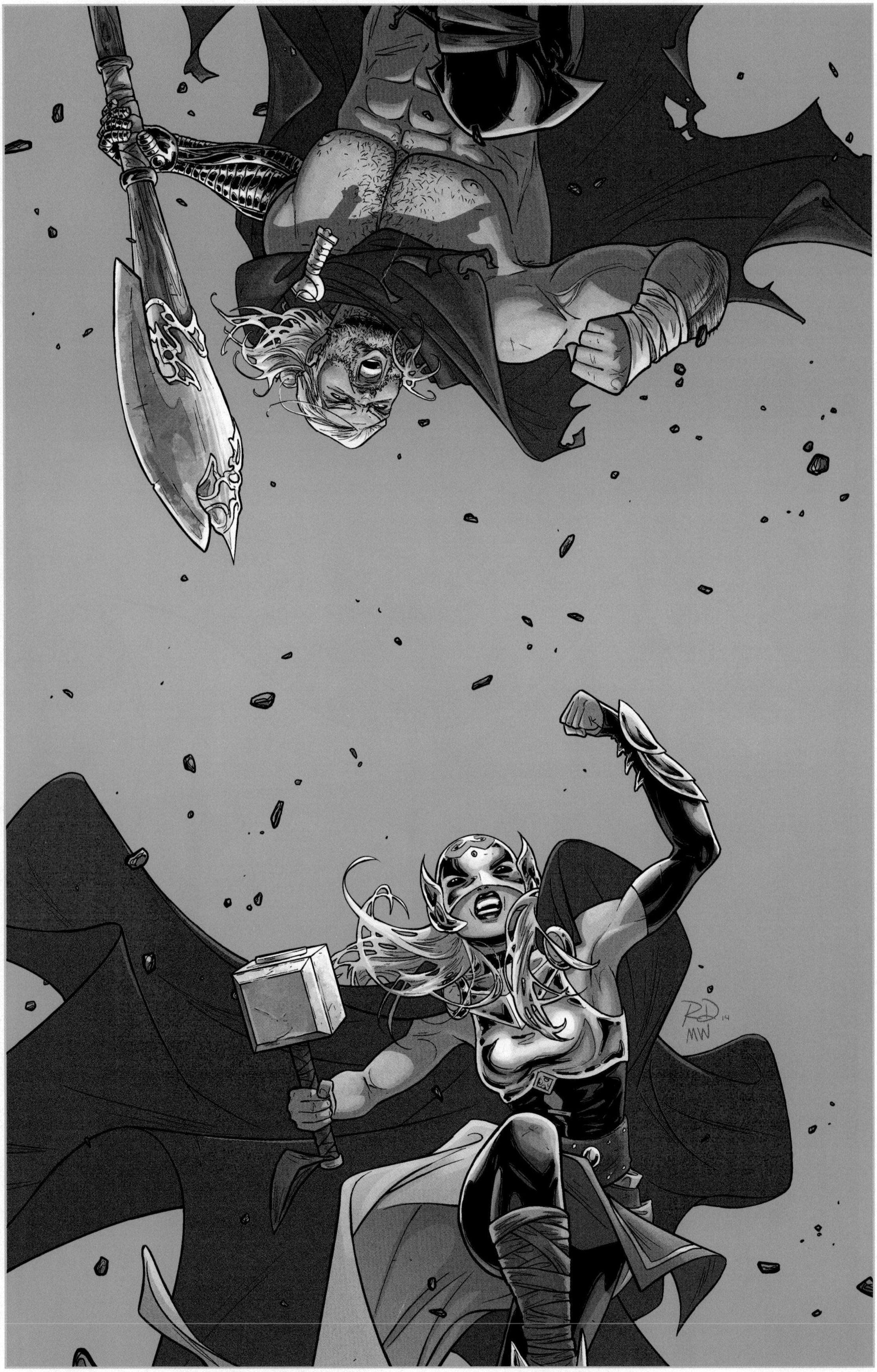
RD '14
MW

THOR VS. THOR

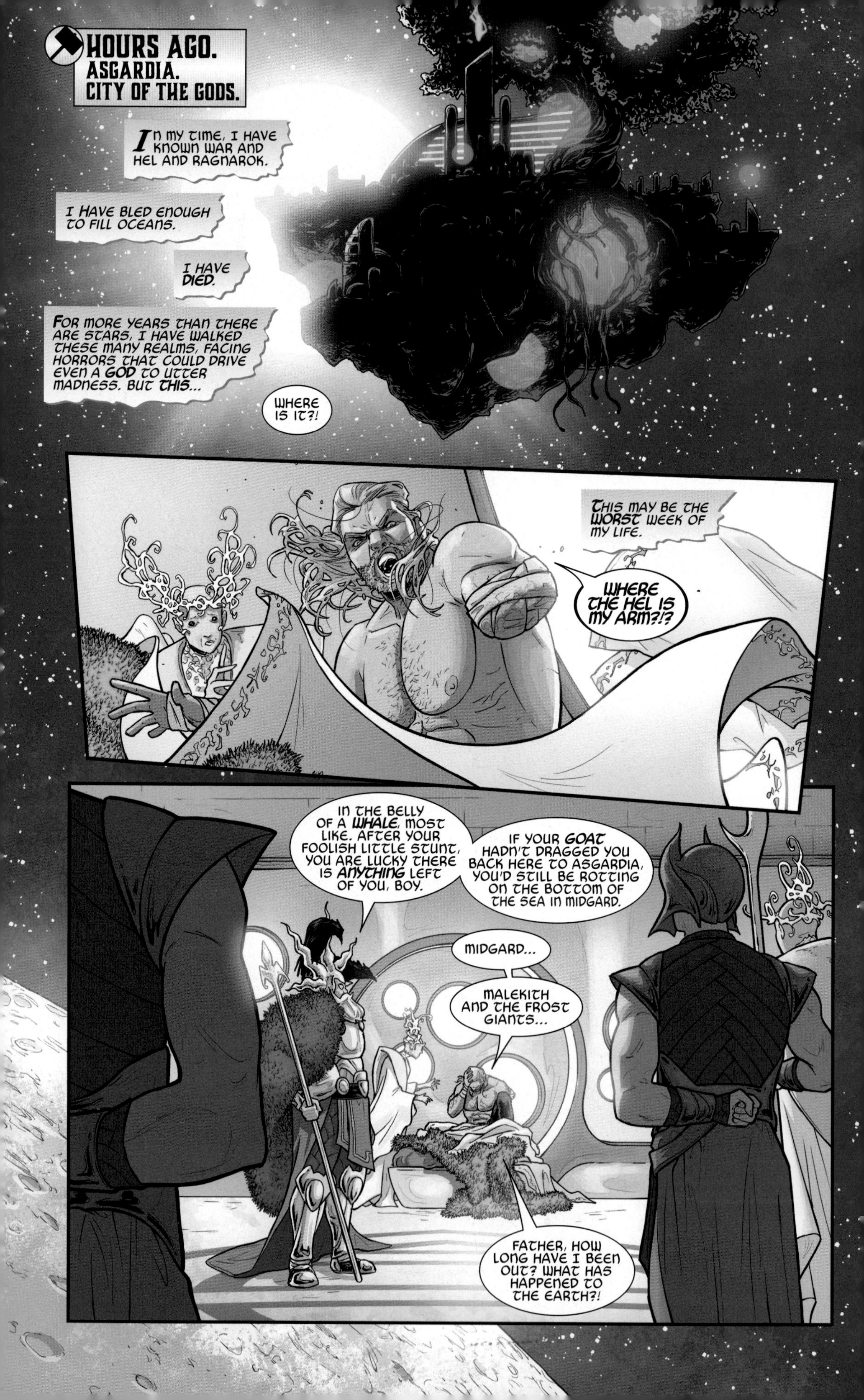
HOURS AGO. ASGARDIA. CITY OF THE GODS.
In my time, I have known war and Hel and Ragnarok.
I have bled enough to fill oceans.
I have died.
For more years than there are stars, I have walked these many realms, facing horrors that could drive even a god to utter madness. But this...
Where is it?!
This may be the worst week of my life.
Where the Hel is my arm?!?
In the belly of a whale, most like. After your foolish little stunt, you are lucky there is anything left of you, boy.
If your goat hadn't dragged you back here to Asgardia, you'd still be rotting on the bottom of the sea in Midgard.
Midgard...
Malekith and the frost giants...
Father, how long have I been out? What has happened to the Earth?!

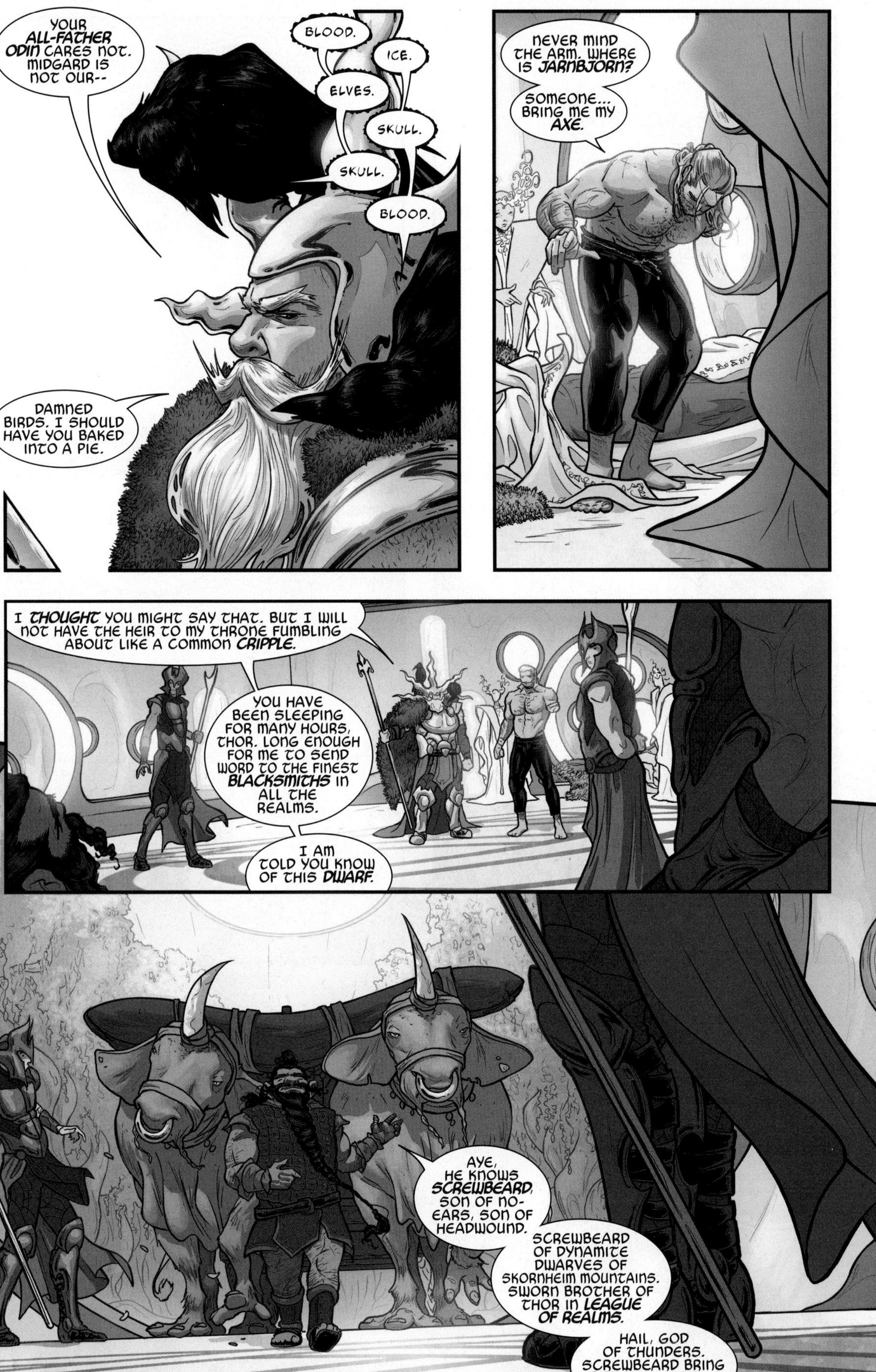
YOUR ALL-FATHER ODIN CARES NOT. MIDGARD IS NOT OUR--
BLOOD.
ICE.
ELVES.
SKULL.
SKULL.
BLOOD.
DAMNED BIRDS. I SHOULD HAVE YOU BAKED INTO A PIE.
NEVER MIND THE ARM. WHERE IS JARNBJORN?
SOMEONE... BRING ME MY AXE.
I THOUGHT YOU MIGHT SAY THAT. BUT I WILL NOT HAVE THE HEIR TO MY THRONE FUMBLING ABOUT LIKE A COMMON CRIPPLE.
YOU HAVE BEEN SLEEPING FOR MANY HOURS, THOR. LONG ENOUGH FOR ME TO SEND WORD TO THE FINEST BLACKSMITHS IN ALL THE REALMS.
I AM TOLD YOU KNOW OF THIS DWARF.
AYE, HE KNOWS SCREWBEARD, SON OF NO-EARS, SON OF HEADWOUND.
SCREWBEARD OF DYNAMITE DWARVES OF SKORNHEIM MOUNTAINS. SWORN BROTHER OF THOR IN LEAGUE OF REALMS.
HAIL, GOD OF THUNDERS. SCREWBEARD BRING GIFT FROM DWARVES OF NIDAVELLIR.

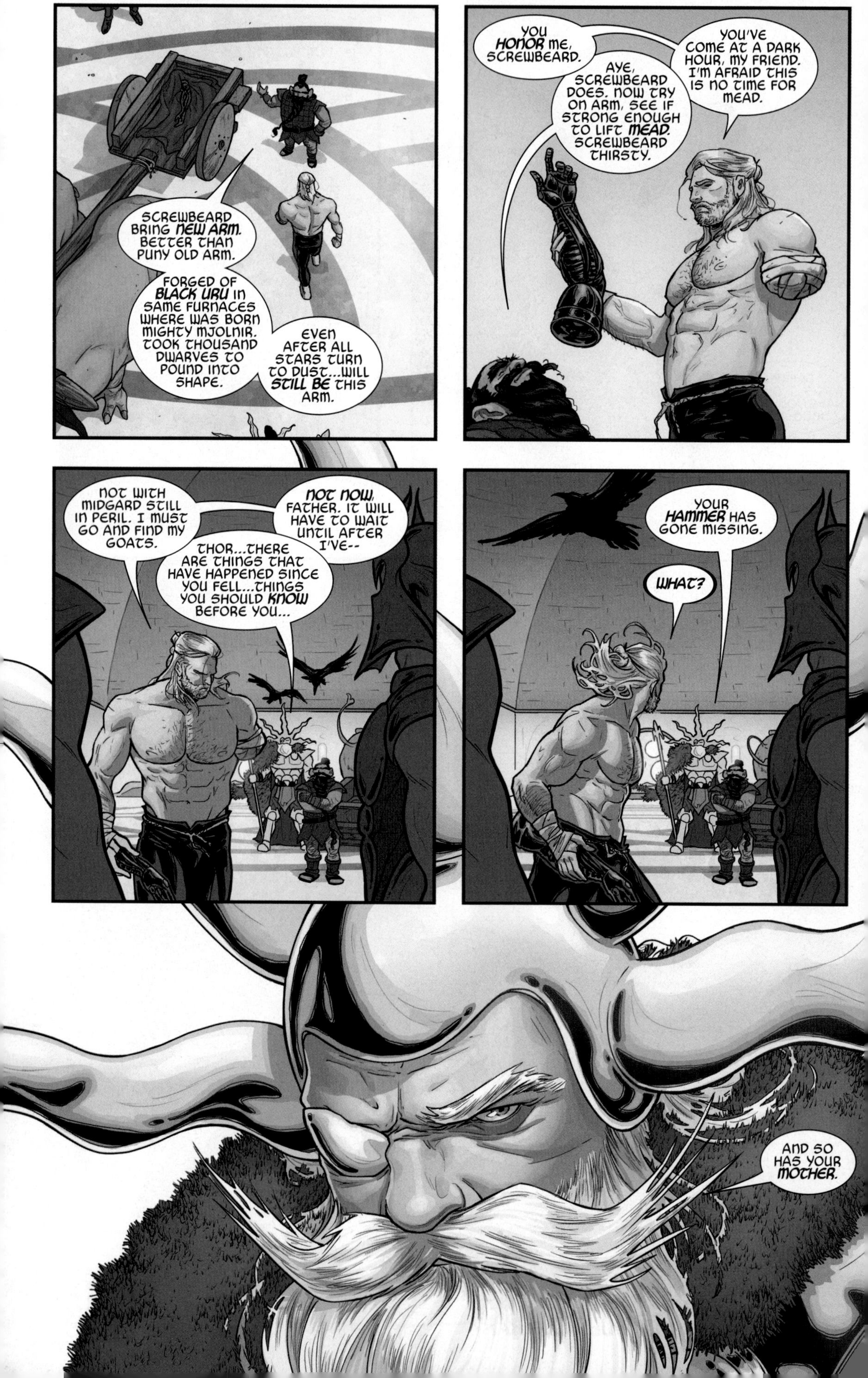
SCREWBEARD BRING NEW ARM. BETTER THAN PUNY OLD ARM.
FORGED OF BLACK URU IN SAME FURNACES WHERE WAS BORN MIGHTY MJOLNIR. TOOK THOUSAND DWARVES TO POUND INTO SHAPE.
EVEN AFTER ALL STARS TURN TO DUST...WILL STILL BE THIS ARM.
YOU HONOR ME, SCREWBEARD.
YOU'VE COME AT A DARK HOUR, MY FRIEND. I'M AFRAID THIS IS NO TIME FOR MEAD.
AYE, SCREWBEARD DOES. NOW TRY ON ARM, SEE IF STRONG ENOUGH TO LIFT MEAD. SCREWBEARD THIRSTY.
NOT WITH MIDGARD STILL IN PERIL. I MUST GO AND FIND MY GOATS.
NOT NOW, FATHER. IT WILL HAVE TO WAIT UNTIL AFTER I'VE--
THOR...THERE ARE THINGS THAT HAVE HAPPENED SINCE YOU FELL...THINGS YOU SHOULD KNOW BEFORE YOU...
YOUR HAMMER HAS GONE MISSING.
WHAT?
AND SO HAS YOUR MOTHER.

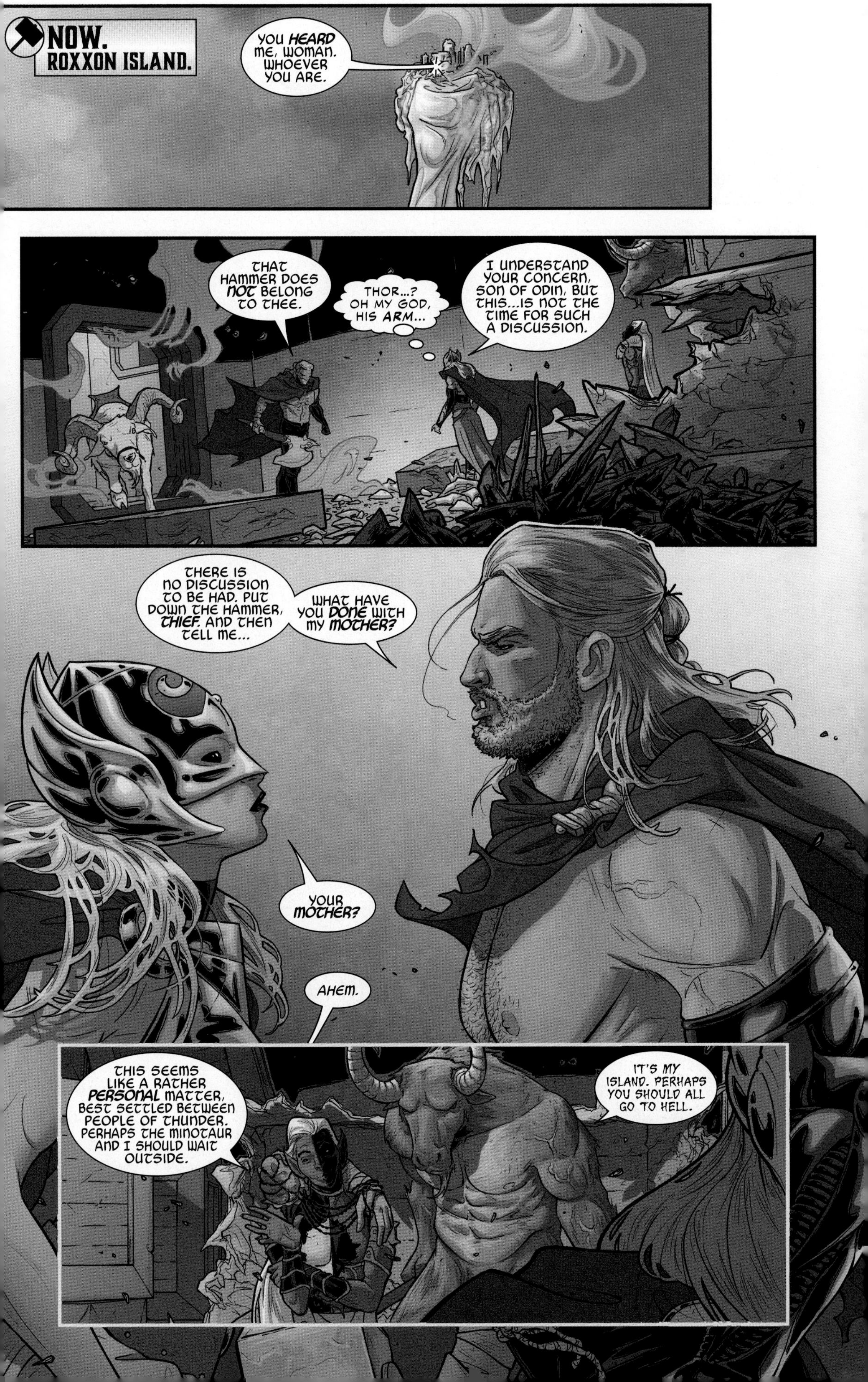
NOW.
ROXXON ISLAND.
YOU HEARD ME, WOMAN. WHOEVER YOU ARE.
THAT HAMMER DOES NOT BELONG TO THEE.
THOR...? OH MY GOD, HIS ARM...
I UNDERSTAND YOUR CONCERN, SON OF ODIN, BUT THIS...IS NOT THE TIME FOR SUCH A DISCUSSION.
THERE IS NO DISCUSSION TO BE HAD. PUT DOWN THE HAMMER, THIEF. AND THEN TELL ME...
WHAT HAVE YOU DONE WITH MY MOTHER?
YOUR MOTHER?
AHEM.
THIS SEEMS LIKE A RATHER PERSONAL MATTER, BEST SETTLED BETWEEN PEOPLE OF THUNDER. PERHAPS THE MINOTAUR AND I SHOULD WAIT OUTSIDE.
IT'S MY ISLAND. PERHAPS YOU SHOULD ALL GO TO HELL.

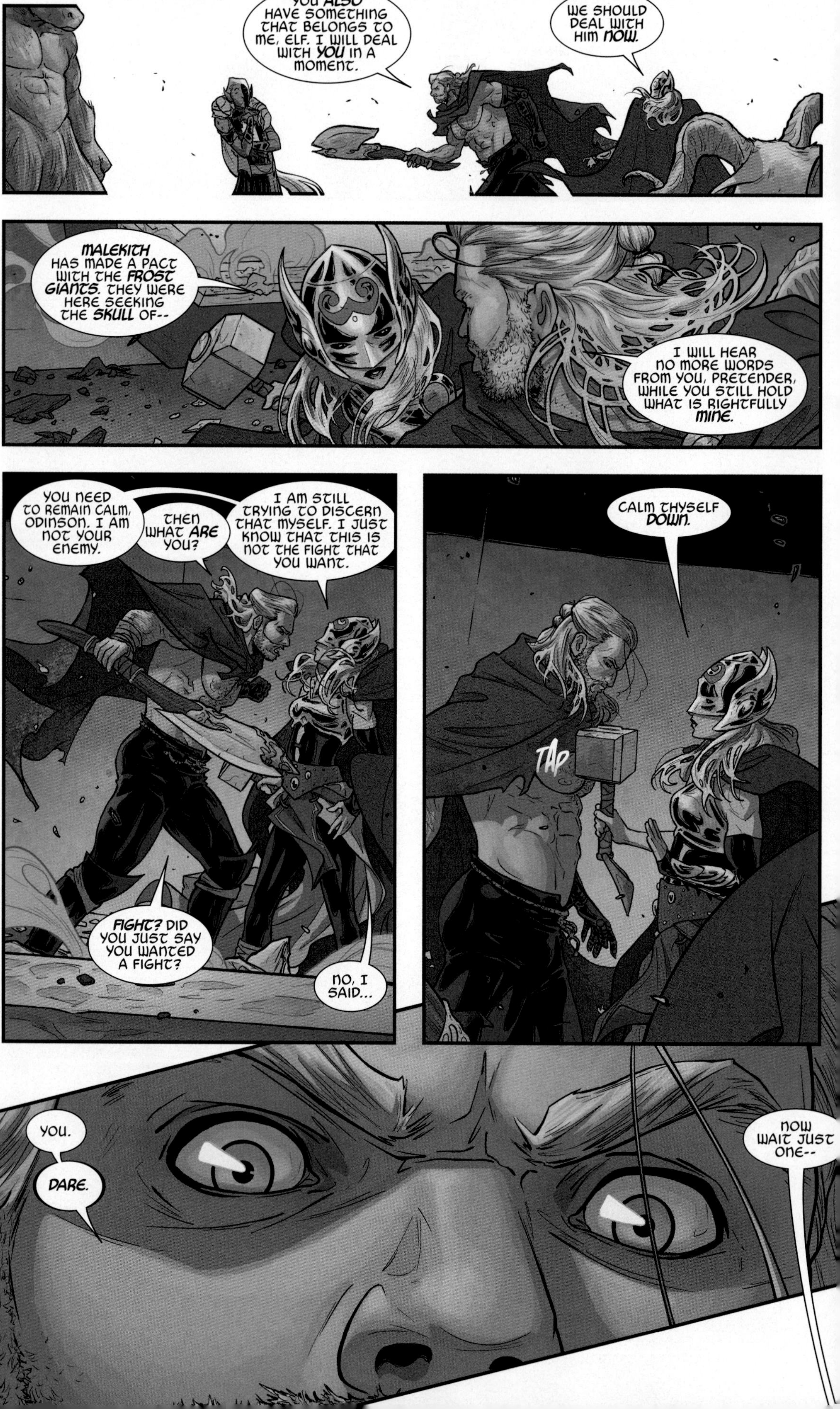
YOU ALSO HAVE SOMETHING THAT BELONGS TO ME, ELF. I WILL DEAL WITH YOU IN A MOMENT.
WE SHOULD DEAL WITH HIM NOW.
MALEKITH HAS MADE A PACT WITH THE FROST GIANTS. THEY WERE HERE SEEKING THE SKULL OF--
I WILL HEAR NO MORE WORDS FROM YOU, PRETENDER, WHILE YOU STILL HOLD WHAT IS RIGHTFULLY MINE.
YOU NEED TO REMAIN CALM, ODINSON. I AM NOT YOUR ENEMY.
THEN WHAT ARE YOU?
I AM STILL TRYING TO DISCERN THAT MYSELF. I JUST KNOW THAT THIS IS NOT THE FIGHT THAT YOU WANT.
FIGHT? DID YOU JUST SAY YOU WANTED A FIGHT?
NO, I SAID...
CALM THYSELF DOWN.
TAP
YOU.
DARE.
NOW WAIT JUST ONE--

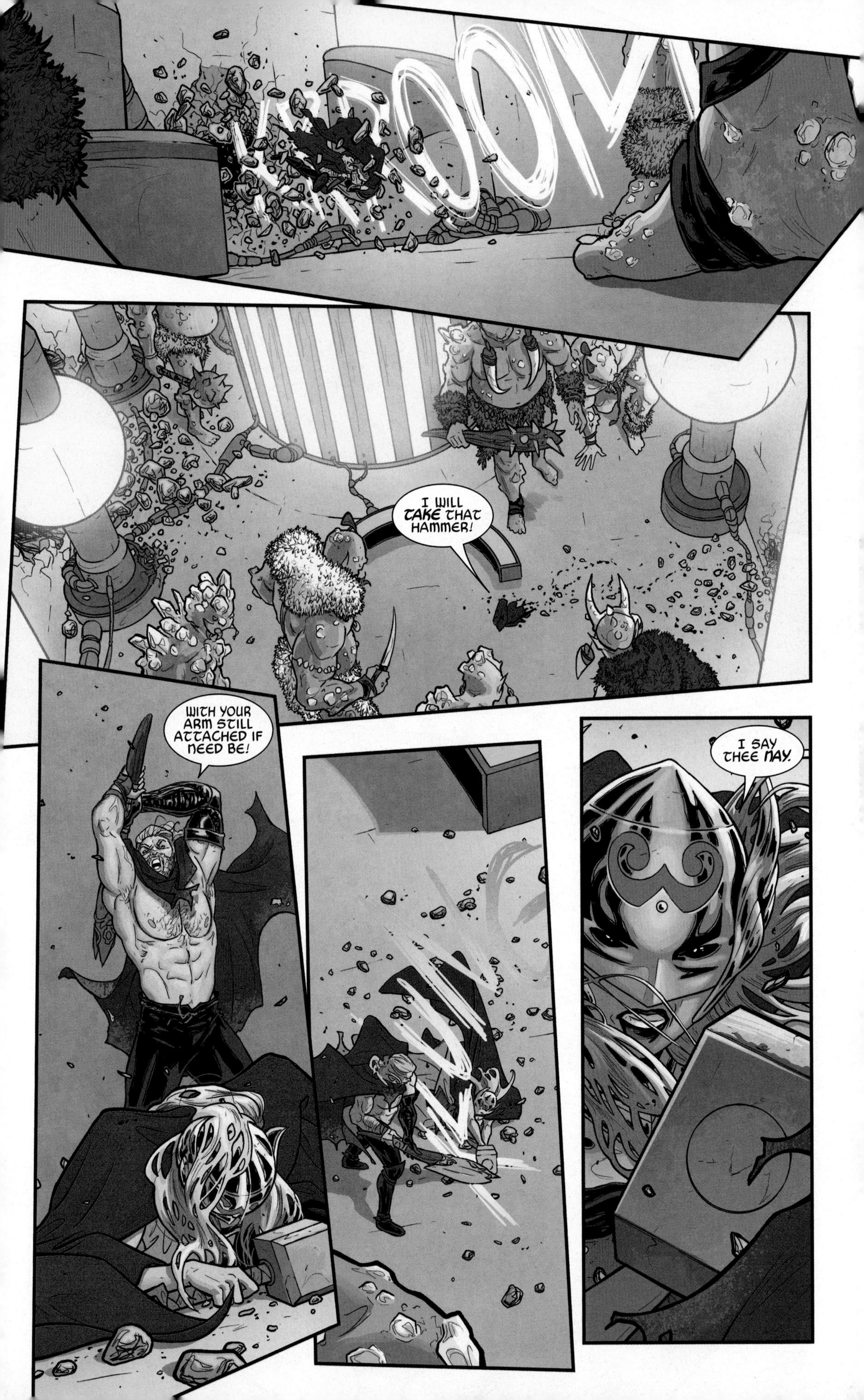
KRAAOOM
I WILL TAKE THAT HAMMER!
WITH YOUR ARM STILL ATTACHED IF NEED BE!
I SAY THEE NAY.

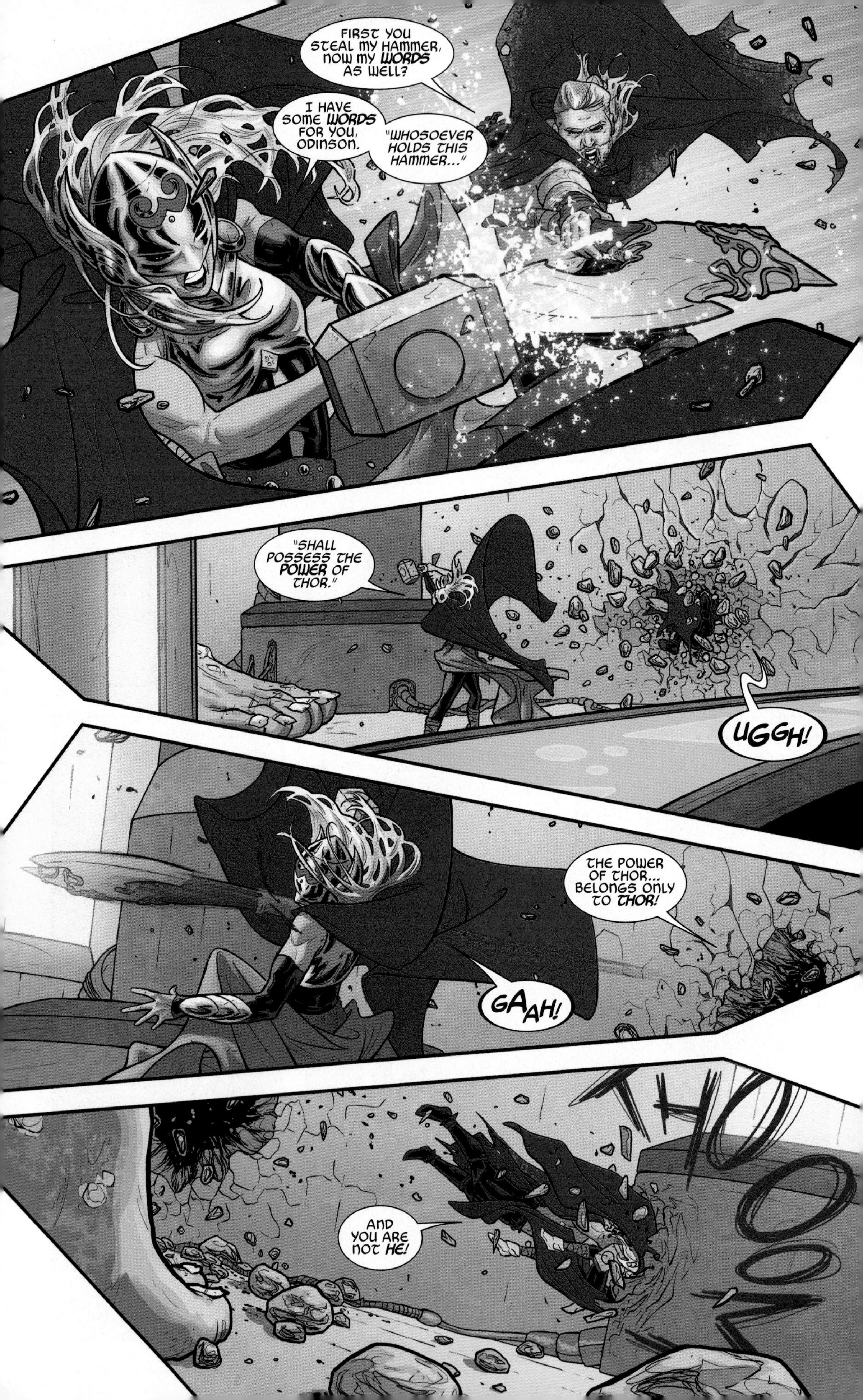

FIRST YOU STEAL MY HAMMER, NOW MY WORDS AS WELL?
I HAVE SOME WORDS FOR YOU, ODINSON.
"WHOSOEVER HOLDS THIS HAMMER..."
"SHALL POSSESS THE POWER OF THOR."
UGGH!
THE POWER OF THOR... BELONGS ONLY TO THOR!
GAAH!
AND YOU ARE NOT HE!
THOOOM

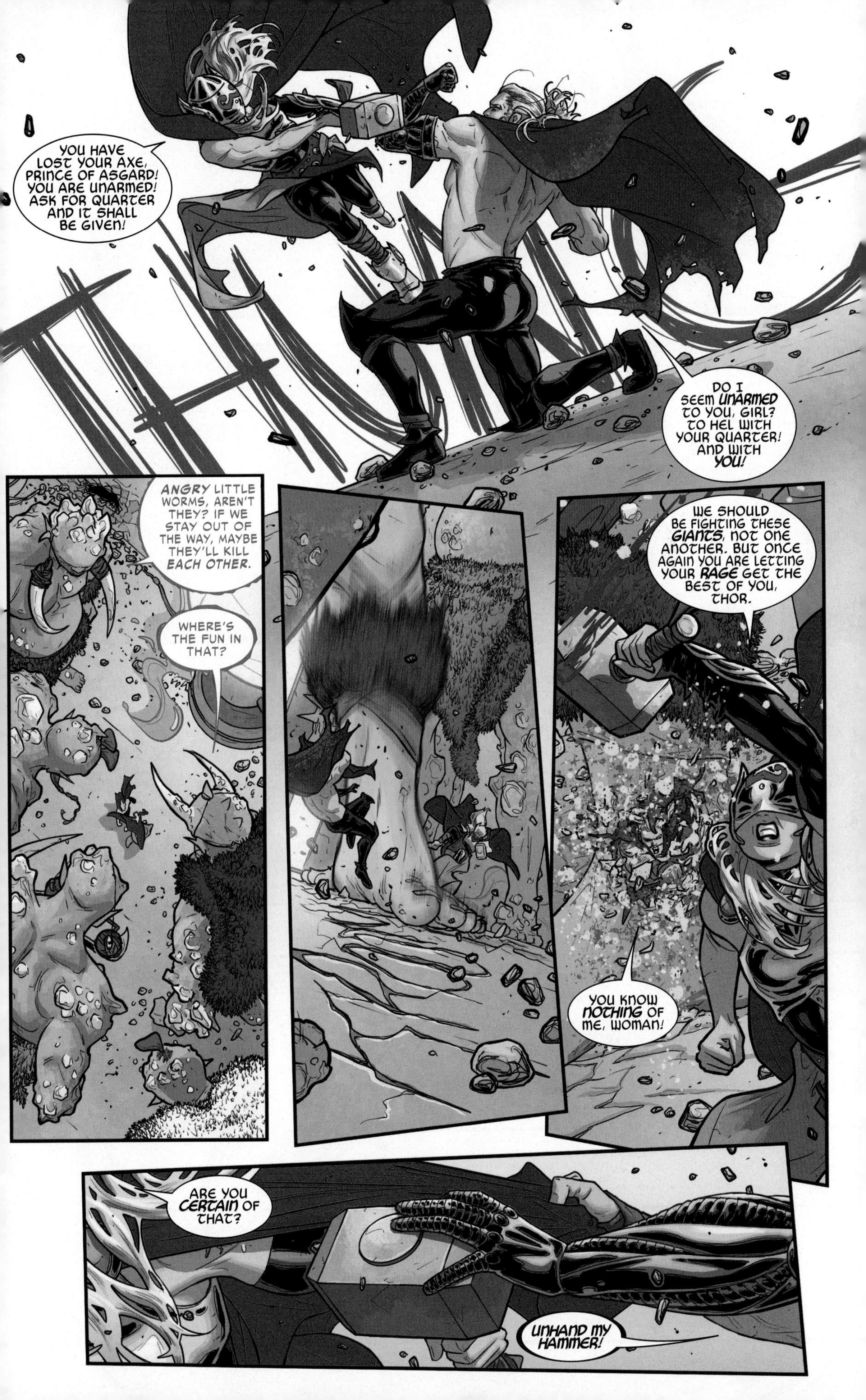

YOU HAVE LOST YOUR AXE, PRINCE OF ASGARD! YOU ARE UNARMED! ASK FOR QUARTER AND IT SHALL BE GIVEN!
THANG
DO I SEEM UNARMED TO YOU, GIRL? TO HEL WITH YOUR QUARTER! AND WITH YOU!
ANGRY LITTLE WORMS, AREN'T THEY? IF WE STAY OUT OF THE WAY, MAYBE THEY'LL KILL EACH OTHER.
WHERE'S THE FUN IN THAT?
WE SHOULD BE FIGHTING THESE GIANTS, NOT ONE ANOTHER. BUT ONCE AGAIN YOU ARE LETTING YOUR RAGE GET THE BEST OF YOU, THOR.
YOU KNOW NOTHING OF ME, WOMAN!
ARE YOU CERTAIN OF THAT?
UNHAND MY HAMMER!

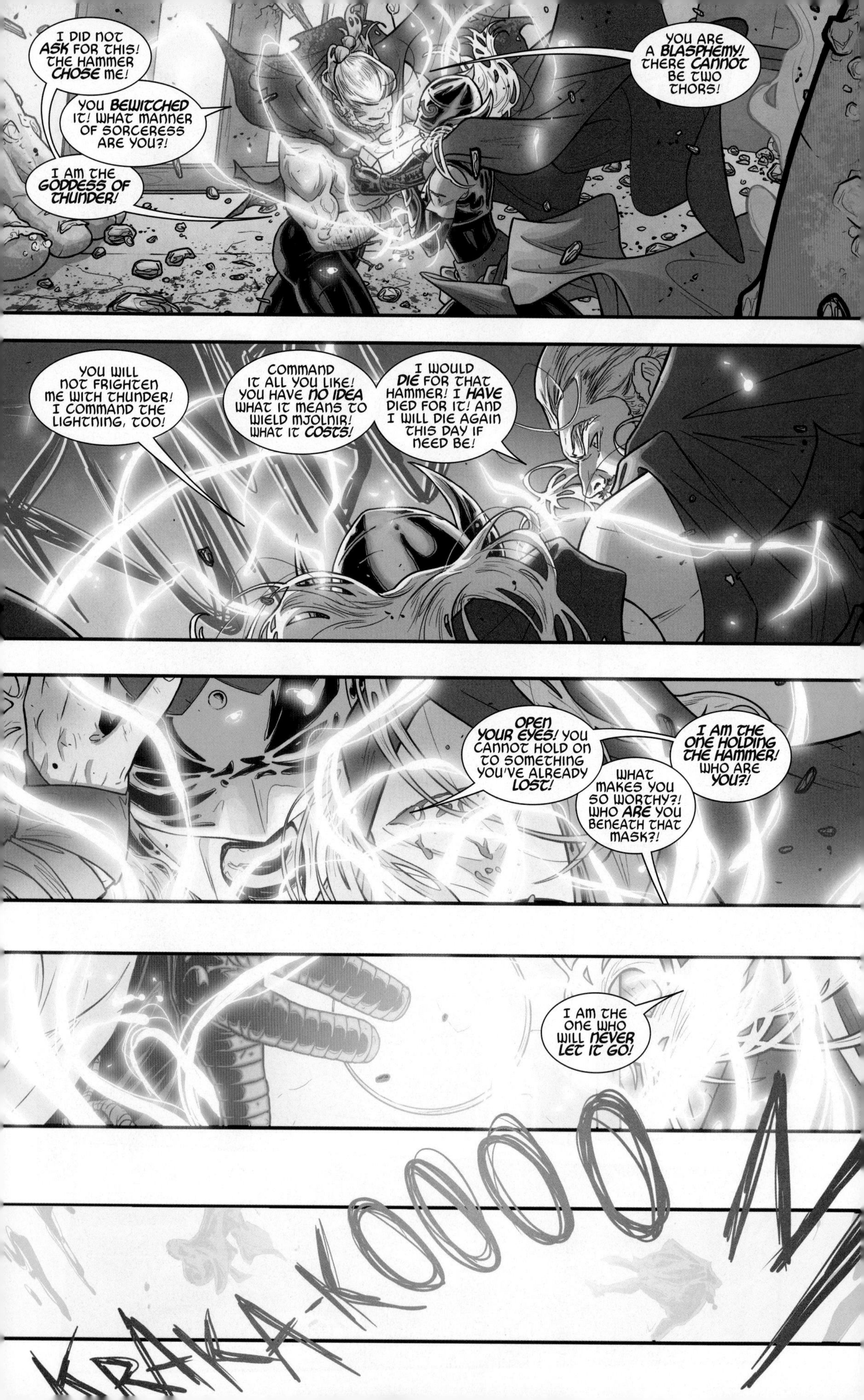
I DID NOT ASK FOR THIS! THE HAMMER CHOSE ME!
YOU BEWITCHED IT! WHAT MANNER OF SORCERESS ARE YOU?!
YOU ARE A BLASPHEMY! THERE CANNOT BE TWO THORS!
I AM THE GODDESS OF THUNDER!
YOU WILL NOT FRIGHTEN ME WITH THUNDER! I COMMAND THE LIGHTNING, TOO!
COMMAND IT ALL YOU LIKE! YOU HAVE NO IDEA WHAT IT MEANS TO WIELD MJOLNIR! WHAT IT COSTS!
I WOULD DIE FOR THAT HAMMER! I HAVE DIED FOR IT! AND I WILL DIE AGAIN THIS DAY IF NEED BE!
OPEN YOUR EYES! YOU CANNOT HOLD ON TO SOMETHING YOU'VE ALREADY LOST!
I AM THE ONE HOLDING THE HAMMER! WHO ARE YOU?!
WHAT MAKES YOU SO WORTHY?! WHO ARE YOU BENEATH THAT MASK?!
I AM THE ONE WHO WILL NEVER LET IT GO!
KRAKA-KOOOOOM

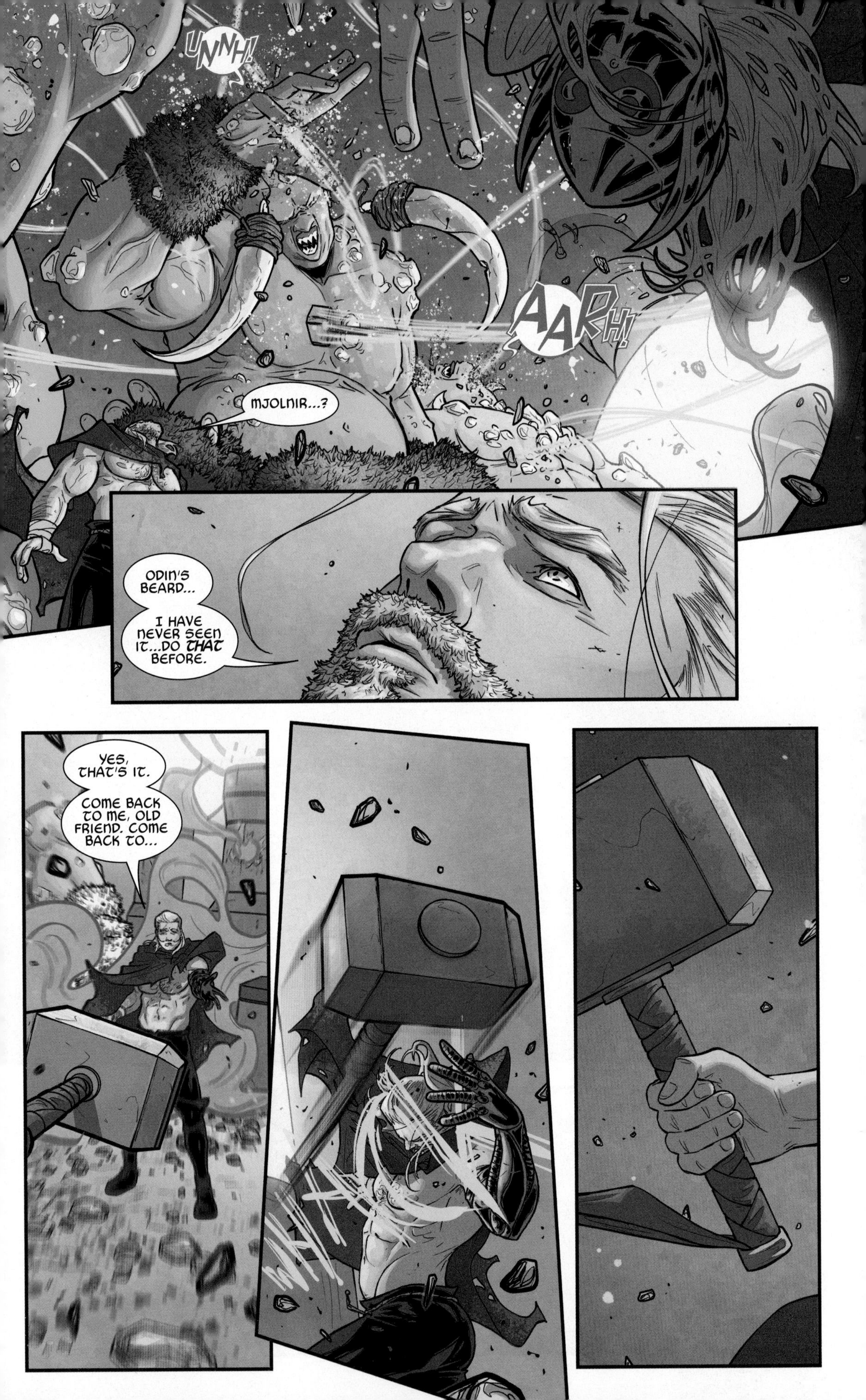
UNNH!
AARH!
MJOLNIR...?
ODIN'S BEARD...
I HAVE NEVER SEEN IT...DO *THAT* BEFORE.
YES, THAT'S IT.
COME BACK TO ME, OLD FRIEND. COME BACK TO...

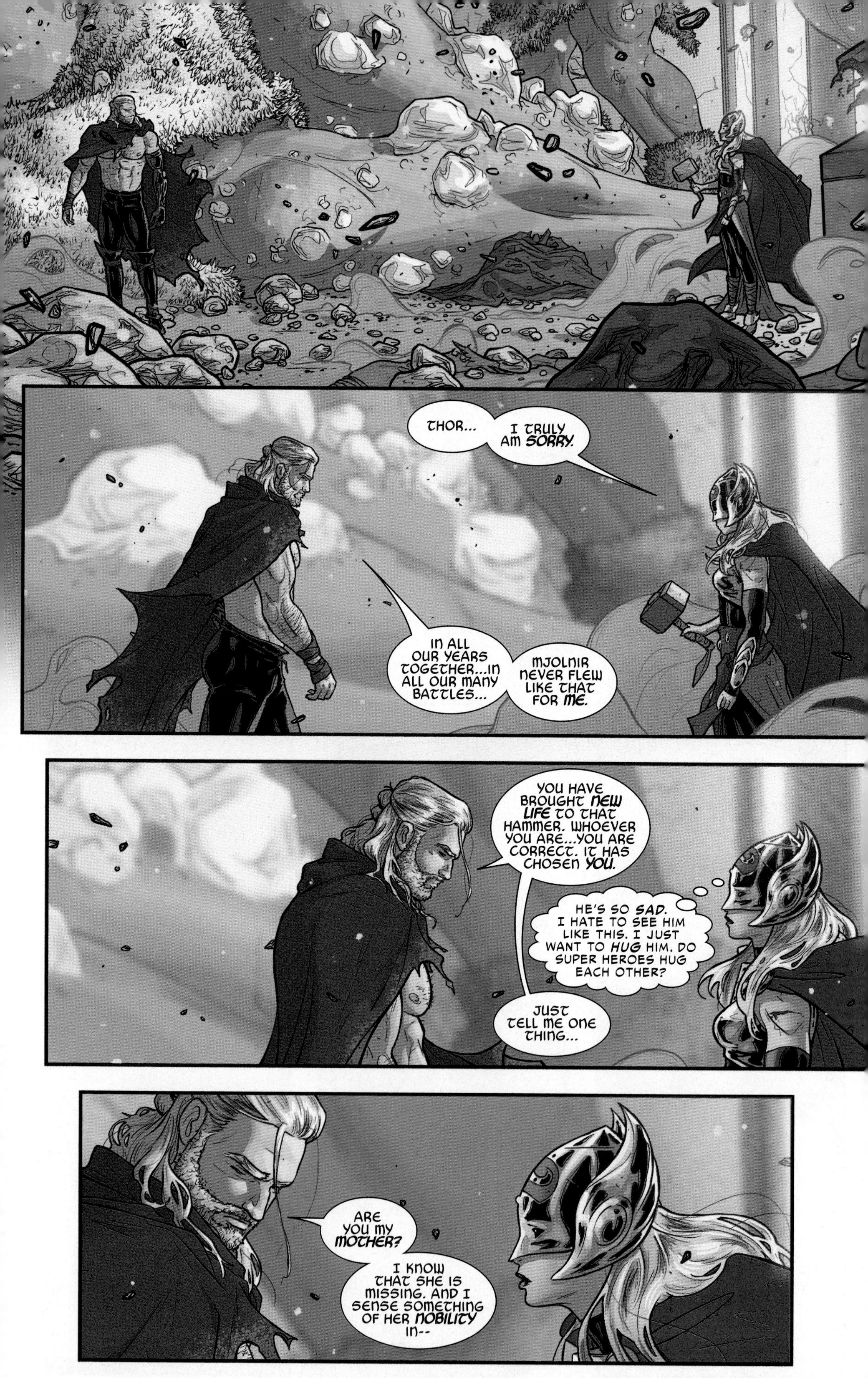
THOR...
I TRULY AM SORRY.
IN ALL OUR YEARS TOGETHER...IN ALL OUR MANY BATTLES...
MJOLNIR NEVER FLEW LIKE THAT FOR ME.
YOU HAVE BROUGHT NEW LIFE TO THAT HAMMER. WHOEVER YOU ARE...YOU ARE CORRECT. IT HAS CHOSEN YOU.
HE'S SO SAD. I HATE TO SEE HIM LIKE THIS. I JUST WANT TO HUG HIM. DO SUPER HEROES HUG EACH OTHER?
JUST TELL ME ONE THING...
ARE YOU MY MOTHER?
I KNOW THAT SHE IS MISSING. AND I SENSE SOMETHING OF HER NOBILITY IN--

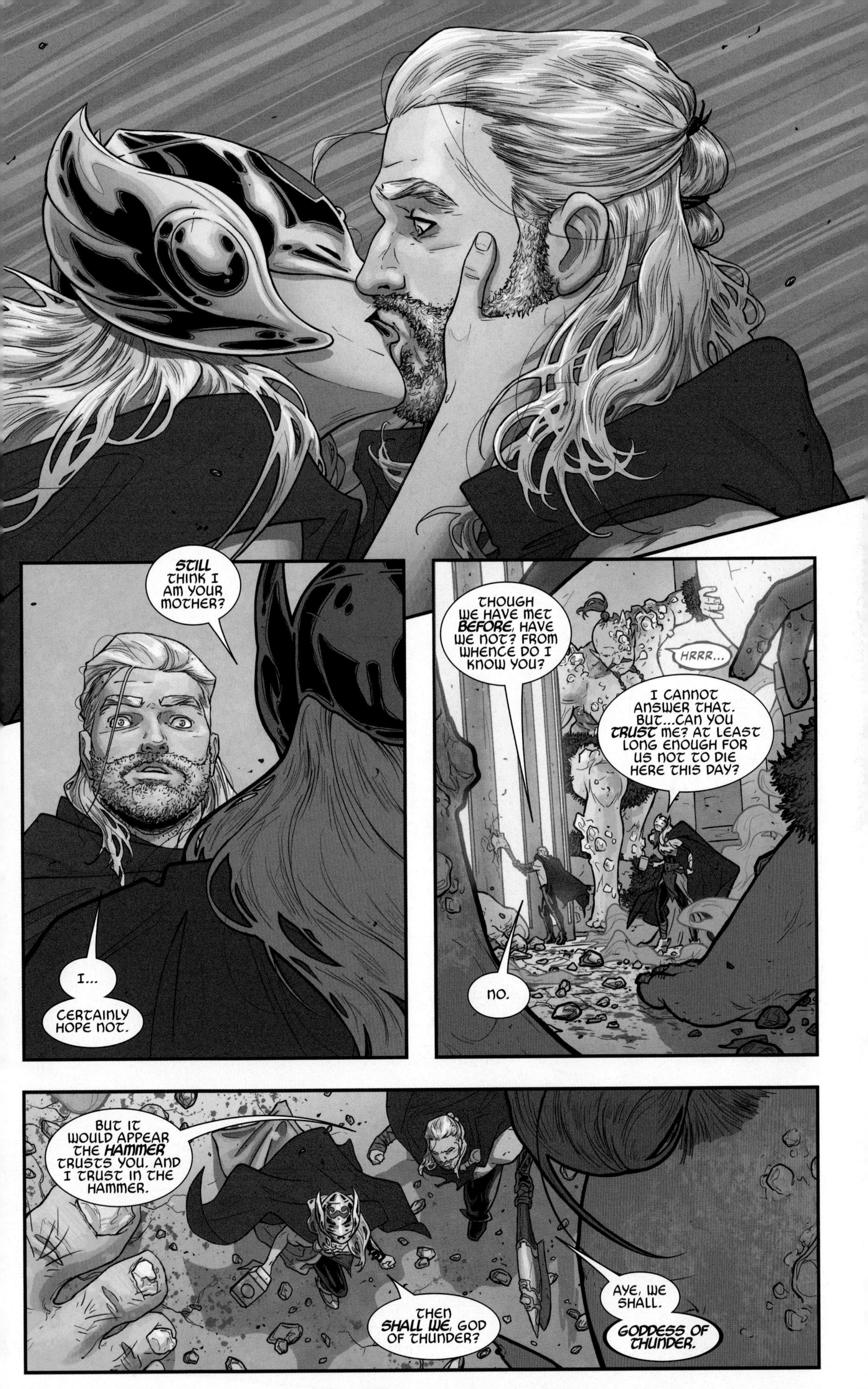
STILL THINK I AM YOUR MOTHER?
I... CERTAINLY HOPE NOT.
THOUGH WE HAVE MET BEFORE, HAVE WE NOT? FROM WHENCE DO I KNOW YOU?
HRRR...
I CANNOT ANSWER THAT. BUT...CAN YOU TRUST ME? AT LEAST LONG ENOUGH FOR US NOT TO DIE HERE THIS DAY?
NO.
BUT IT WOULD APPEAR THE HAMMER TRUSTS YOU. AND I TRUST IN THE HAMMER.
THEN SHALL WE, GOD OF THUNDER?
AYE, WE SHALL.
GODDESS OF THUNDER.

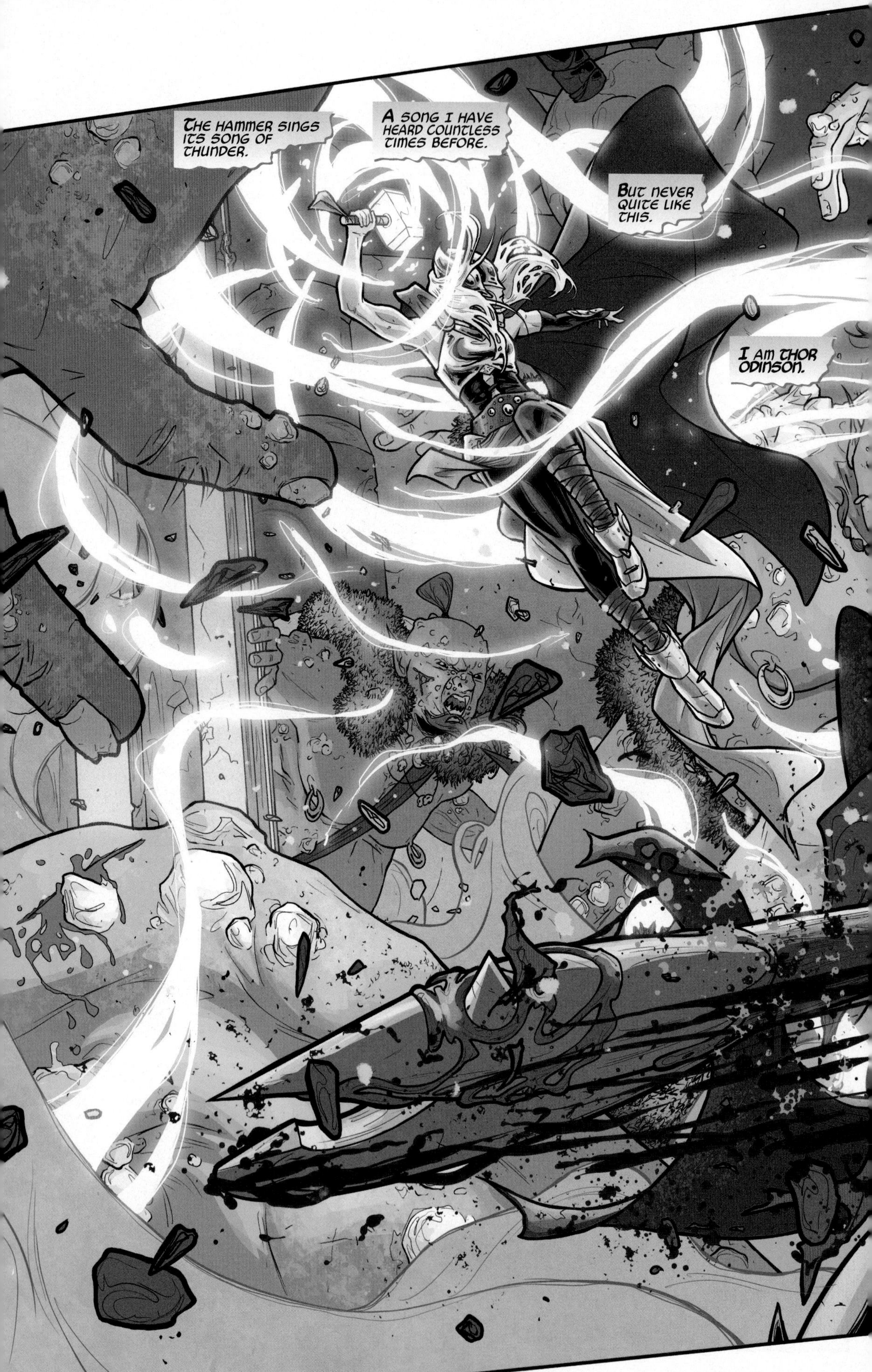
THE HAMMER SINGS ITS SONG OF THUNDER.
A SONG I HAVE HEARD COUNTLESS TIMES BEFORE.
BUT NEVER QUITE LIKE THIS.
I AM THOR ODINSON.

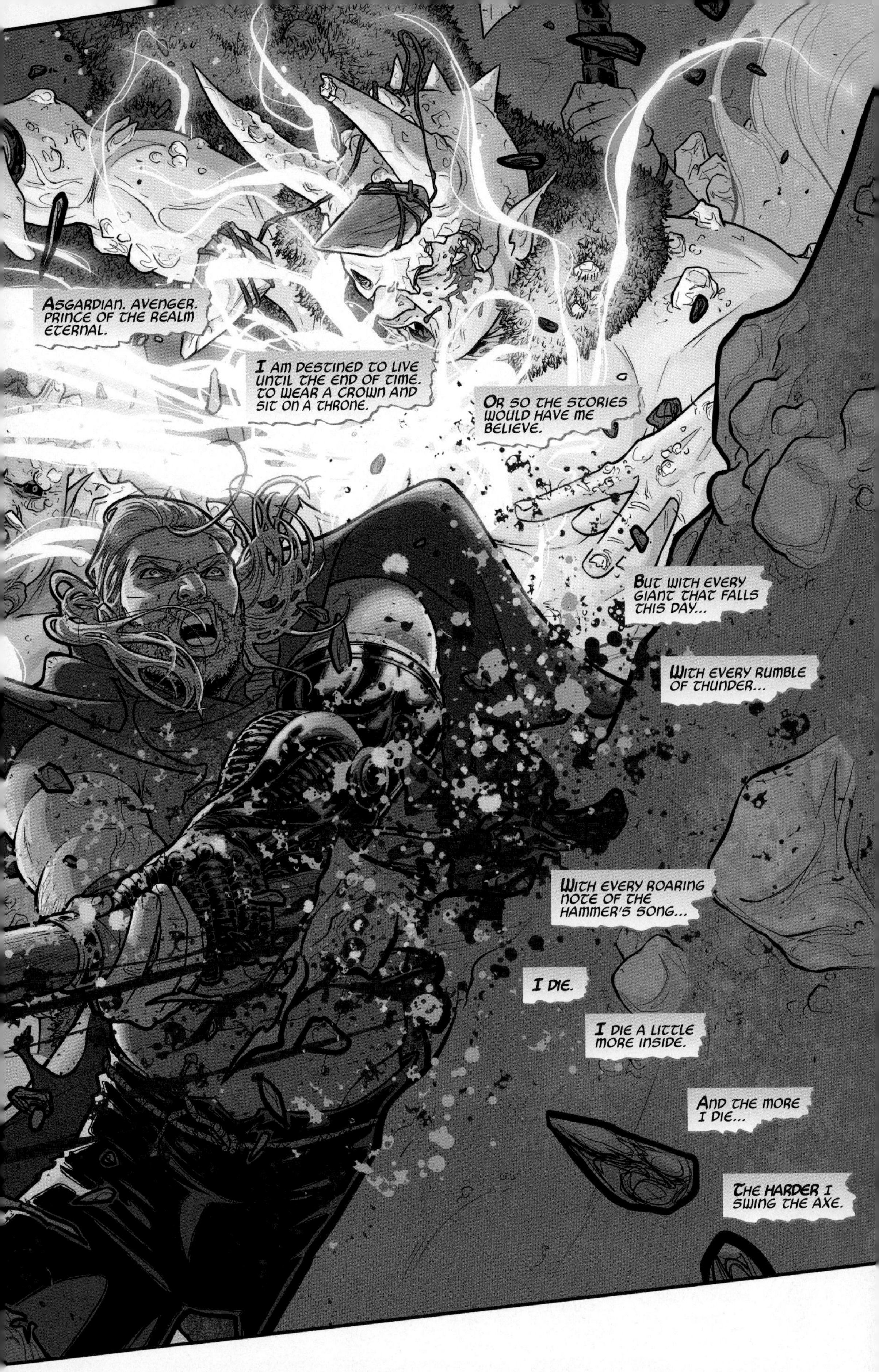

ASGARDIAN. AVENGER. PRINCE OF THE REALM ETERNAL.
I AM DESTINED TO LIVE UNTIL THE END OF TIME. TO WEAR A CROWN AND SIT ON A THRONE.
OR SO THE STORIES WOULD HAVE ME BELIEVE.
BUT WITH EVERY GIANT THAT FALLS THIS DAY...
WITH EVERY RUMBLE OF THUNDER...
WITH EVERY ROARING NOTE OF THE HAMMER'S SONG...
I DIE.
I DIE A LITTLE MORE INSIDE.
AND THE MORE I DIE...
THE HARDER I SWING THE AXE.

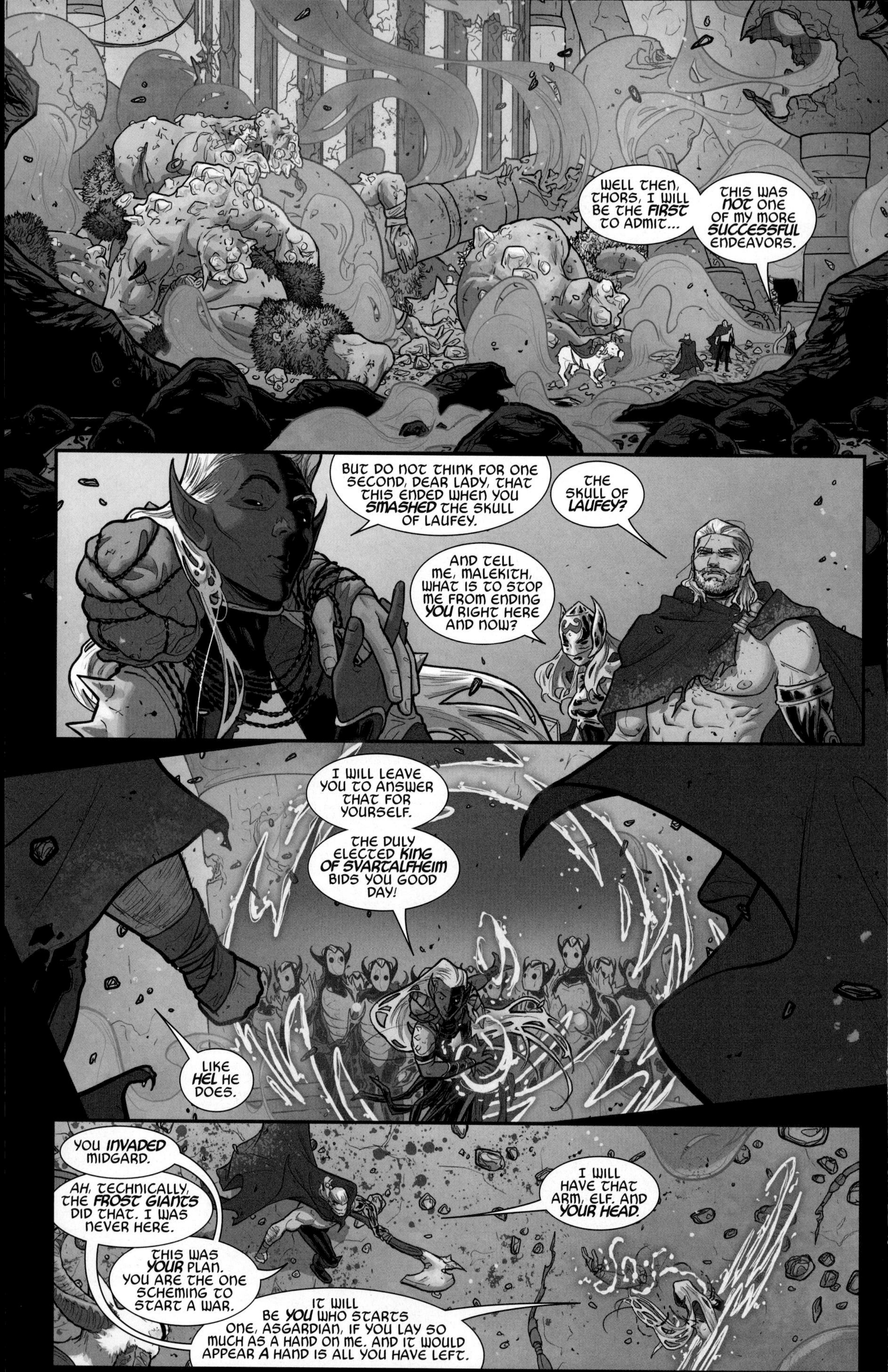

WELL THEN, THORS, I WILL BE THE FIRST TO ADMIT...
THIS WAS NOT ONE OF MY MORE SUCCESSFUL ENDEAVORS.
BUT DO NOT THINK FOR ONE SECOND, DEAR LADY, THAT THIS ENDED WHEN YOU SMASHED THE SKULL OF LAUFEY.
THE SKULL OF LAUFEY?
AND TELL ME, MALEKITH, WHAT IS TO STOP ME FROM ENDING YOU RIGHT HERE AND NOW?
I WILL LEAVE YOU TO ANSWER THAT FOR YOURSELF.
THE DULY ELECTED KING OF SVARTALFHEIM BIDS YOU GOOD DAY!
LIKE HEL HE DOES.
YOU INVADED MIDGARD.
AH, TECHNICALLY, THE FROST GIANTS DID THAT. I WAS NEVER HERE.
I WILL HAVE THAT ARM, ELF. AND YOUR HEAD.
THIS WAS YOUR PLAN. YOU ARE THE ONE SCHEMING TO START A WAR.
IT WILL BE YOU WHO STARTS ONE, ASGARDIAN, IF YOU LAY SO MUCH AS A HAND ON ME. AND IT WOULD APPEAR A HAND IS ALL YOU HAVE LEFT.

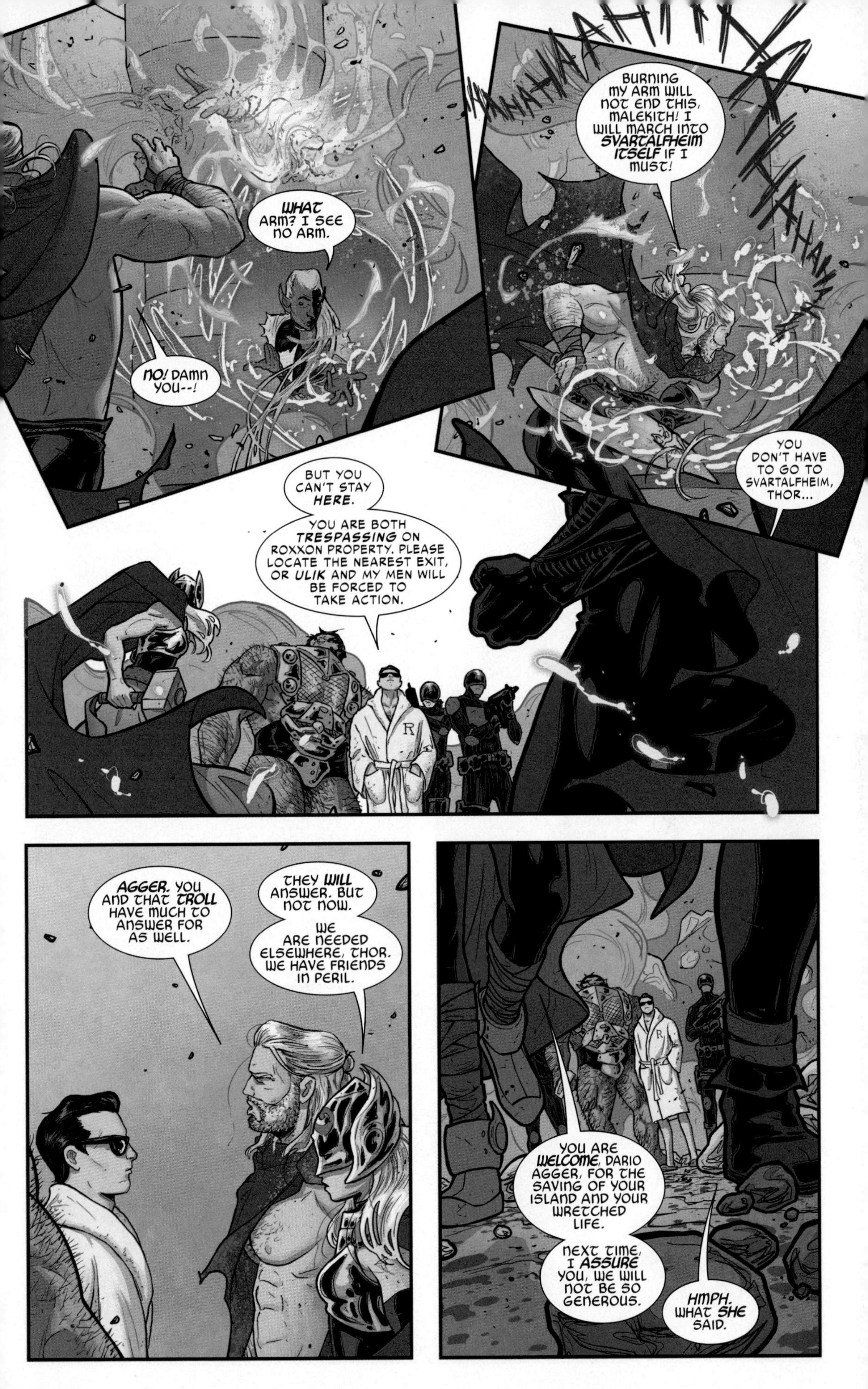
WHAT ARM? I SEE NO ARM.
NO! DAMN YOU--!
BURNING MY ARM WILL NOT END THIS, MALEKITH! I WILL MARCH INTO SVARTALFHEIM ITSELF IF I MUST!
HAHAHAHAHAHAHAHAHA
YOU DON'T HAVE TO GO TO SVARTALFHEIM, THOR...
BUT YOU CAN'T STAY HERE.
YOU ARE BOTH TRESPASSING ON ROXXON PROPERTY. PLEASE LOCATE THE NEAREST EXIT, OR ULIK AND MY MEN WILL BE FORCED TO TAKE ACTION.
AGGER. YOU AND THAT TROLL HAVE MUCH TO ANSWER FOR AS WELL.
THEY WILL ANSWER. BUT NOT NOW.
WE ARE NEEDED ELSEWHERE, THOR. WE HAVE FRIENDS IN PERIL.
YOU ARE WELCOME, DARIO AGGER, FOR THE SAVING OF YOUR ISLAND AND YOUR WRETCHED LIFE.
NEXT TIME, I ASSURE YOU, WE WILL NOT BE SO GENEROUS.
HMPH. WHAT SHE SAID.

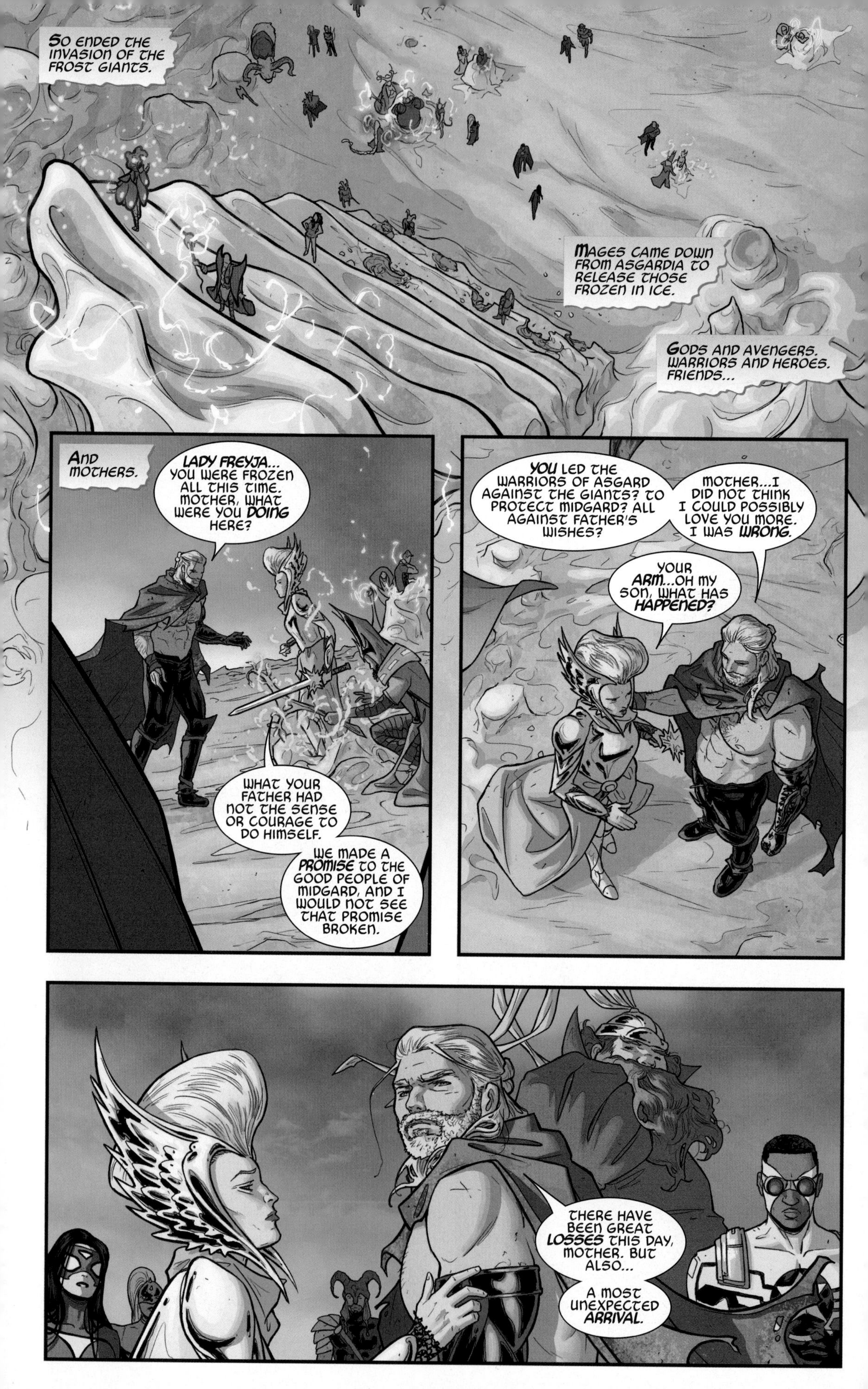

SO ENDED THE INVASION OF THE FROST GIANTS.
MAGES CAME DOWN FROM ASGARDIA TO RELEASE THOSE FROZEN IN ICE.
GODS AND AVENGERS. WARRIORS AND HEROES. FRIENDS...
AND MOTHERS.
LADY FREYJA... YOU WERE FROZEN ALL THIS TIME. MOTHER, WHAT WERE YOU DOING HERE?
WHAT YOUR FATHER HAD NOT THE SENSE OR COURAGE TO DO HIMSELF.
WE MADE A PROMISE TO THE GOOD PEOPLE OF MIDGARD, AND I WOULD NOT SEE THAT PROMISE BROKEN.
YOU LED THE WARRIORS OF ASGARD AGAINST THE GIANTS? TO PROTECT MIDGARD? ALL AGAINST FATHER'S WISHES?
MOTHER...I DID NOT THINK I COULD POSSIBLY LOVE YOU MORE. I WAS WRONG.
YOUR ARM...OH MY SON, WHAT HAS HAPPENED?
THERE HAVE BEEN GREAT LOSSES THIS DAY, MOTHER. BUT ALSO...
A MOST UNEXPECTED ARRIVAL.

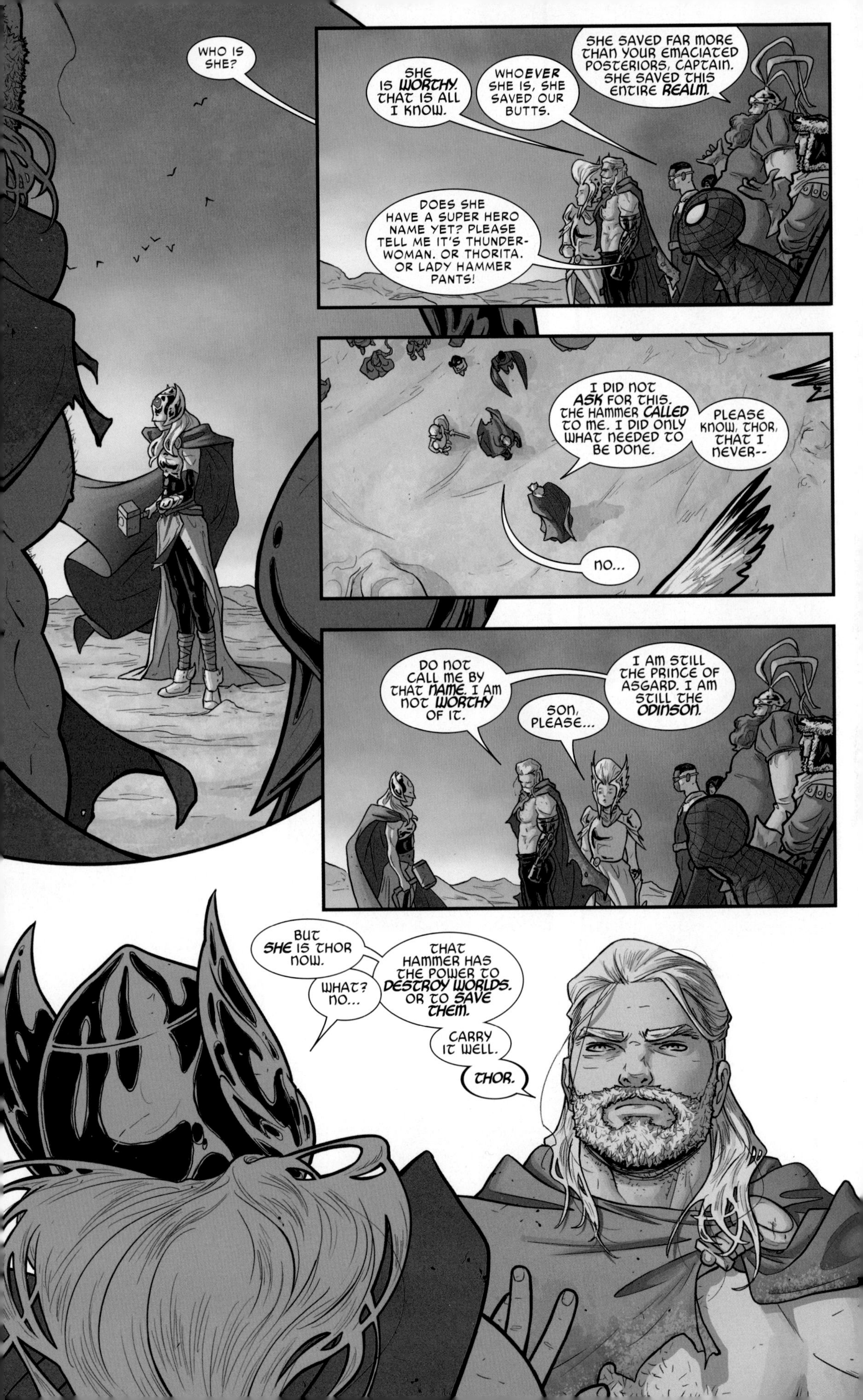

WHO IS SHE?
SHE IS WORTHY. THAT IS ALL I KNOW.
WHOEVER SHE IS, SHE SAVED OUR BUTTS.
SHE SAVED FAR MORE THAN YOUR EMACIATED POSTERIORS, CAPTAIN. SHE SAVED THIS ENTIRE REALM.
DOES SHE HAVE A SUPER HERO NAME YET? PLEASE TELL ME IT'S THUNDER-WOMAN. OR THORITA. OR LADY HAMMER PANTS!
I DID NOT ASK FOR THIS. THE HAMMER CALLED TO ME. I DID ONLY WHAT NEEDED TO BE DONE.
PLEASE KNOW, THOR, THAT I NEVER--
NO...
DO NOT CALL ME BY THAT NAME. I AM NOT WORTHY OF IT.
SON, PLEASE...
I AM STILL THE PRINCE OF ASGARD. I AM STILL THE ODINSON.
BUT SHE IS THOR NOW.
WHAT? NO...
THAT HAMMER HAS THE POWER TO DESTROY WORLDS. OR TO SAVE THEM.
CARRY IT WELL.
THOR.

I...DO NOT KNOW WHAT TO SAY... EXCEPT...

AYE.

I WILL CARRY IT.

I AM...

THE MIGHTY THOR.

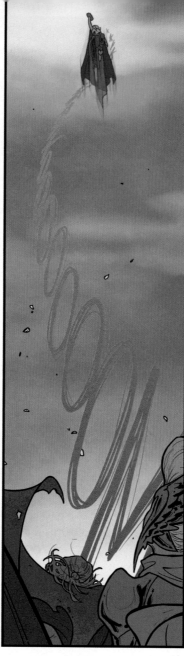

I AM THE ODINSON. I AM THE UNWORTHY. AND THIS IS THE STORY OF HOW I LOST MY HAMMER.

BUT THIS IS NOT THE END OF MY TALE.

YOUR FATHER WILL HATE THIS.

WHICH MAKES ME LIKE IT ALL THE MORE.

THERE IS SOMETHING FAMILIAR ABOUT HER...DO YOU KNOW WHO SHE IS?

NO.

"BUT I LOOK FORWARD TO FINDING OUT."

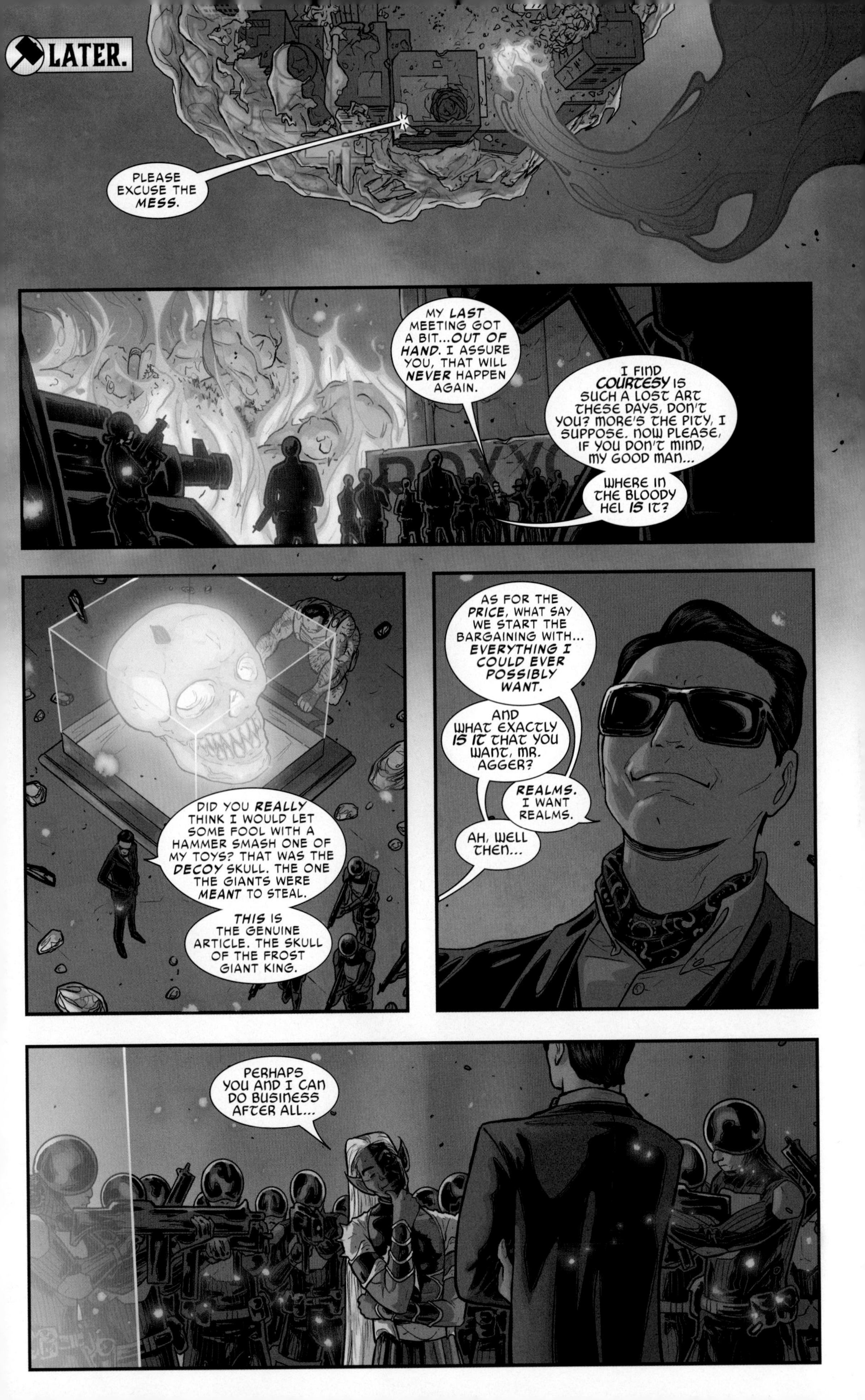
LATER.
PLEASE EXCUSE THE MESS.
MY LAST MEETING GOT A BIT...OUT OF HAND. I ASSURE YOU, THAT WILL NEVER HAPPEN AGAIN.
I FIND COURTESY IS SUCH A LOST ART THESE DAYS, DON'T YOU? MORE'S THE PITY, I SUPPOSE. NOW PLEASE, IF YOU DON'T MIND, MY GOOD MAN...
WHERE IN THE BLOODY HEL IS IT?
DID YOU REALLY THINK I WOULD LET SOME FOOL WITH A HAMMER SMASH ONE OF MY TOYS? THAT WAS THE DECOY SKULL. THE ONE THE GIANTS WERE MEANT TO STEAL.
THIS IS THE GENUINE ARTICLE. THE SKULL OF THE FROST GIANT KING.
AS FOR THE PRICE, WHAT SAY WE START THE BARGAINING WITH... EVERYTHING I COULD EVER POSSIBLY WANT.
AND WHAT EXACTLY IS IT THAT YOU WANT, MR. AGGER?
REALMS. I WANT REALMS.
AH, WELL THEN...
PERHAPS YOU AND I CAN DO BUSINESS AFTER ALL...

5

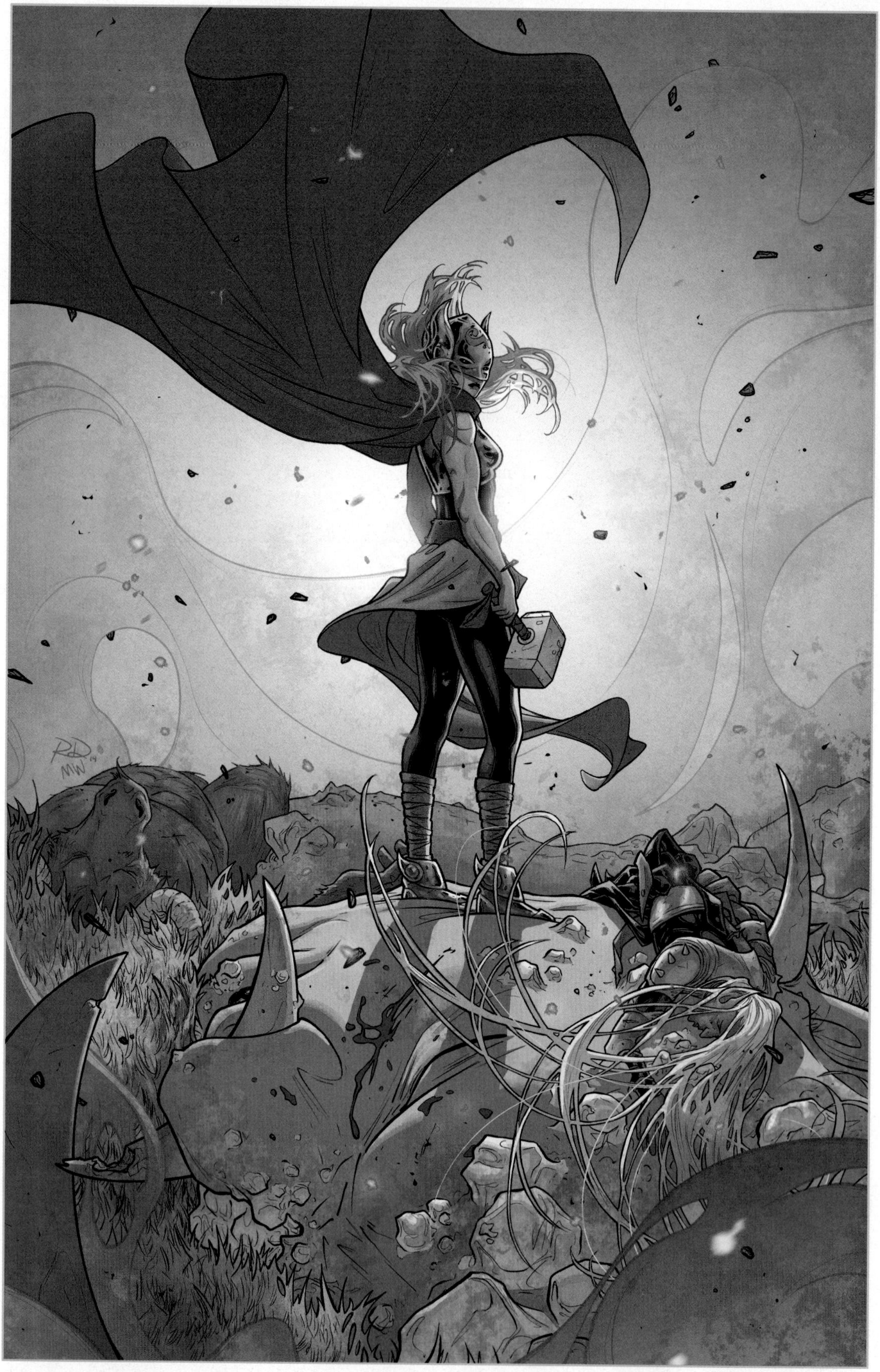

BEHOLD, A NEW AGE OF THUNDER

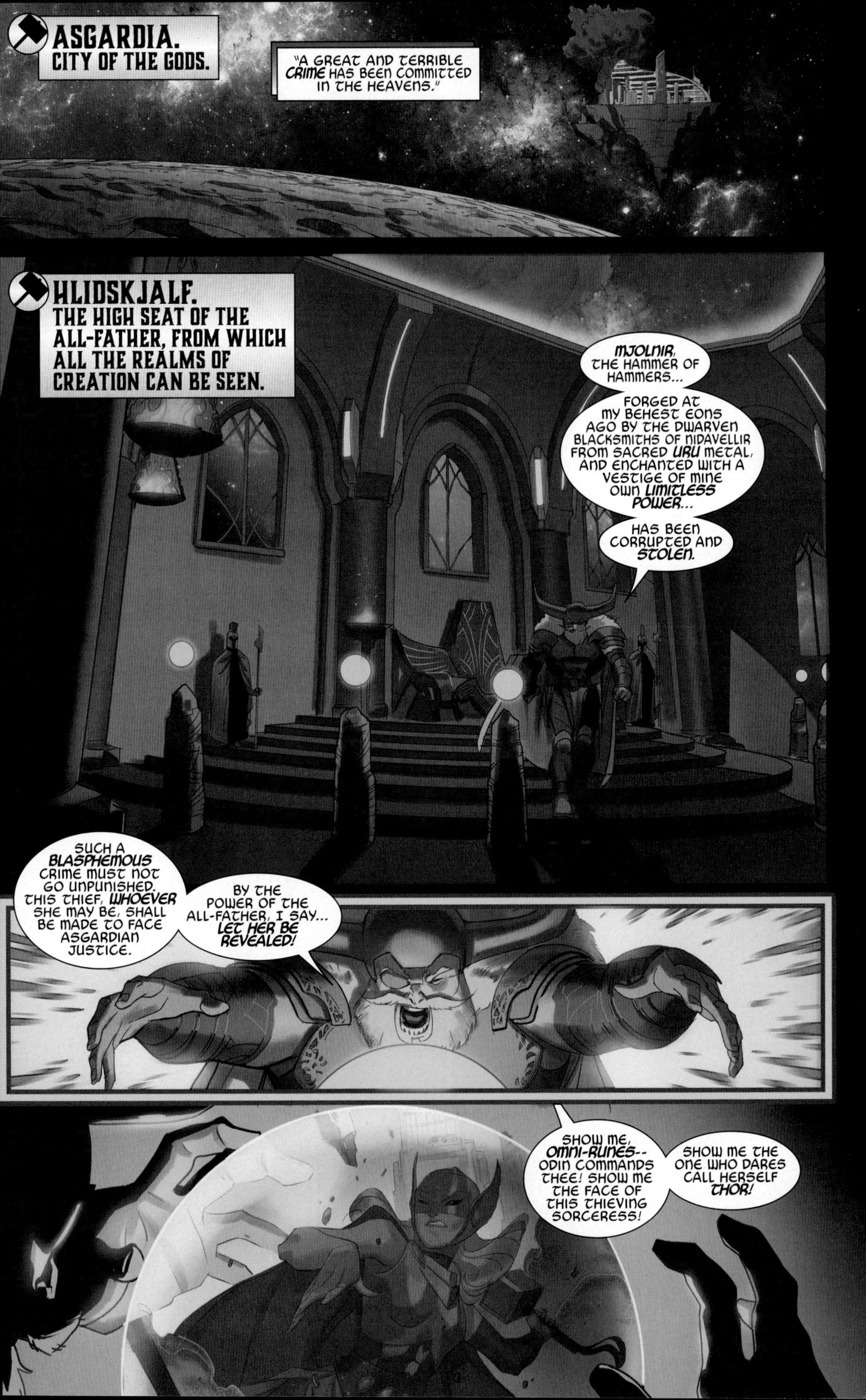
ASGARDIA.
CITY OF THE GODS.
"A GREAT AND TERRIBLE CRIME HAS BEEN COMMITTED IN THE HEAVENS."
HLIDSKJALF.
THE HIGH SEAT OF THE ALL-FATHER, FROM WHICH ALL THE REALMS OF CREATION CAN BE SEEN.
MJOLNIR, THE HAMMER OF HAMMERS...
FORGED AT MY BEHEST EONS AGO BY THE DWARVEN BLACKSMITHS OF NIDAVELLIR FROM SACRED URU METAL, AND ENCHANTED WITH A VESTIGE OF MINE OWN LIMITLESS POWER...
HAS BEEN CORRUPTED AND STOLEN.
SUCH A BLASPHEMOUS CRIME MUST NOT GO UNPUNISHED. THIS THIEF, WHOEVER SHE MAY BE, SHALL BE MADE TO FACE ASGARDIAN JUSTICE.
BY THE POWER OF THE ALL-FATHER, I SAY... LET HER BE REVEALED!
SHOW ME, OMNI-RUNES-- ODIN COMMANDS THEE! SHOW ME THE FACE OF THIS THIEVING SORCERESS!
SHOW ME THE ONE WHO DARES CALL HERSELF THOR!

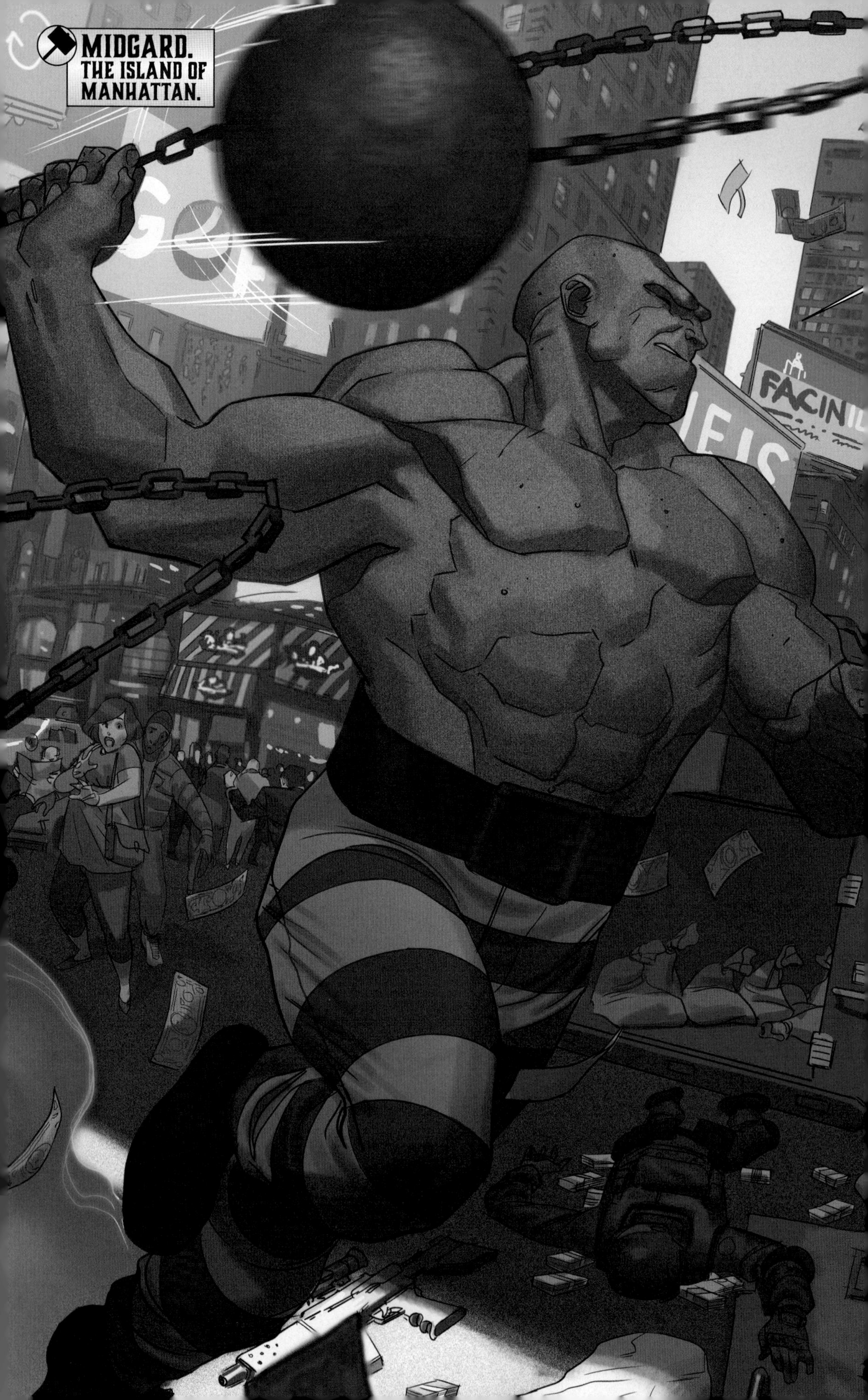
MIDGARD. THE ISLAND OF MANHATTAN.

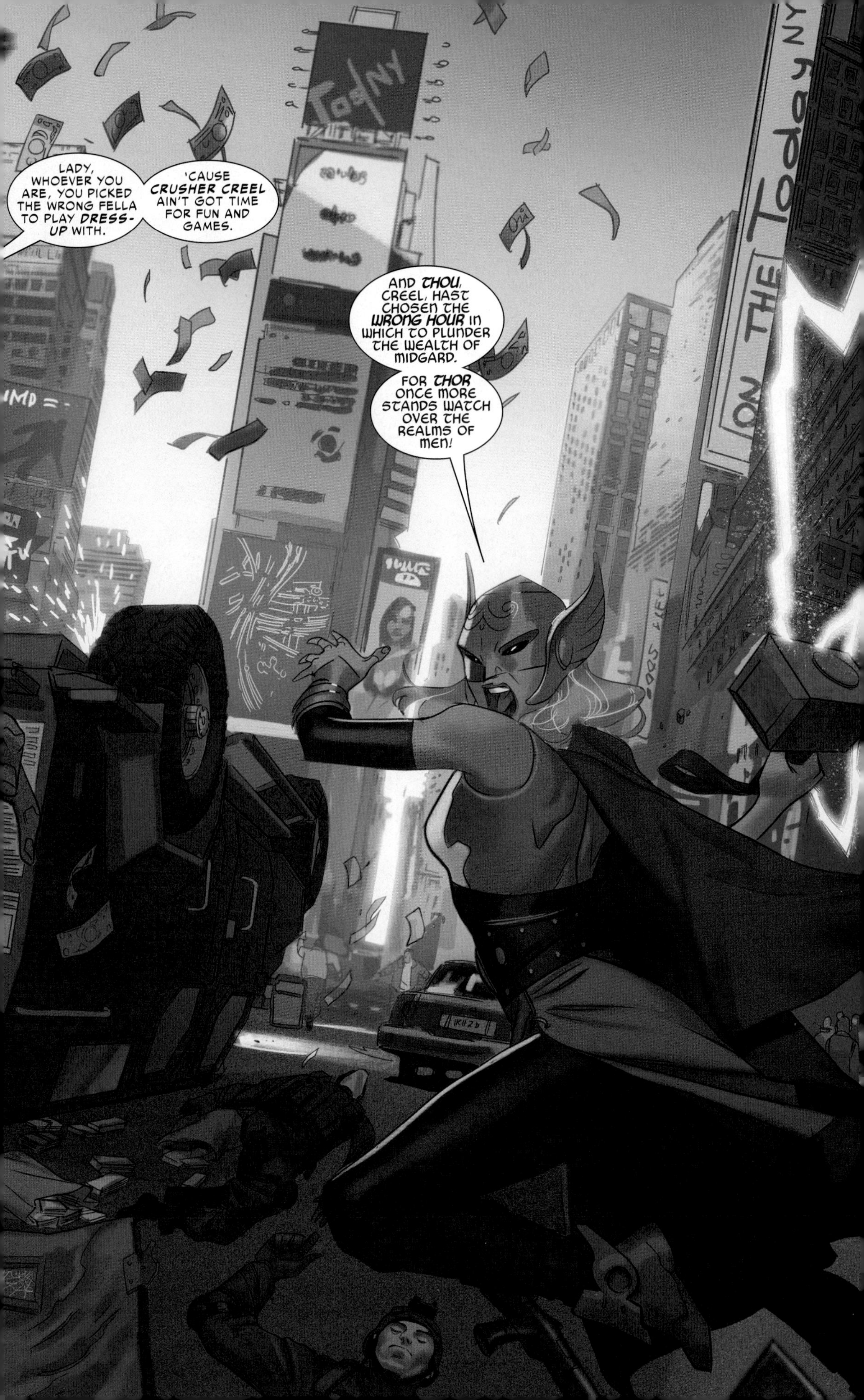
LADY, WHOEVER YOU ARE, YOU PICKED THE WRONG FELLA TO PLAY DRESS-UP WITH.
'CAUSE CRUSHER CREEL AIN'T GOT TIME FOR FUN AND GAMES.
AND THOU, CREEL, HAST CHOSEN THE WRONG HOUR IN WHICH TO PLUNDER THE WEALTH OF MIDGARD.
FOR THOR ONCE MORE STANDS WATCH OVER THE REALMS OF MEN!
ON THE Today NY

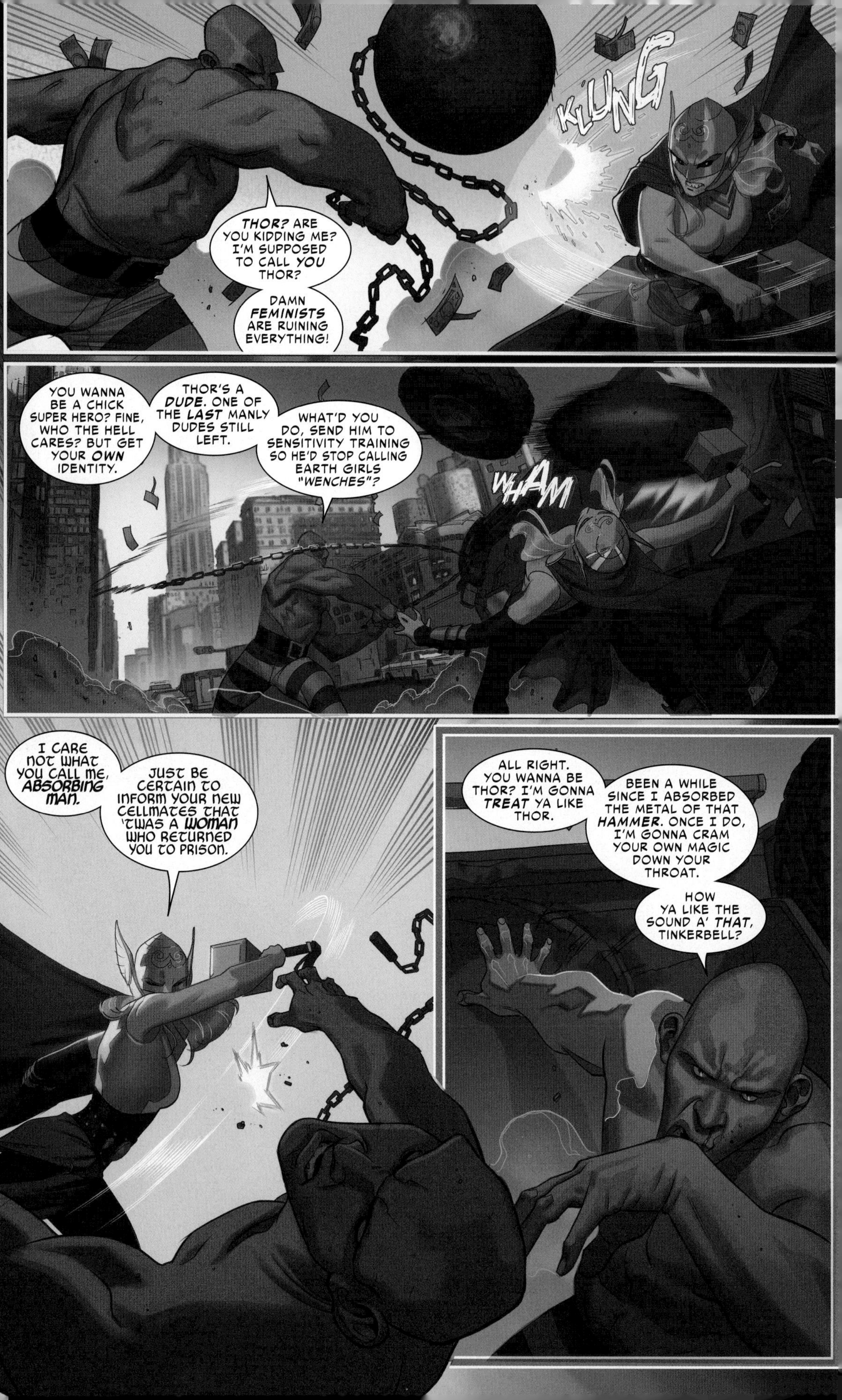
KLUNG
THOR? ARE YOU KIDDING ME? I'M SUPPOSED TO CALL YOU THOR?
DAMN FEMINISTS ARE RUINING EVERYTHING!
YOU WANNA BE A CHICK SUPER HERO? FINE, WHO THE HELL CARES? BUT GET YOUR OWN IDENTITY.
THOR'S A DUDE. ONE OF THE LAST MANLY DUDES STILL LEFT.
WHAT'D YOU DO, SEND HIM TO SENSITIVITY TRAINING SO HE'D STOP CALLING EARTH GIRLS "WENCHES"?
WHAM
I CARE NOT WHAT YOU CALL ME, ABSORBING MAN.
JUST BE CERTAIN TO INFORM YOUR NEW CELLMATES THAT 'TWAS A WOMAN WHO RETURNED YOU TO PRISON.
ALL RIGHT. YOU WANNA BE THOR? I'M GONNA TREAT YA LIKE THOR.
BEEN A WHILE SINCE I ABSORBED THE METAL OF THAT HAMMER. ONCE I DO, I'M GONNA CRAM YOUR OWN MAGIC DOWN YOUR THROAT.
HOW YA LIKE THE SOUND A' THAT, TINKERBELL?

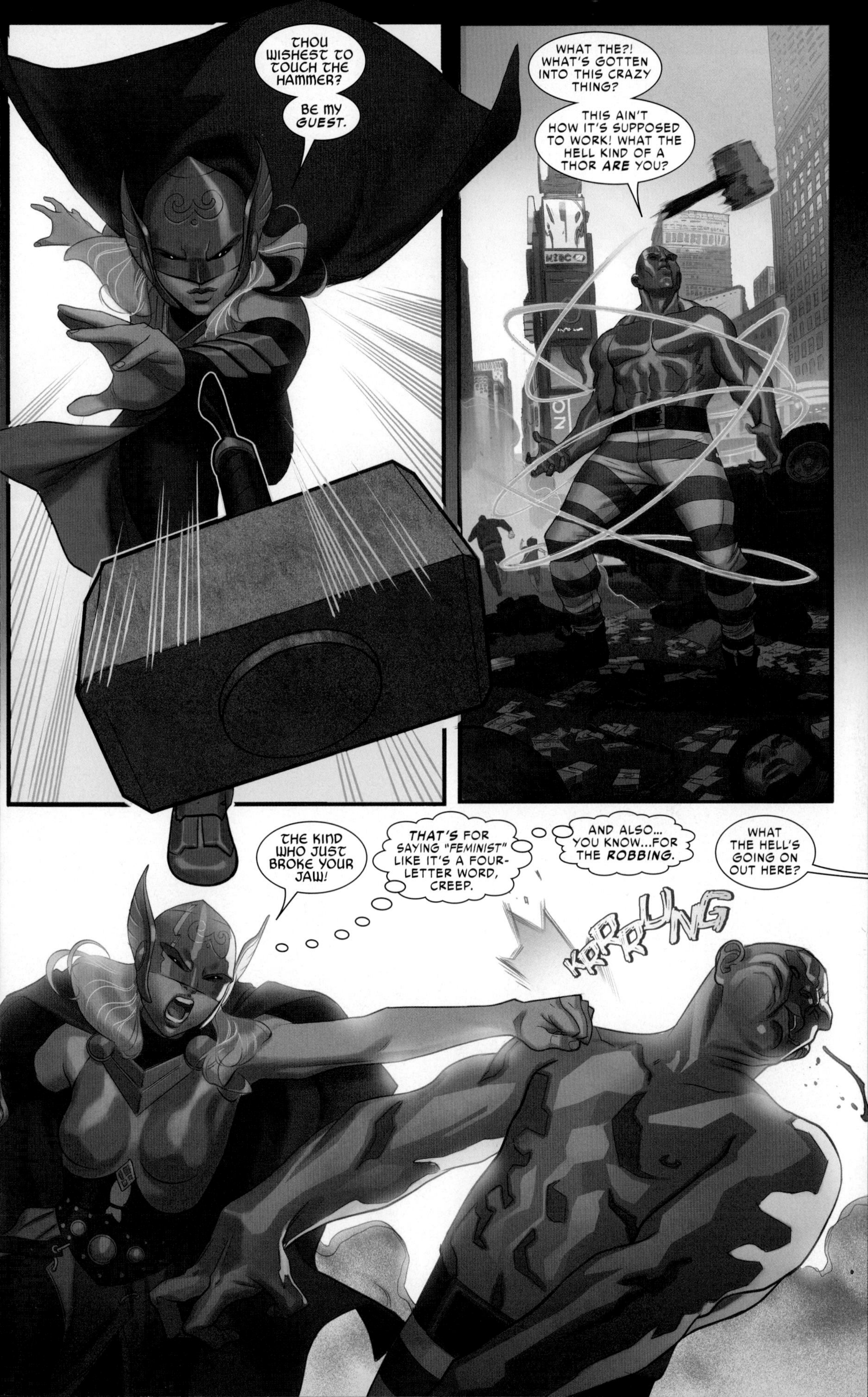

THOU WISHEST TO TOUCH THE HAMMER?
BE MY GUEST.
WHAT THE?! WHAT'S GOTTEN INTO THIS CRAZY THING?
THIS AIN'T HOW IT'S SUPPOSED TO WORK! WHAT THE HELL KIND OF A THOR ARE YOU?
THE KIND WHO JUST BROKE YOUR JAW!
THAT'S FOR SAYING "FEMINIST" LIKE IT'S A FOUR-LETTER WORD, CREEP.
AND ALSO... YOU KNOW...FOR THE ROBBING.
WHAT THE HELL'S GOING ON OUT HERE?
KRRRUNG

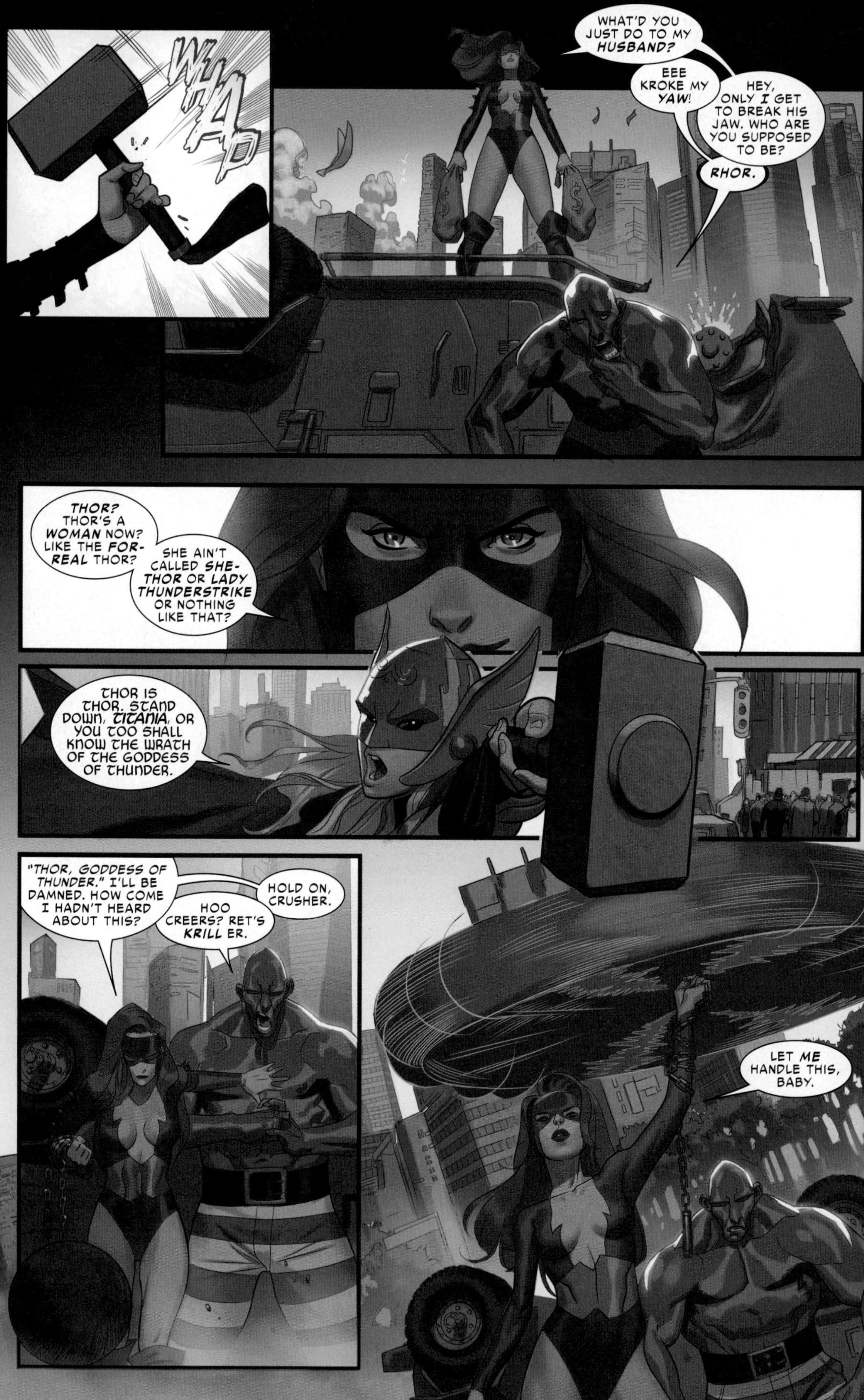
WHAP
WHAT'D YOU JUST DO TO MY HUSBAND?
EEE KROKE MY YAW!
HEY, ONLY I GET TO BREAK HIS JAW. WHO ARE YOU SUPPOSED TO BE?
RHOR.
THOR? THOR'S A WOMAN NOW? LIKE THE FOR-REAL THOR?
SHE AIN'T CALLED SHE-THOR OR LADY THUNDERSTRIKE OR NOTHING LIKE THAT?
THOR IS THOR. STAND DOWN, TITANIA, OR YOU TOO SHALL KNOW THE WRATH OF THE GODDESS OF THUNDER.
"THOR, GODDESS OF THUNDER." I'LL BE DAMNED. HOW COME I HADN'T HEARD ABOUT THIS?
HOO CREERS? RET'S KRILL ER.
HOLD ON, CRUSHER.
LET ME HANDLE THIS, BABY.

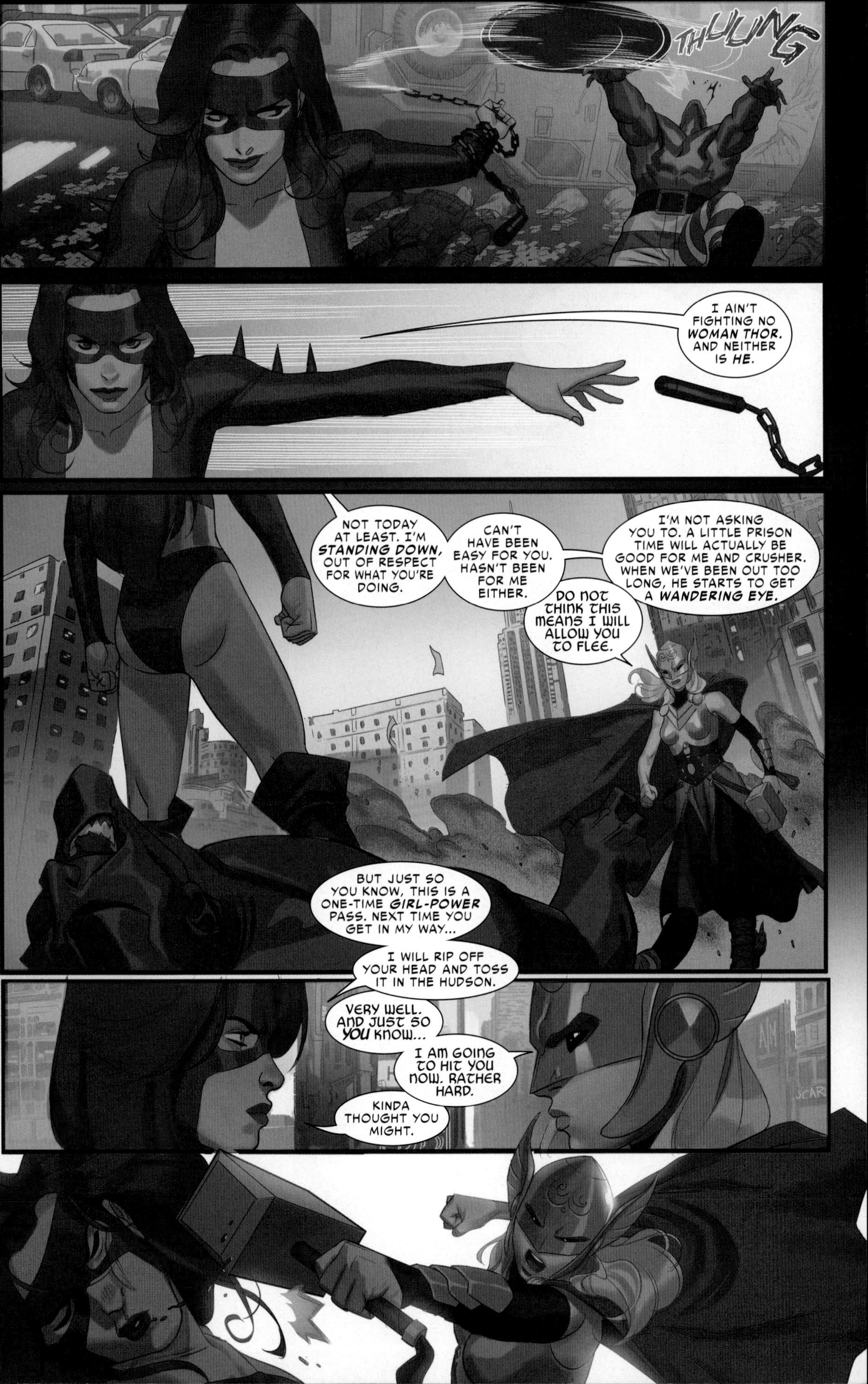
THUUNG
I AIN'T FIGHTING NO WOMAN THOR. AND NEITHER IS HE.
NOT TODAY AT LEAST. I'M STANDING DOWN, OUT OF RESPECT FOR WHAT YOU'RE DOING.
CAN'T HAVE BEEN EASY FOR YOU. HASN'T BEEN FOR ME EITHER.
I'M NOT ASKING YOU TO. A LITTLE PRISON TIME WILL ACTUALLY BE GOOD FOR ME AND CRUSHER. WHEN WE'VE BEEN OUT TOO LONG, HE STARTS TO GET A WANDERING EYE.
DO NOT THINK THIS MEANS I WILL ALLOW YOU TO FLEE.
BUT JUST SO YOU KNOW, THIS IS A ONE-TIME GIRL-POWER PASS. NEXT TIME YOU GET IN MY WAY...
I WILL RIP OFF YOUR HEAD AND TOSS IT IN THE HUDSON.
VERY WELL. AND JUST SO YOU KNOW...
I AM GOING TO HIT YOU NOW. RATHER HARD.
KINDA THOUGHT YOU MIGHT.

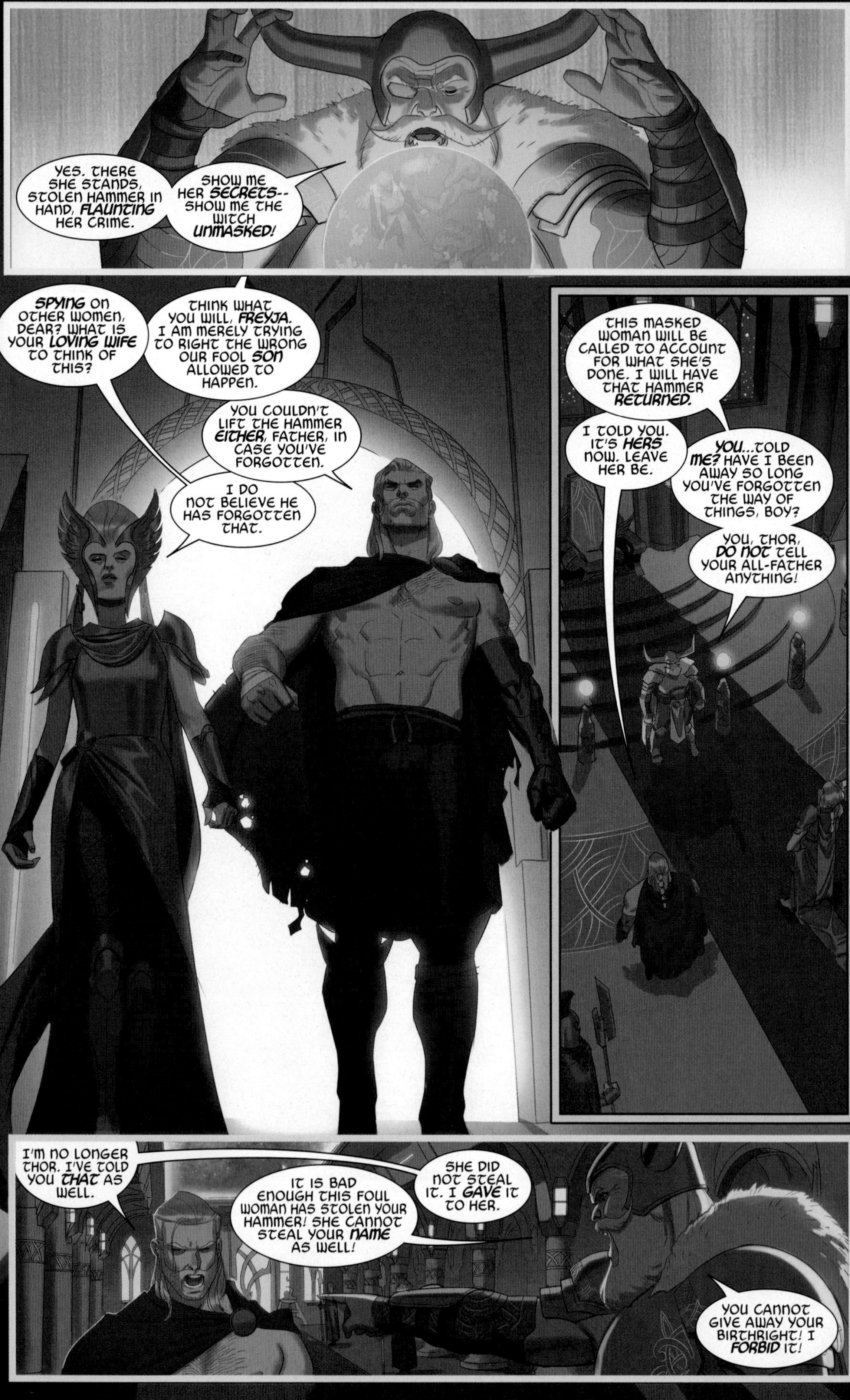

YES. THERE SHE STANDS, STOLEN HAMMER IN HAND, FLAUNTING HER CRIME.
SHOW ME HER SECRETS-- SHOW ME THE WITCH UNMASKED!
SPYING ON OTHER WOMEN, DEAR? WHAT IS YOUR LOVING WIFE TO THINK OF THIS?
THINK WHAT YOU WILL, FREYJA. I AM MERELY TRYING TO RIGHT THE WRONG OUR FOOL SON ALLOWED TO HAPPEN.
YOU COULDN'T LIFT THE HAMMER EITHER, FATHER, IN CASE YOU'VE FORGOTTEN.
I DO NOT BELIEVE HE HAS FORGOTTEN THAT.
THIS MASKED WOMAN WILL BE CALLED TO ACCOUNT FOR WHAT SHE'S DONE. I WILL HAVE THAT HAMMER RETURNED.
I TOLD YOU. IT'S HERS NOW. LEAVE HER BE.
YOU...TOLD ME? HAVE I BEEN AWAY SO LONG YOU'VE FORGOTTEN THE WAY OF THINGS, BOY?
YOU, THOR, DO NOT TELL YOUR ALL-FATHER ANYTHING!
I'M NO LONGER THOR. I'VE TOLD YOU THAT AS WELL.
IT IS BAD ENOUGH THIS FOUL WOMAN HAS STOLEN YOUR HAMMER! SHE CANNOT STEAL YOUR NAME AS WELL!
SHE DID NOT STEAL IT. I GAVE IT TO HER.
YOU CANNOT GIVE AWAY YOUR BIRTHRIGHT! I FORBID IT!

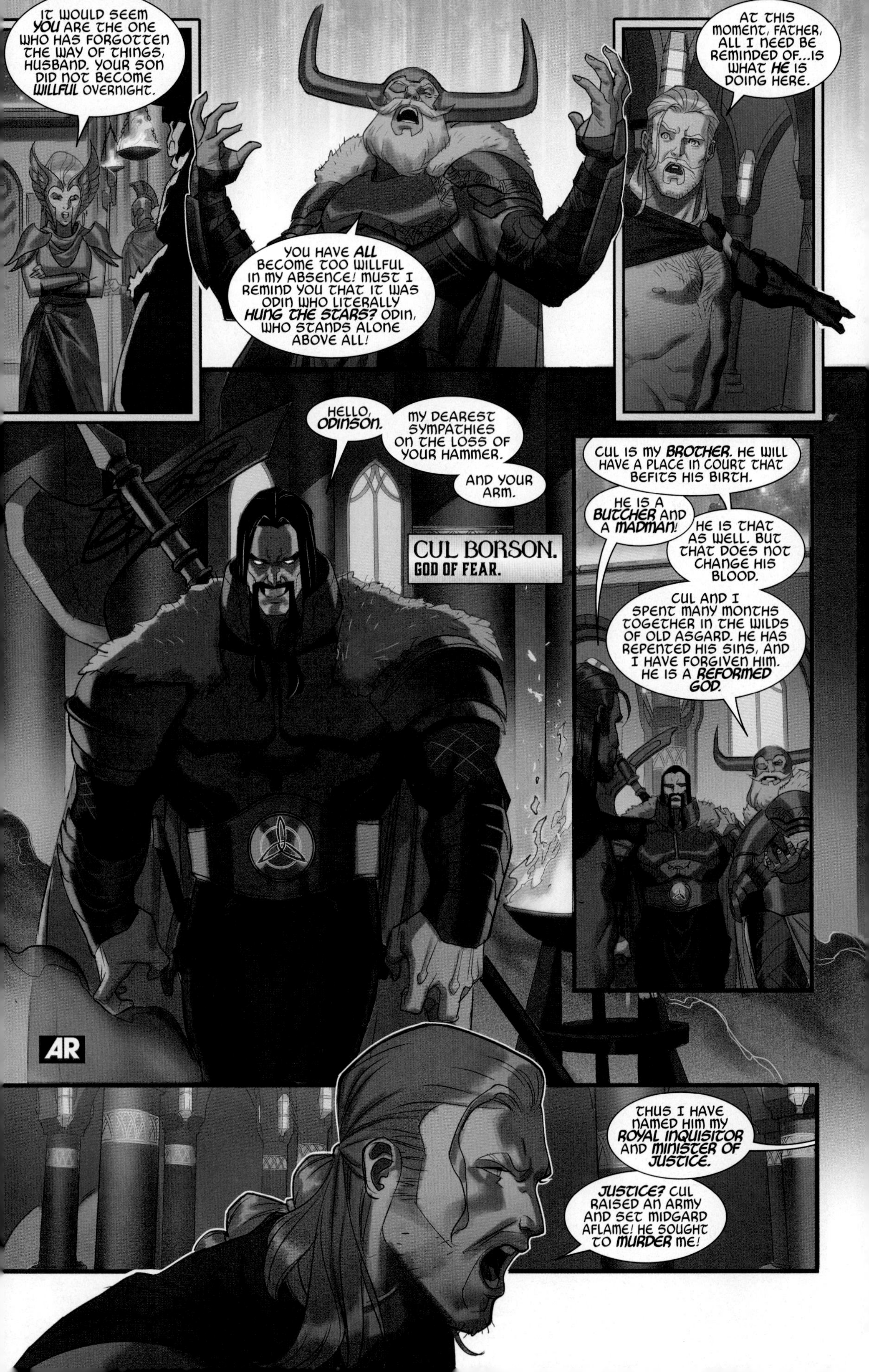
IT WOULD SEEM YOU ARE THE ONE WHO HAS FORGOTTEN THE WAY OF THINGS, HUSBAND. YOUR SON DID NOT BECOME WILLFUL OVERNIGHT.
YOU HAVE ALL BECOME TOO WILLFUL IN MY ABSENCE! MUST I REMIND YOU THAT IT WAS ODIN WHO LITERALLY HUNG THE STARS? ODIN, WHO STANDS ALONE ABOVE ALL!
AT THIS MOMENT, FATHER, ALL I NEED BE REMINDED OF... IS WHAT HE IS DOING HERE.
HELLO, ODINSON.
MY DEAREST SYMPATHIES ON THE LOSS OF YOUR HAMMER.
AND YOUR ARM.
CUL BORSON.
GOD OF FEAR.
CUL IS MY BROTHER. HE WILL HAVE A PLACE IN COURT THAT BEFITS HIS BIRTH.
HE IS A BUTCHER AND A MADMAN!
HE IS THAT AS WELL. BUT THAT DOES NOT CHANGE HIS BLOOD.
CUL AND I SPENT MANY MONTHS TOGETHER IN THE WILDS OF OLD ASGARD. HE HAS REPENTED HIS SINS, AND I HAVE FORGIVEN HIM. HE IS A REFORMED GOD.
AR
THUS I HAVE NAMED HIM MY ROYAL INQUISITOR AND MINISTER OF JUSTICE.
JUSTICE? CUL RAISED AN ARMY AND SET MIDGARD AFLAME! HE SOUGHT TO MURDER ME!

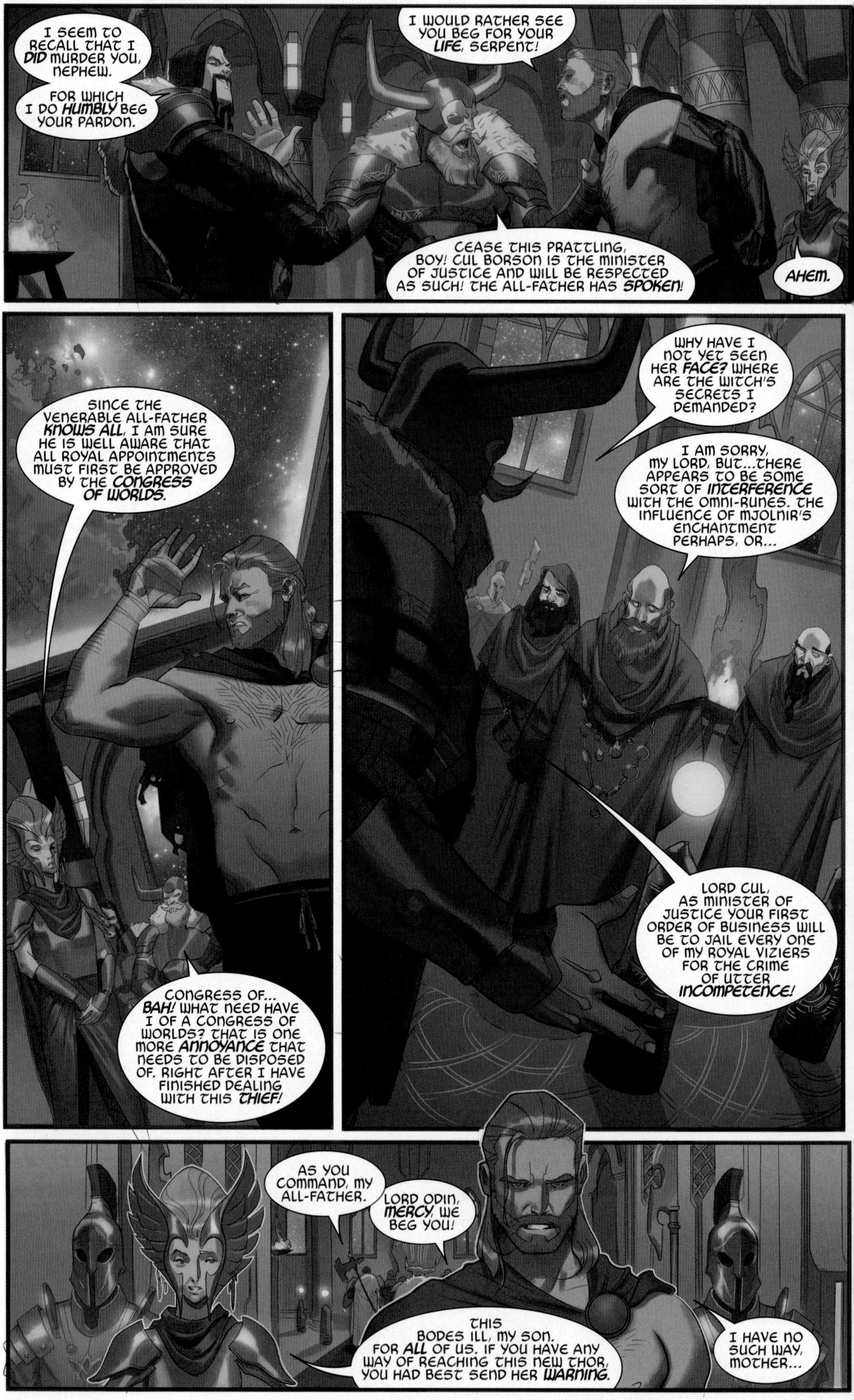
I SEEM TO RECALL THAT I DID MURDER YOU, NEPHEW.
FOR WHICH I DO HUMBLY BEG YOUR PARDON.
I WOULD RATHER SEE YOU BEG FOR YOUR LIFE, SERPENT!
CEASE THIS PRATTLING, BOY! CUL BORSON IS THE MINISTER OF JUSTICE AND WILL BE RESPECTED AS SUCH! THE ALL-FATHER HAS SPOKEN!
AHEM.
SINCE THE VENERABLE ALL-FATHER KNOWS ALL, I AM SURE HE IS WELL AWARE THAT ALL ROYAL APPOINTMENTS MUST FIRST BE APPROVED BY THE CONGRESS OF WORLDS.
CONGRESS OF... BAH! WHAT NEED HAVE I OF A CONGRESS OF WORLDS? THAT IS ONE MORE ANNOYANCE THAT NEEDS TO BE DISPOSED OF. RIGHT AFTER I HAVE FINISHED DEALING WITH THIS THIEF!
WHY HAVE I NOT YET SEEN HER FACE? WHERE ARE THE WITCH'S SECRETS I DEMANDED?
I AM SORRY, MY LORD, BUT...THERE APPEARS TO BE SOME SORT OF INTERFERENCE WITH THE OMNI-RUNES. THE INFLUENCE OF MJOLNIR'S ENCHANTMENT PERHAPS, OR...
LORD CUL, AS MINISTER OF JUSTICE YOUR FIRST ORDER OF BUSINESS WILL BE TO JAIL EVERY ONE OF MY ROYAL VIZIERS FOR THE CRIME OF UTTER INCOMPETENCE!
AS YOU COMMAND, MY ALL-FATHER.
LORD ODIN, MERCY, WE BEG YOU!
THIS BODES ILL, MY SON. FOR ALL OF US. IF YOU HAVE ANY WAY OF REACHING THIS NEW THOR, YOU HAD BEST SEND HER WARNING.
I HAVE NO SUCH WAY, MOTHER...

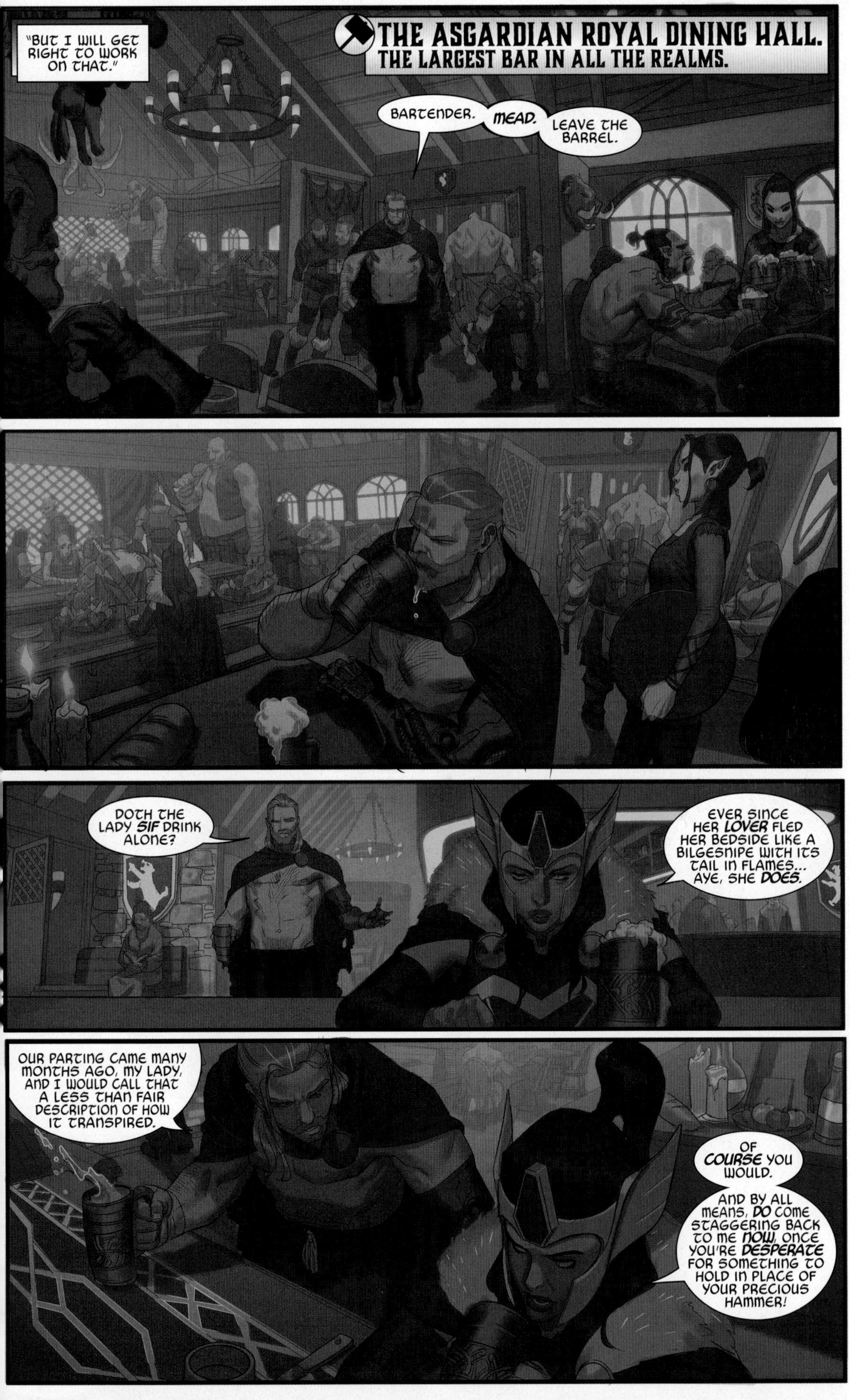
"BUT I WILL GET RIGHT TO WORK ON THAT."
THE ASGARDIAN ROYAL DINING HALL.
THE LARGEST BAR IN ALL THE REALMS.
BARTENDER.
MEAD.
LEAVE THE BARREL.
DOTH THE LADY SIF DRINK ALONE?
EVER SINCE HER LOVER FLED HER BEDSIDE LIKE A BILGESNIPE WITH ITS TAIL IN FLAMES... AYE, SHE DOES.
OUR PARTING CAME MANY MONTHS AGO, MY LADY, AND I WOULD CALL THAT A LESS THAN FAIR DESCRIPTION OF HOW IT TRANSPIRED.
OF COURSE YOU WOULD.
AND BY ALL MEANS, DO COME STAGGERING BACK TO ME NOW, ONCE YOU'RE DESPERATE FOR SOMETHING TO HOLD IN PLACE OF YOUR PRECIOUS HAMMER!

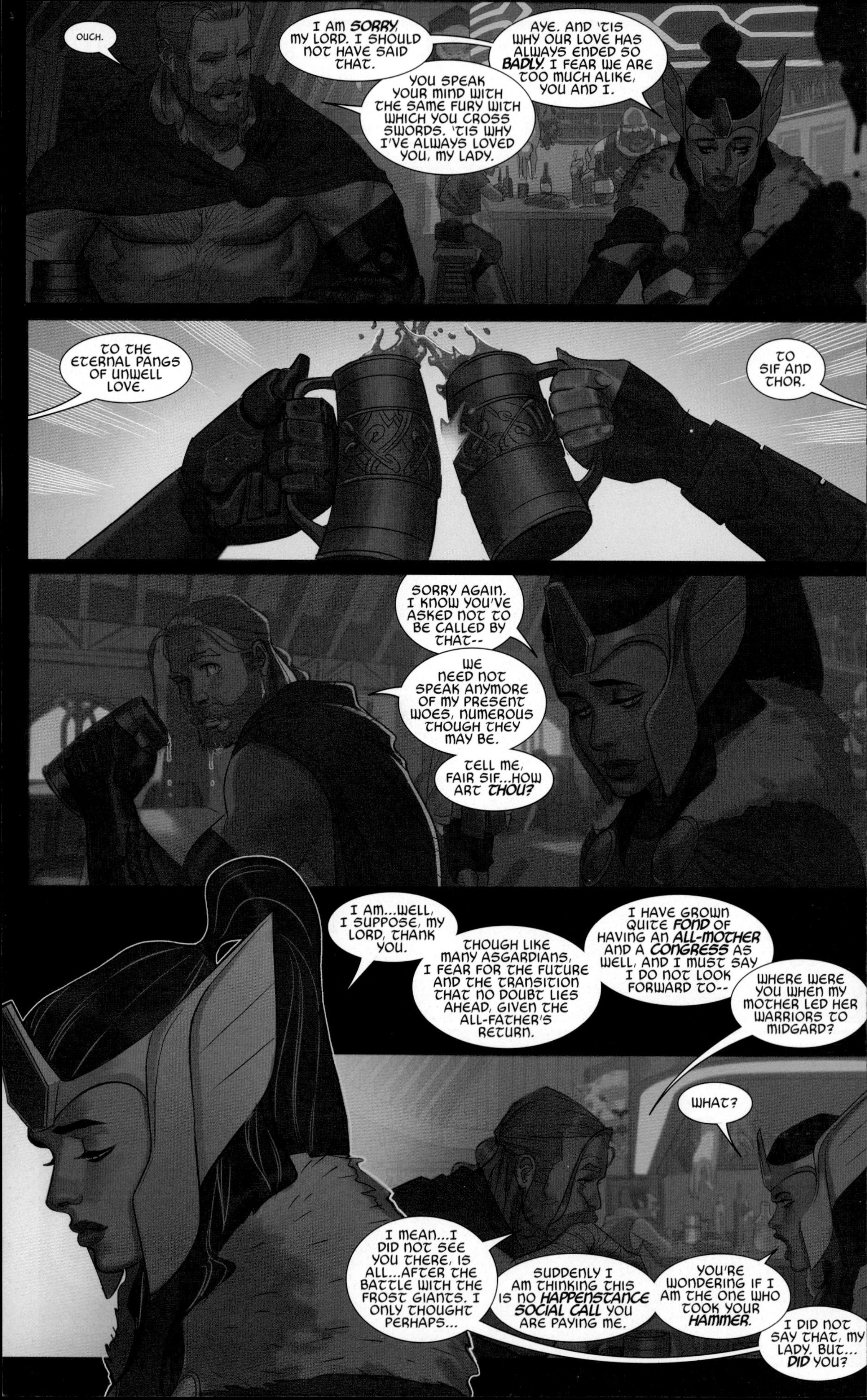

OUCH.
I AM SORRY, MY LORD. I SHOULD NOT HAVE SAID THAT.
AYE. AND 'TIS WHY OUR LOVE HAS ALWAYS ENDED SO BADLY. I FEAR WE ARE TOO MUCH ALIKE, YOU AND I.
YOU SPEAK YOUR MIND WITH THE SAME FURY WITH WHICH YOU CROSS SWORDS. 'TIS WHY I'VE ALWAYS LOVED YOU, MY LADY.
TO THE ETERNAL PANGS OF UNWELL LOVE.
TO SIF AND THOR.
SORRY AGAIN. I KNOW YOU'VE ASKED NOT TO BE CALLED BY THAT--
WE NEED NOT SPEAK ANYMORE OF MY PRESENT WOES, NUMEROUS THOUGH THEY MAY BE.
TELL ME, FAIR SIF...HOW ART THOU?
I AM...WELL, I SUPPOSE, MY LORD, THANK YOU.
THOUGH LIKE MANY ASGARDIANS, I FEAR FOR THE FUTURE AND THE TRANSITION THAT NO DOUBT LIES AHEAD, GIVEN THE ALL-FATHER'S RETURN.
I HAVE GROWN QUITE FOND OF HAVING AN ALL-MOTHER AND A CONGRESS AS WELL, AND I MUST SAY I DO NOT LOOK FORWARD TO--
WHERE WERE YOU WHEN MY MOTHER LED HER WARRIORS TO MIDGARD?
WHAT?
I MEAN...I DID NOT SEE YOU THERE, IS ALL...AFTER THE BATTLE WITH THE FROST GIANTS. I ONLY THOUGHT PERHAPS...
SUDDENLY I AM THINKING THIS IS NO HAPPENSTANCE SOCIAL CALL YOU ARE PAYING ME.
YOU'RE WONDERING IF I AM THE ONE WHO TOOK YOUR HAMMER.
I DID NOT SAY THAT, MY LADY. BUT... DID YOU?

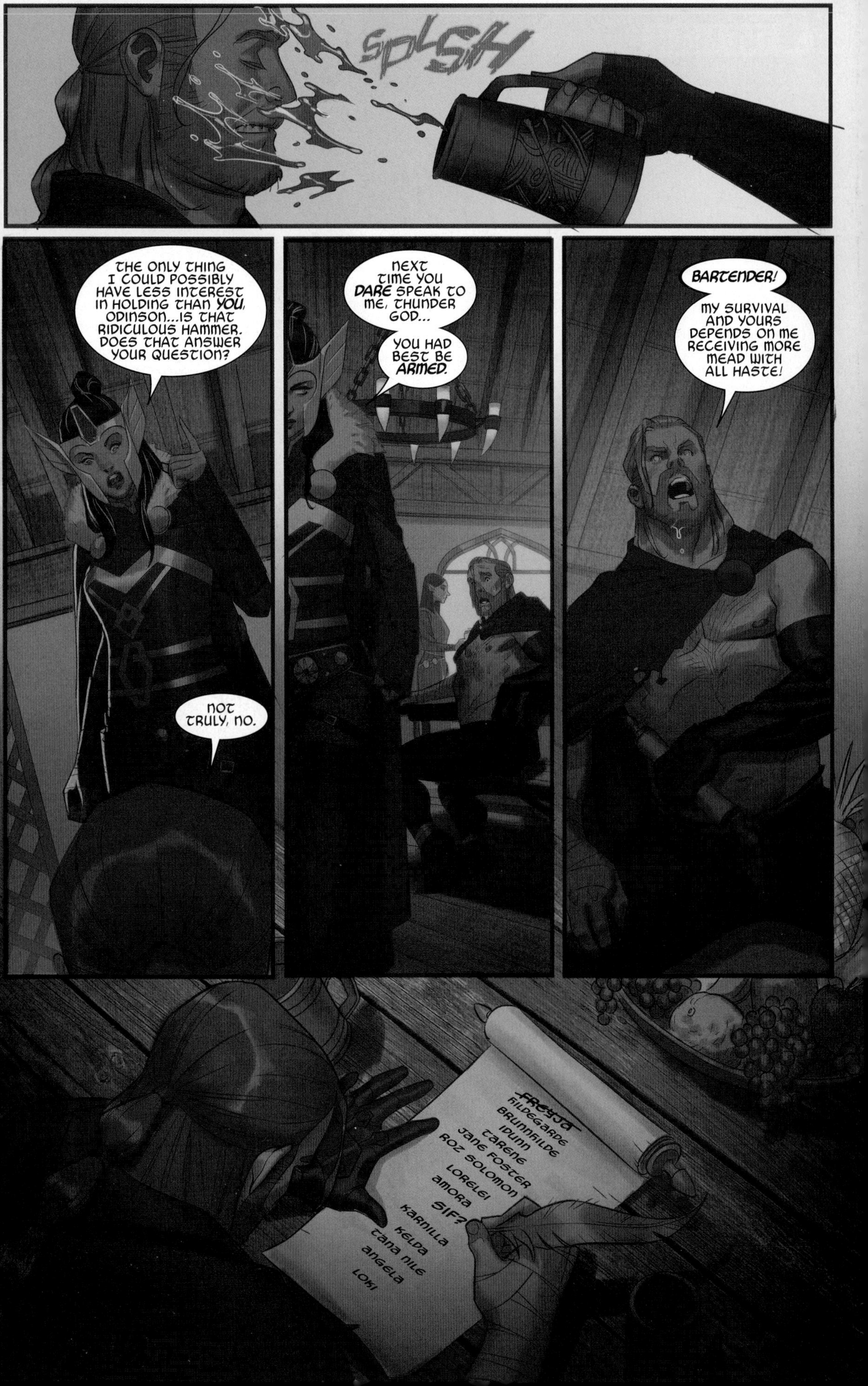
SPLSH
THE ONLY THING I COULD POSSIBLY HAVE LESS INTEREST IN HOLDING THAN YOU, ODINSON...IS THAT RIDICULOUS HAMMER. DOES THAT ANSWER YOUR QUESTION?
NOT TRULY, NO.
NEXT TIME YOU DARE SPEAK TO ME, THUNDER GOD...
YOU HAD BEST BE ARMED.
BARTENDER!
MY SURVIVAL AND YOURS DEPENDS ON ME RECEIVING MORE MEAD WITH ALL HASTE!
~~FREYJA~~
HILDEGARDE
BRUNNHILDE
IDUNN
TARENE
JANE FOSTER
ROZ SOLOMON
LORELEI
AMORA
SIF?
KARNILLA
KELDA
TANA NILE
ANGELA
LOKI

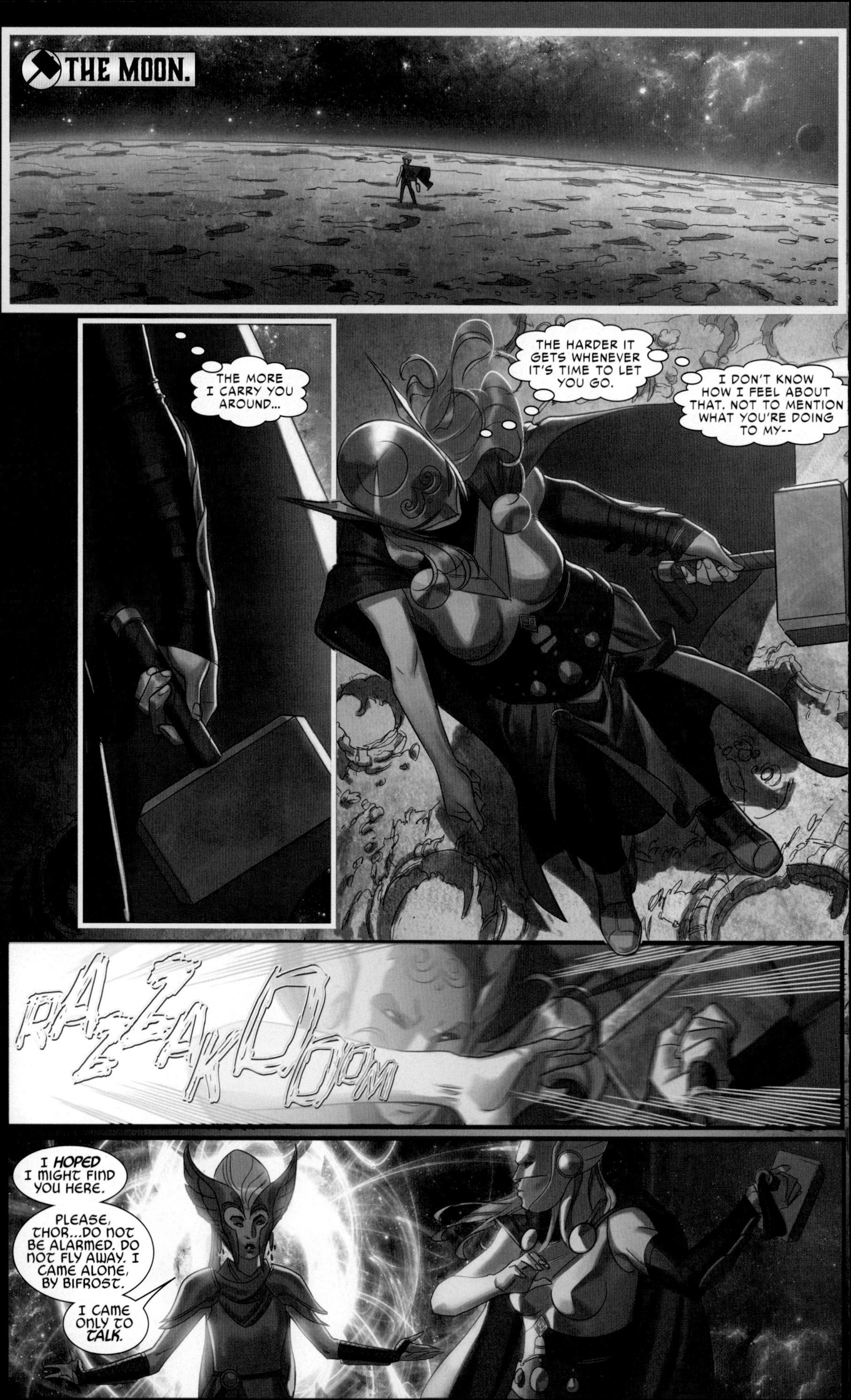
THE MOON.
THE MORE I CARRY YOU AROUND...
THE HARDER IT GETS WHENEVER IT'S TIME TO LET YOU GO.
I DON'T KNOW HOW I FEEL ABOUT THAT. NOT TO MENTION WHAT YOU'RE DOING TO MY--
RAZAKDOOM
I *HOPED* I MIGHT FIND YOU HERE.
PLEASE, THOR...DO NOT BE ALARMED. DO NOT FLY AWAY. I CAME ALONE, BY BIFROST.
I CAME ONLY TO *TALK*.

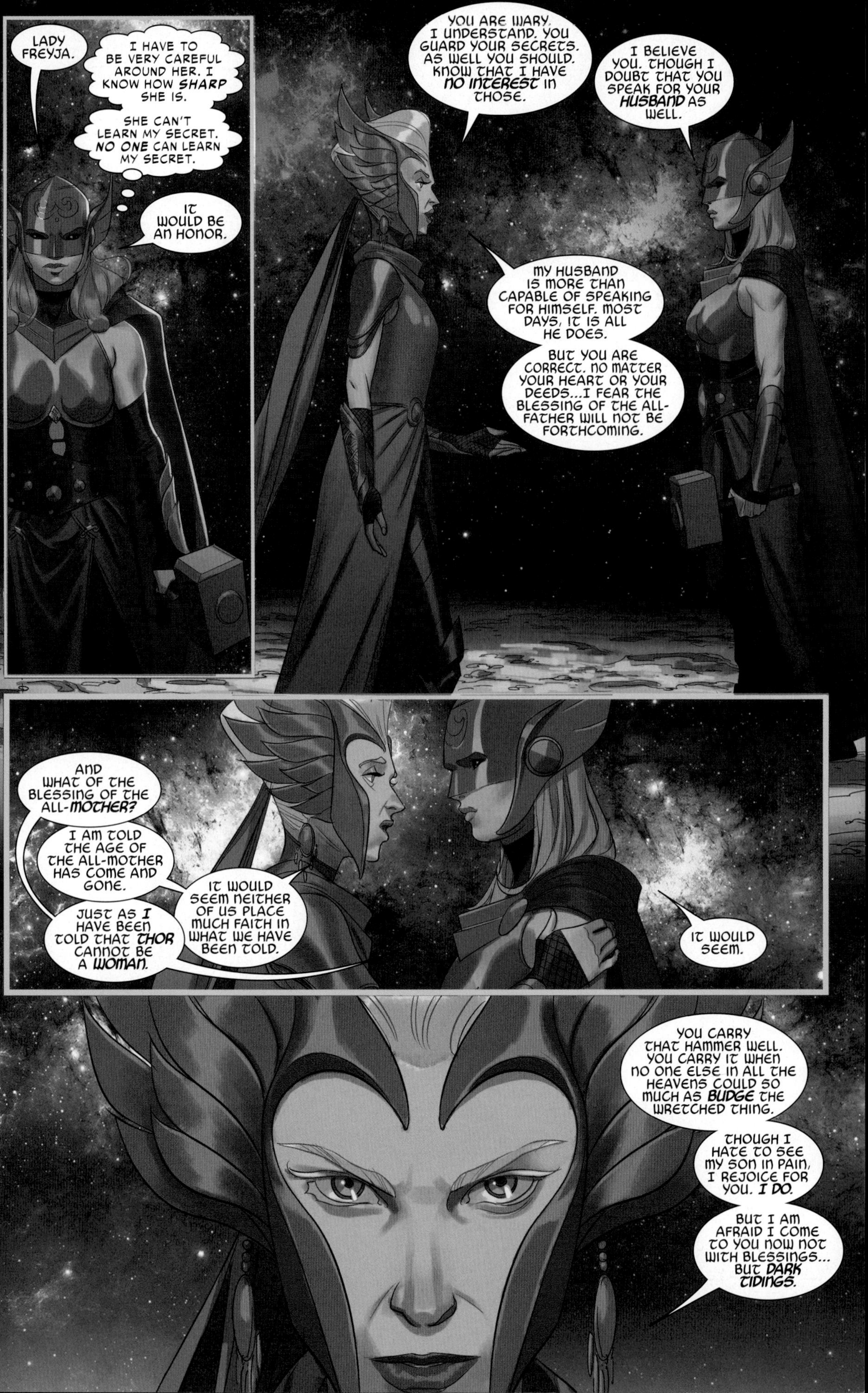
LADY FREYJA.
I HAVE TO BE VERY CAREFUL AROUND HER. I KNOW HOW SHARP SHE IS.
SHE CAN'T LEARN MY SECRET. NO ONE CAN LEARN MY SECRET.
IT WOULD BE AN HONOR.
YOU ARE WARY. I UNDERSTAND. YOU GUARD YOUR SECRETS. AS WELL YOU SHOULD. KNOW THAT I HAVE NO INTEREST IN THOSE.
I BELIEVE YOU. THOUGH I DOUBT THAT YOU SPEAK FOR YOUR HUSBAND AS WELL.
MY HUSBAND IS MORE THAN CAPABLE OF SPEAKING FOR HIMSELF. MOST DAYS, IT IS ALL HE DOES.
BUT YOU ARE CORRECT. NO MATTER YOUR HEART OR YOUR DEEDS...I FEAR THE BLESSING OF THE ALL-FATHER WILL NOT BE FORTHCOMING.
AND WHAT OF THE BLESSING OF THE ALL-MOTHER?
I AM TOLD THE AGE OF THE ALL-MOTHER HAS COME AND GONE.
JUST AS I HAVE BEEN TOLD THAT THOR CANNOT BE A WOMAN.
IT WOULD SEEM NEITHER OF US PLACE MUCH FAITH IN WHAT WE HAVE BEEN TOLD.
IT WOULD SEEM.
YOU CARRY THAT HAMMER WELL. YOU CARRY IT WHEN NO ONE ELSE IN ALL THE HEAVENS COULD SO MUCH AS BUDGE THE WRETCHED THING.
THOUGH I HATE TO SEE MY SON IN PAIN, I REJOICE FOR YOU. I DO.
BUT I AM AFRAID I COME TO YOU NOW NOT WITH BLESSINGS... BUT DARK TIDINGS.

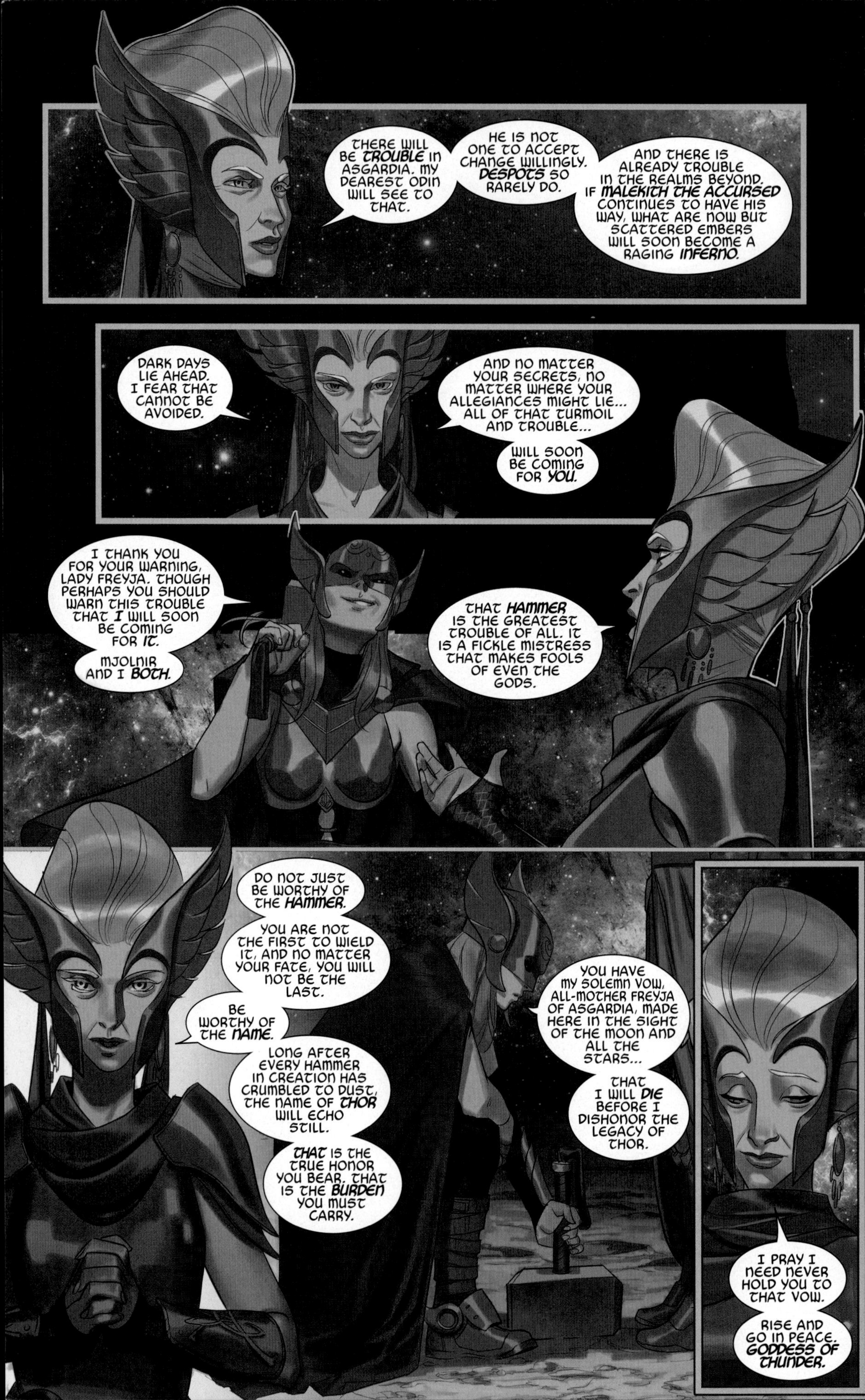
THERE WILL BE TROUBLE IN ASGARDIA. MY DEAREST ODIN WILL SEE TO THAT.
HE IS NOT ONE TO ACCEPT CHANGE WILLINGLY. DESPOTS SO RARELY DO.
AND THERE IS ALREADY TROUBLE IN THE REALMS BEYOND. IF MALEKITH THE ACCURSED CONTINUES TO HAVE HIS WAY, WHAT ARE NOW BUT SCATTERED EMBERS WILL SOON BECOME A RAGING INFERNO.
DARK DAYS LIE AHEAD. I FEAR THAT CANNOT BE AVOIDED.
AND NO MATTER YOUR SECRETS, NO MATTER WHERE YOUR ALLEGIANCES MIGHT LIE... ALL OF THAT TURMOIL AND TROUBLE...
WILL SOON BE COMING FOR YOU.
I THANK YOU FOR YOUR WARNING, LADY FREYJA. THOUGH PERHAPS YOU SHOULD WARN THIS TROUBLE THAT I WILL SOON BE COMING FOR IT.
MJOLNIR AND I BOTH.
THAT HAMMER IS THE GREATEST TROUBLE OF ALL. IT IS A FICKLE MISTRESS THAT MAKES FOOLS OF EVEN THE GODS.
DO NOT JUST BE WORTHY OF THE HAMMER.
YOU ARE NOT THE FIRST TO WIELD IT, AND NO MATTER YOUR FATE, YOU WILL NOT BE THE LAST.
BE WORTHY OF THE NAME.
LONG AFTER EVERY HAMMER IN CREATION HAS CRUMBLED TO DUST, THE NAME OF THOR WILL ECHO STILL.
THAT IS THE TRUE HONOR YOU BEAR. THAT IS THE BURDEN YOU MUST CARRY.
YOU HAVE MY SOLEMN VOW, ALL-MOTHER FREYJA OF ASGARDIA, MADE HERE IN THE SIGHT OF THE MOON AND ALL THE STARS...
THAT I WILL DIE BEFORE I DISHONOR THE LEGACY OF THOR.
I PRAY I NEED NEVER HOLD YOU TO THAT VOW.
RISE AND GO IN PEACE, GODDESS OF THUNDER.

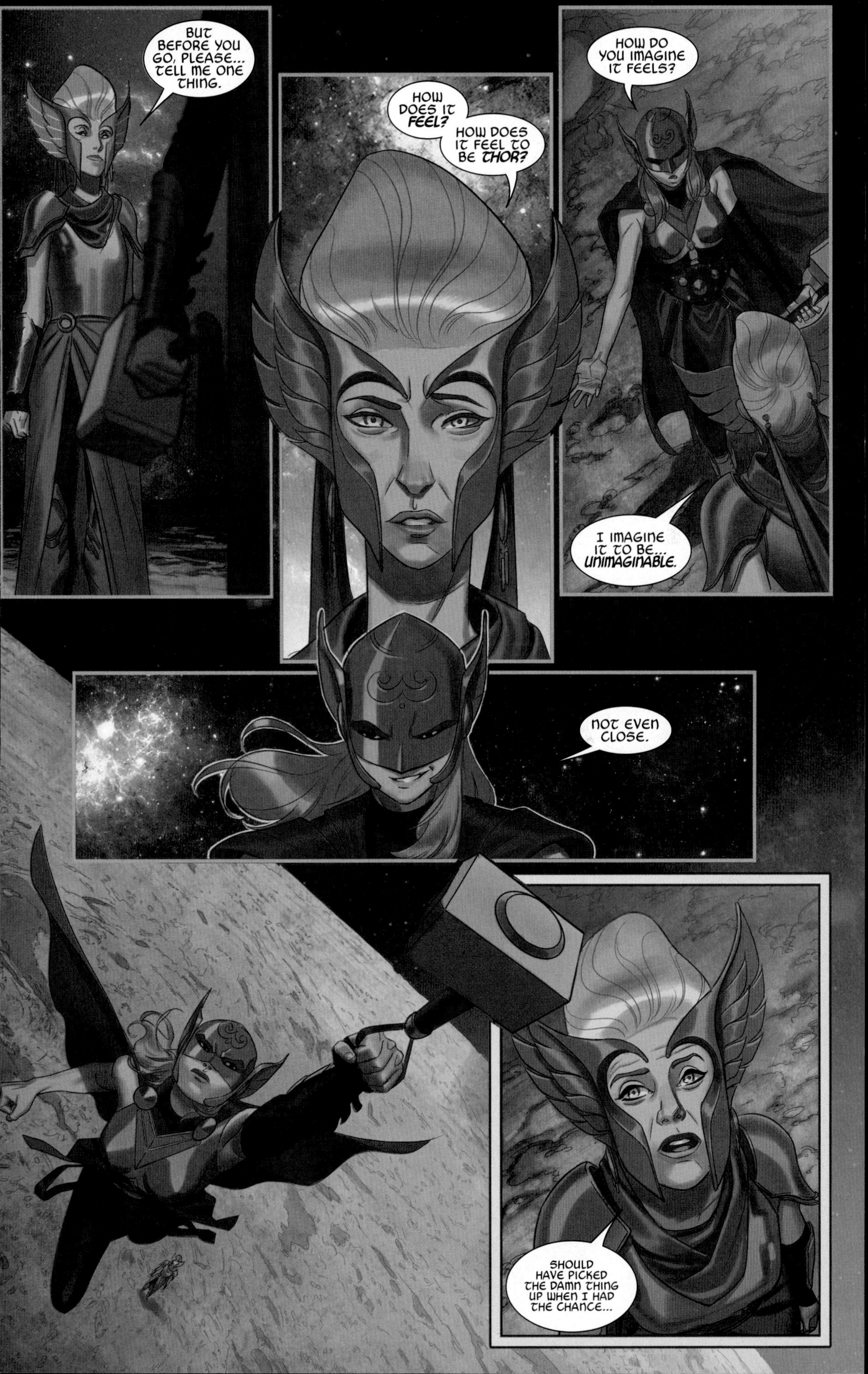
BUT BEFORE YOU GO, PLEASE... TELL ME ONE THING.
HOW DOES IT FEEL?
HOW DOES IT FEEL TO BE THOR?
HOW DO YOU IMAGINE IT FEELS?
I IMAGINE IT TO BE... UNIMAGINABLE.
NOT EVEN CLOSE.
SHOULD HAVE PICKED THE DAMN THING UP WHEN I HAD THE CHANCE...

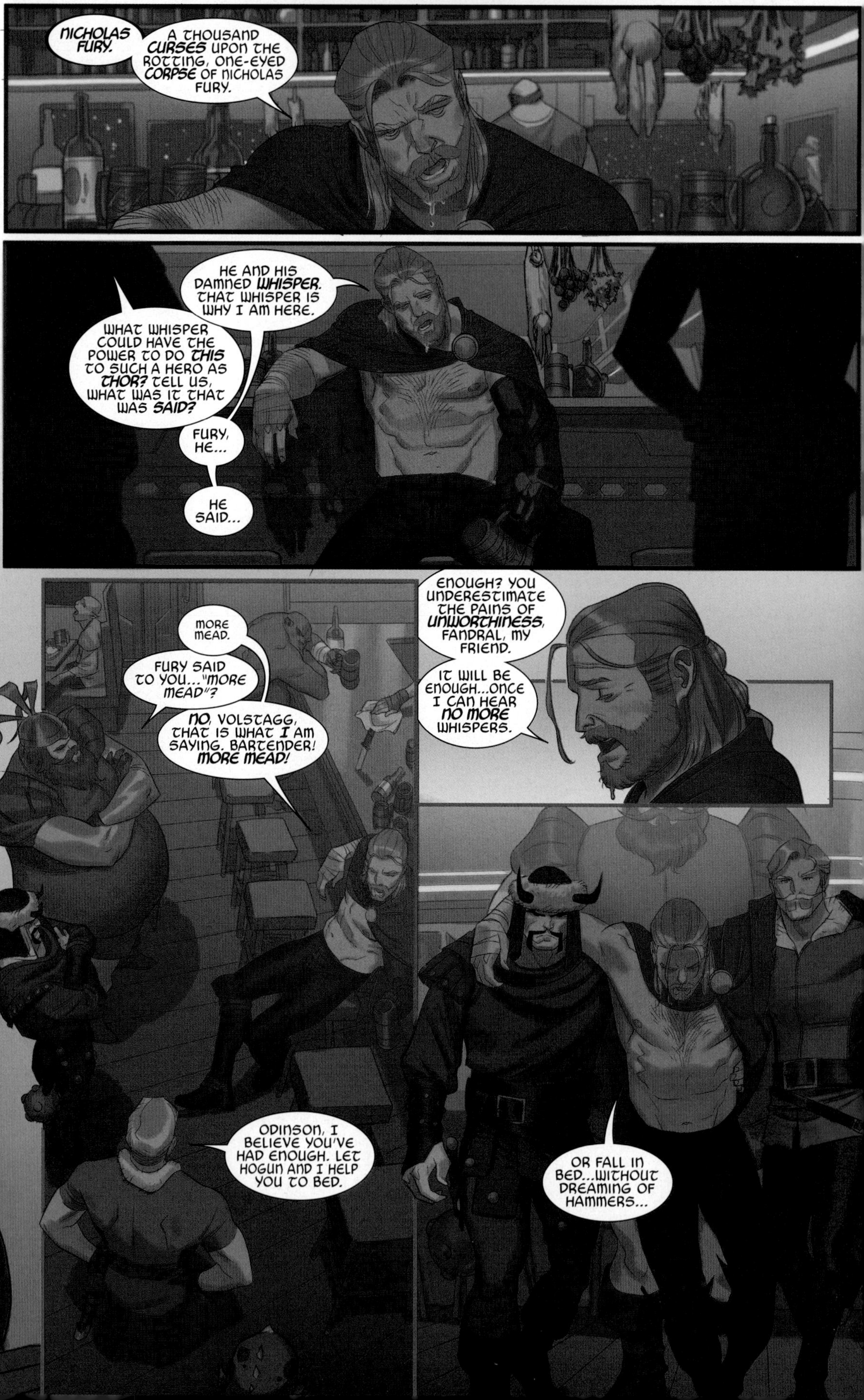
NICHOLAS FURY.
A THOUSAND CURSES UPON THE ROTTING, ONE-EYED CORPSE OF NICHOLAS FURY.
HE AND HIS DAMNED WHISPER. THAT WHISPER IS WHY I AM HERE.
WHAT WHISPER COULD HAVE THE POWER TO DO THIS TO SUCH A HERO AS THOR? TELL US, WHAT WAS IT THAT WAS SAID?
FURY, HE...
HE SAID...
MORE MEAD.
FURY SAID TO YOU..."MORE MEAD"?
NO, VOLSTAGG, THAT IS WHAT I AM SAYING. BARTENDER! MORE MEAD!
ENOUGH? YOU UNDERESTIMATE THE PAINS OF UNWORTHINESS, FANDRAL, MY FRIEND.
IT WILL BE ENOUGH...ONCE I CAN HEAR NO MORE WHISPERS.
ODINSON, I BELIEVE YOU'VE HAD ENOUGH. LET HOGUN AND I HELP YOU TO BED.
OR FALL IN BED...WITHOUT DREAMING OF HAMMERS...

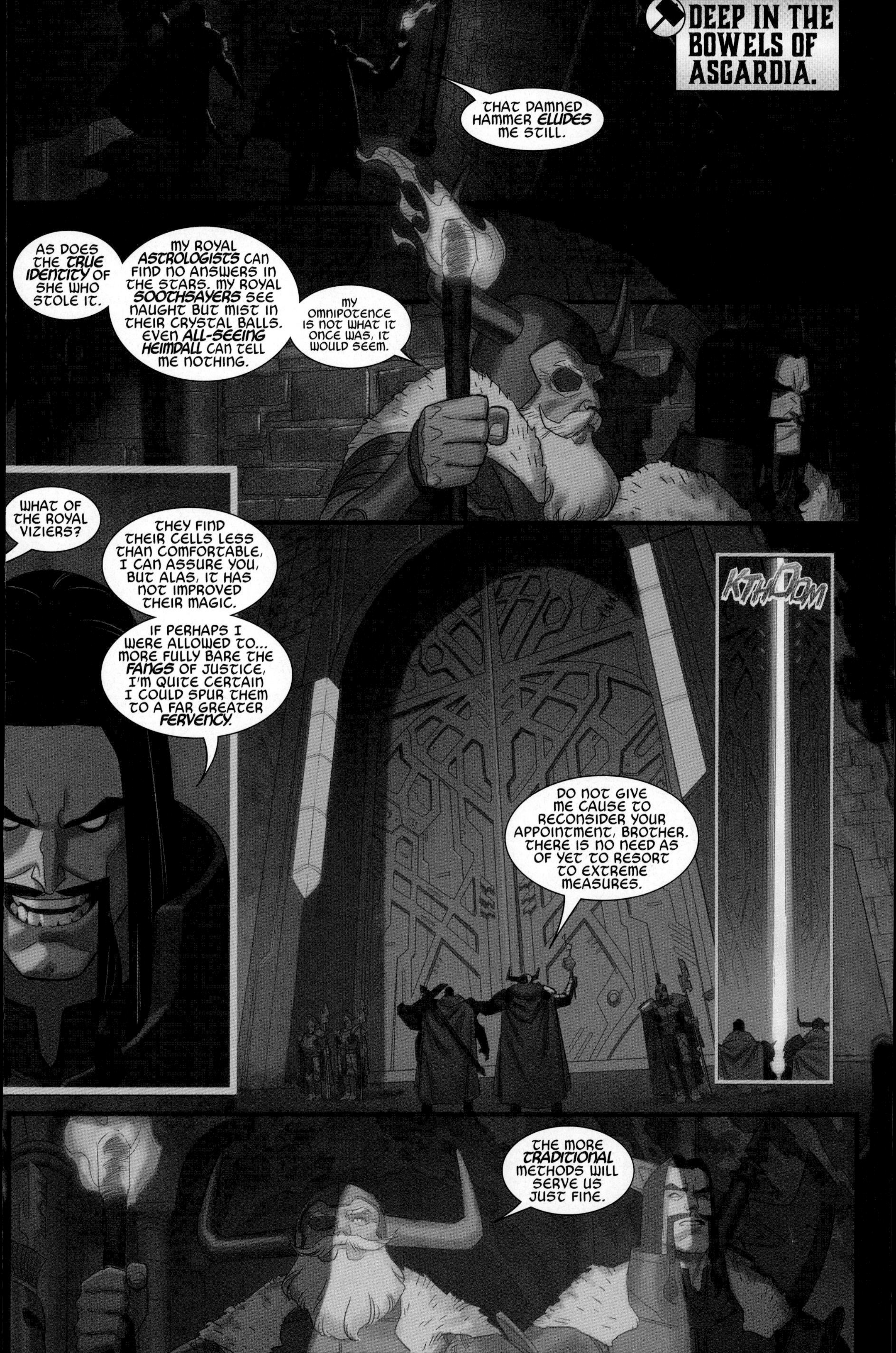
DEEP IN THE BOWELS OF ASGARDIA.
THAT DAMNED HAMMER ELUDES ME STILL.
AS DOES THE TRUE IDENTITY OF SHE WHO STOLE IT.
MY ROYAL ASTROLOGISTS CAN FIND NO ANSWERS IN THE STARS. MY ROYAL SOOTHSAYERS SEE NAUGHT BUT MIST IN THEIR CRYSTAL BALLS. EVEN ALL-SEEING HEIMDALL CAN TELL ME NOTHING.
MY OMNIPOTENCE IS NOT WHAT IT ONCE WAS, IT WOULD SEEM.
WHAT OF THE ROYAL VIZIERS?
THEY FIND THEIR CELLS LESS THAN COMFORTABLE, I CAN ASSURE YOU, BUT ALAS, IT HAS NOT IMPROVED THEIR MAGIC.
IF PERHAPS I WERE ALLOWED TO... MORE FULLY BARE THE FANGS OF JUSTICE, I'M QUITE CERTAIN I COULD SPUR THEM TO A FAR GREATER FERVENCY.
KTHOOM
DO NOT GIVE ME CAUSE TO RECONSIDER YOUR APPOINTMENT, BROTHER. THERE IS NO NEED AS OF YET TO RESORT TO EXTREME MEASURES.
THE MORE TRADITIONAL METHODS WILL SERVE US JUST FINE.

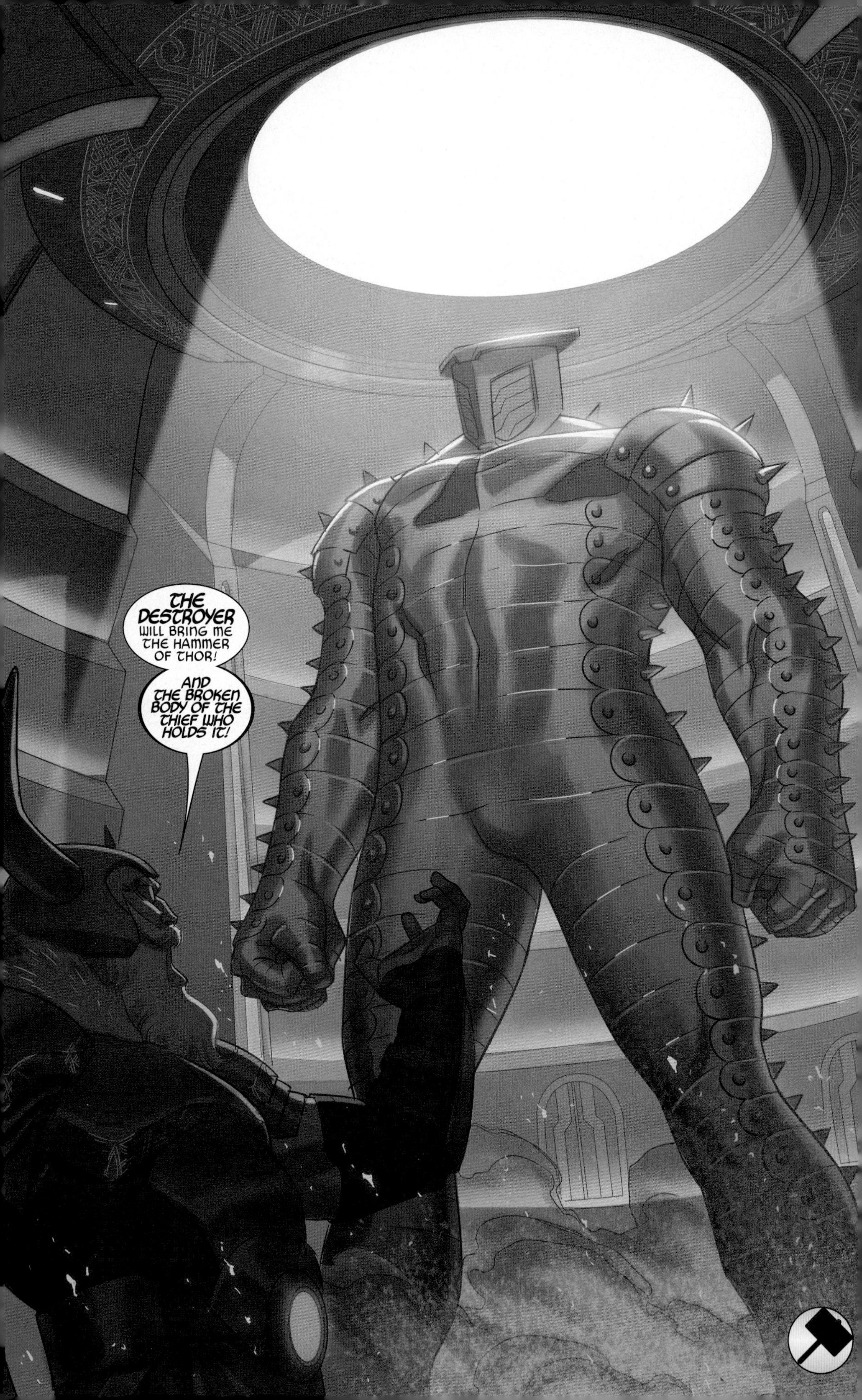
THE DESTROYER WILL BRING ME THE HAMMER OF THOR!
AND THE BROKEN BODY OF THE THIEF WHO HOLDS IT!

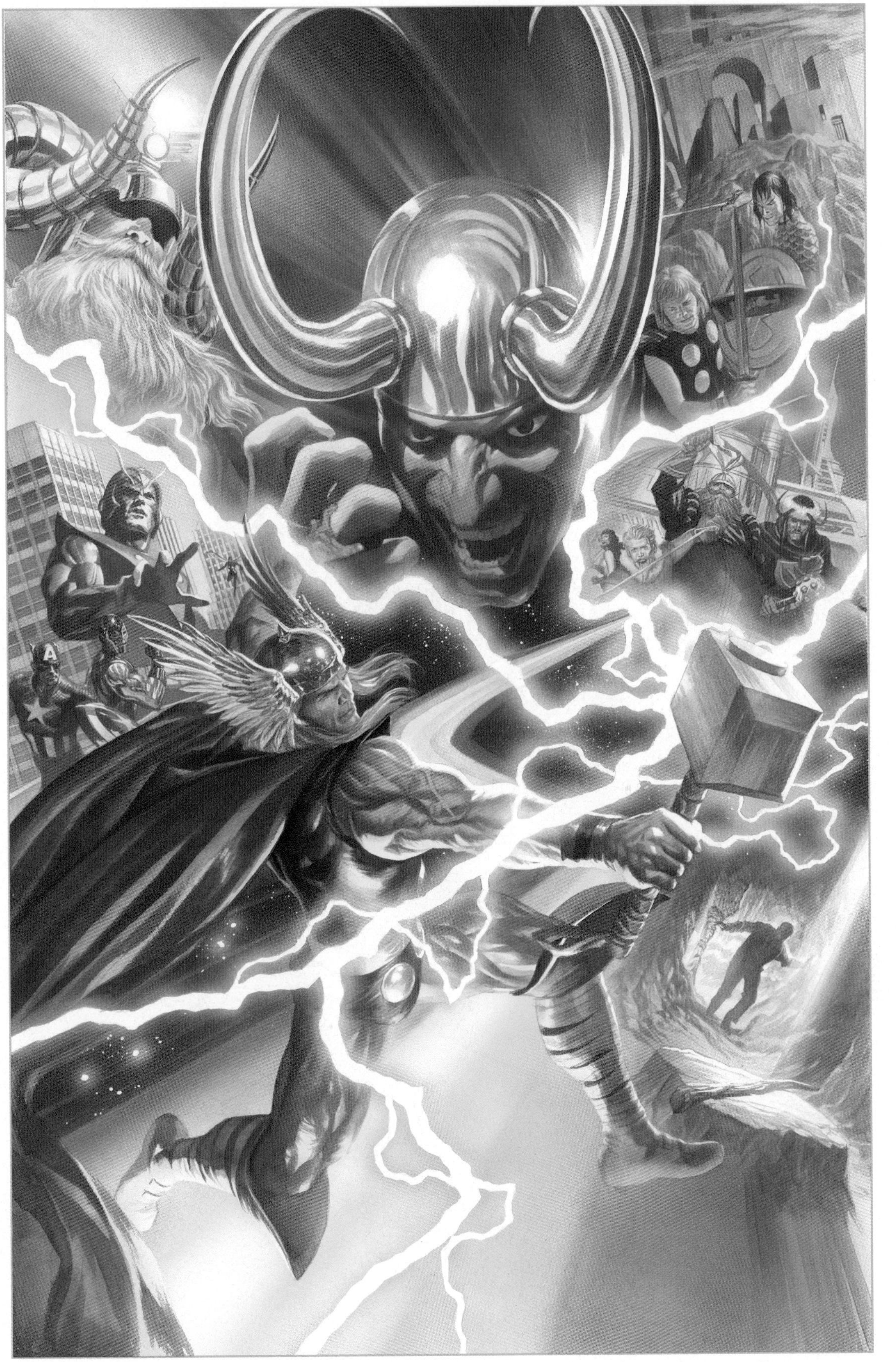

THOR # 1 75TH ANNIVERSARY VARIANT
BY **ALEX ROSS**

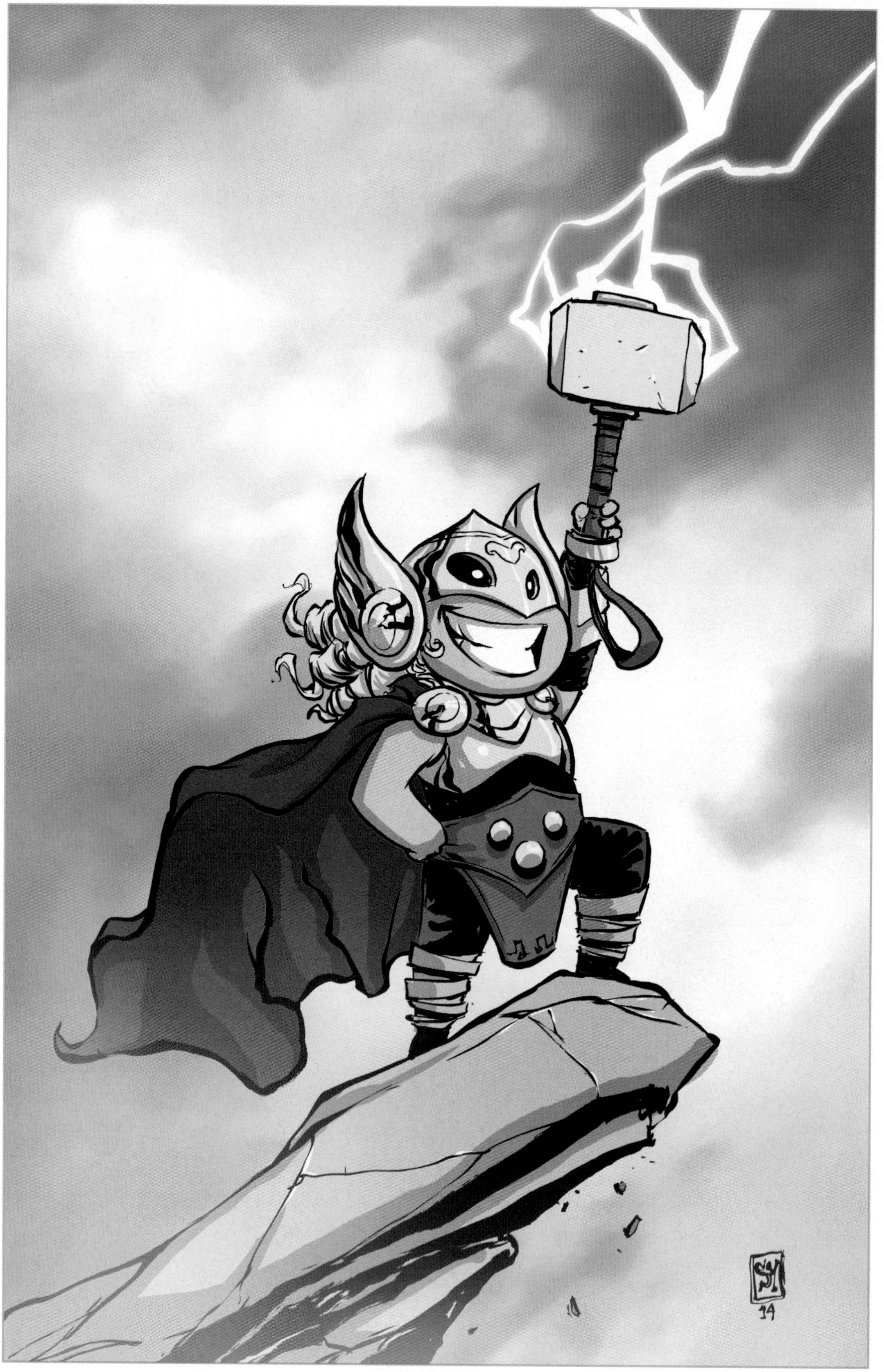

THOR # 1 VARIANT
BY **SKOTTIE YOUNG**

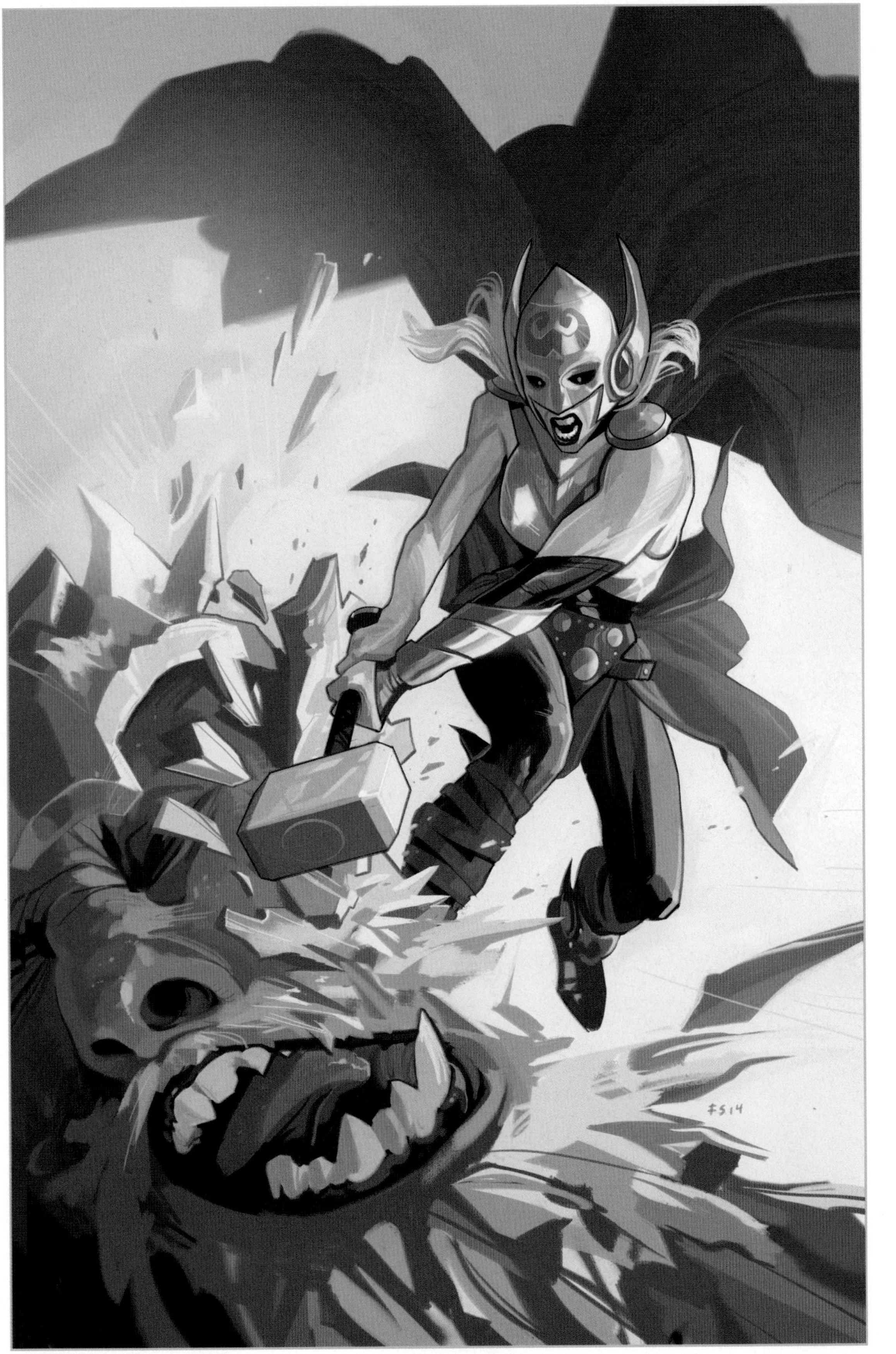
FS14

THOR # 1 VARIANT
BY **FIONA STAPLES**

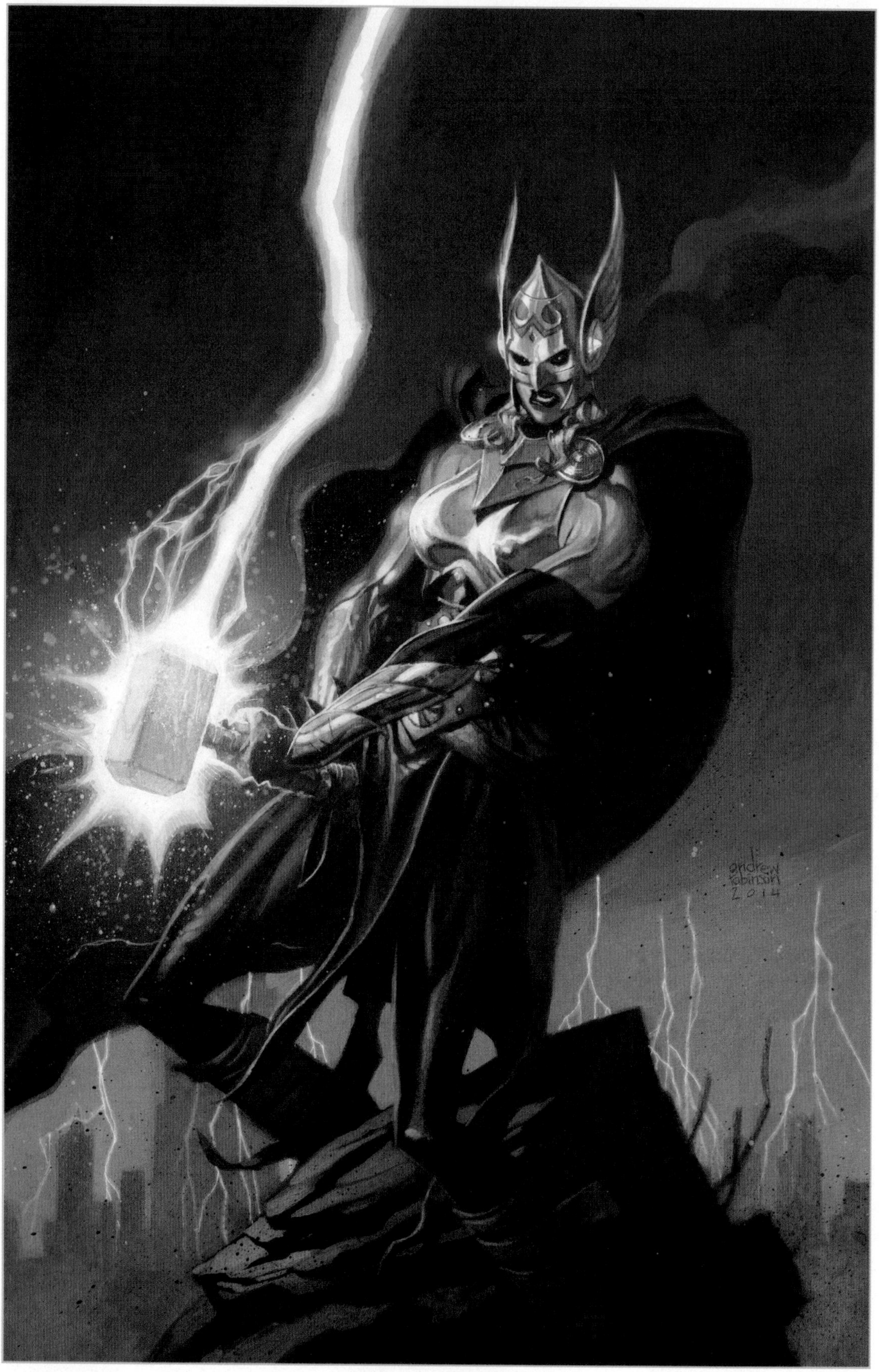
andrew robinson 2014

THOR # 1 VARIANT
BY **ANDREW ROBINSON**

THOR # 1 VARIANT
BY **SARA PICHELLI** & **LAURA MARTIN**

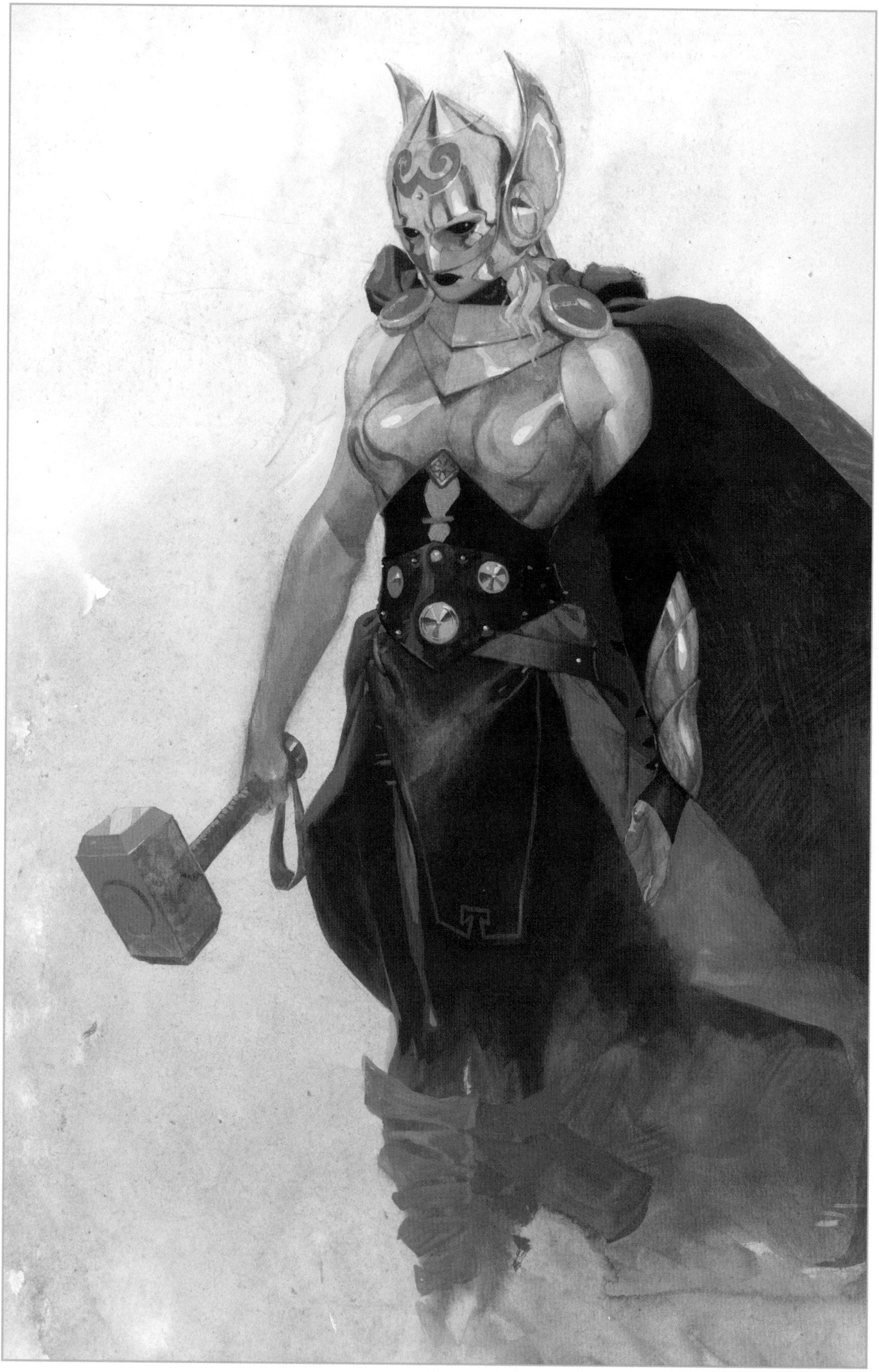

THOR # 1 DESIGN VARIANT
BY **ESAD RIBIC**

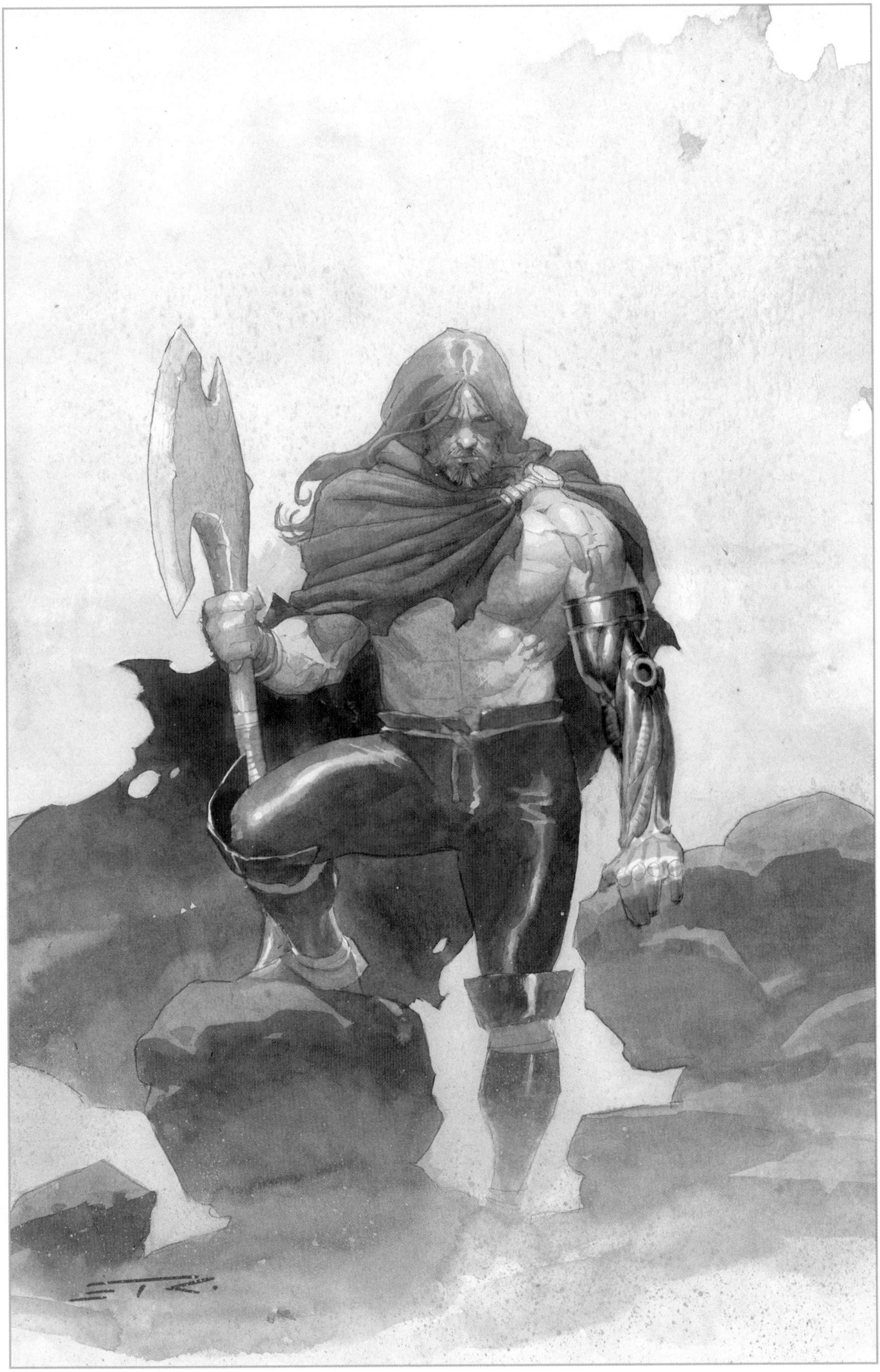

THOR # 2 DESIGN VARIANT
BY **ESAD RIBIC**

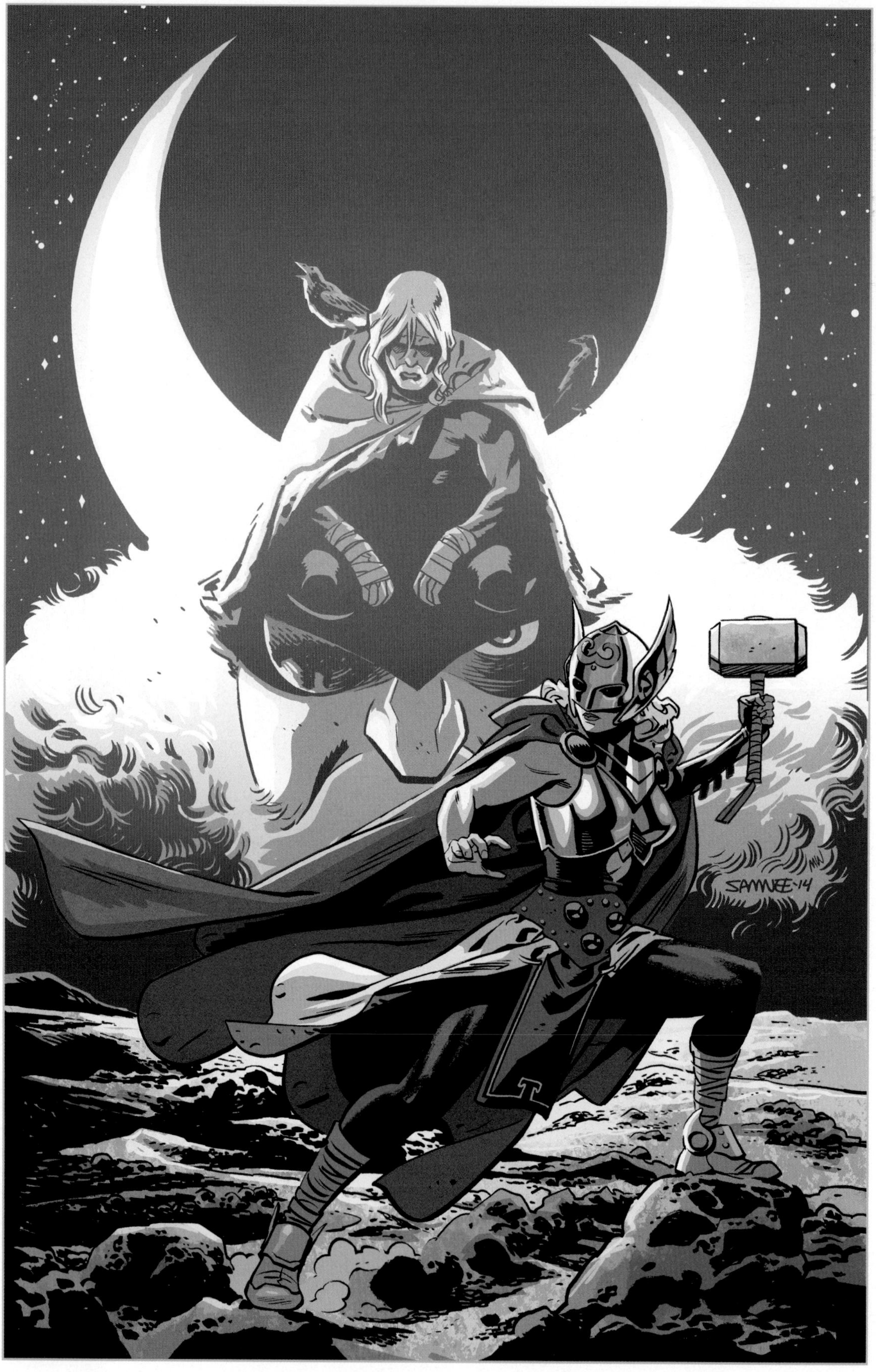
SAMNEE-'14
MW

THOR # 2 VARIANT
BY **CHRIS SAMNEE & MATTHEW WILSON**

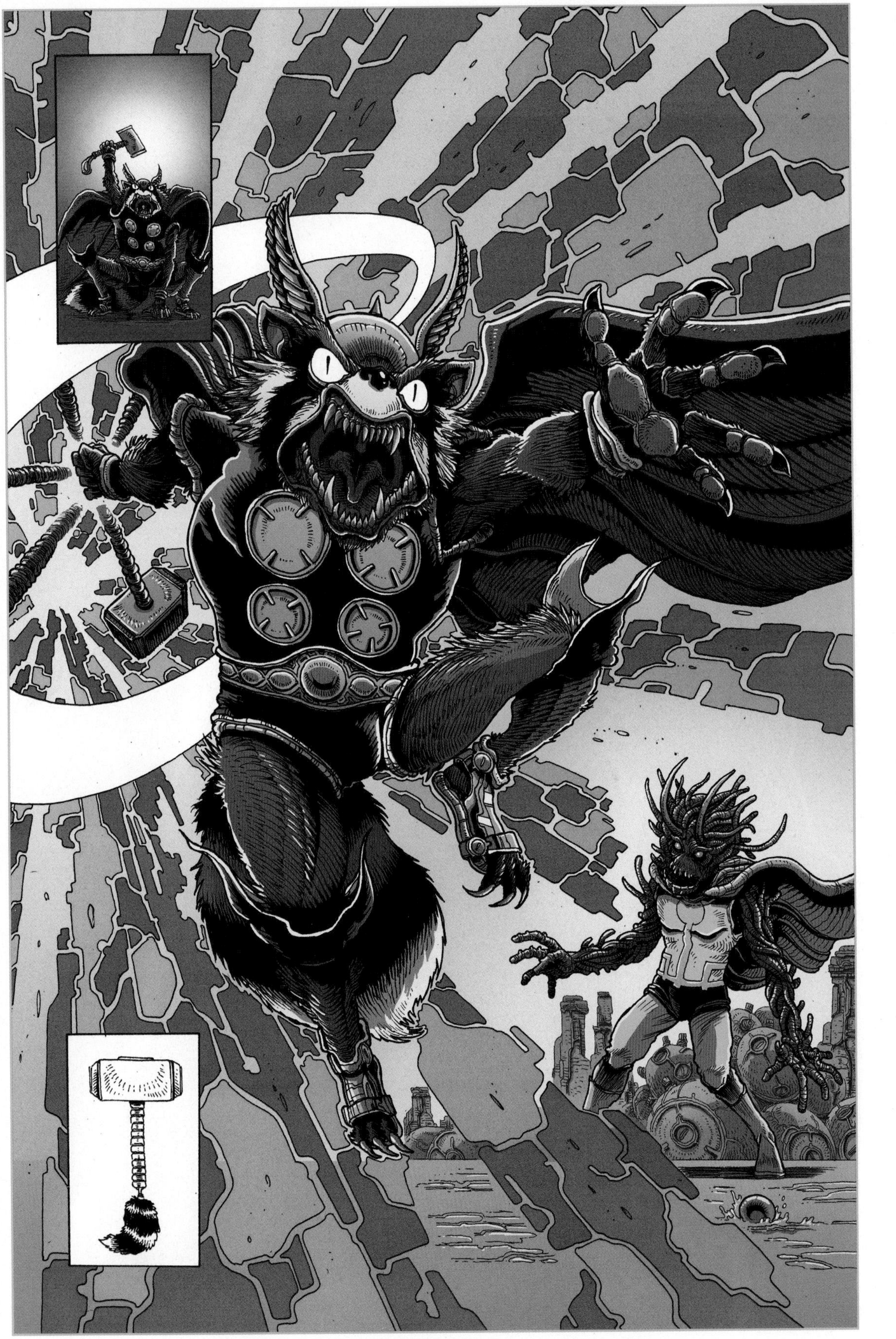

THOR # 2 ROCKET & GROOT VARIANT
BY **JAMES STOKOE**

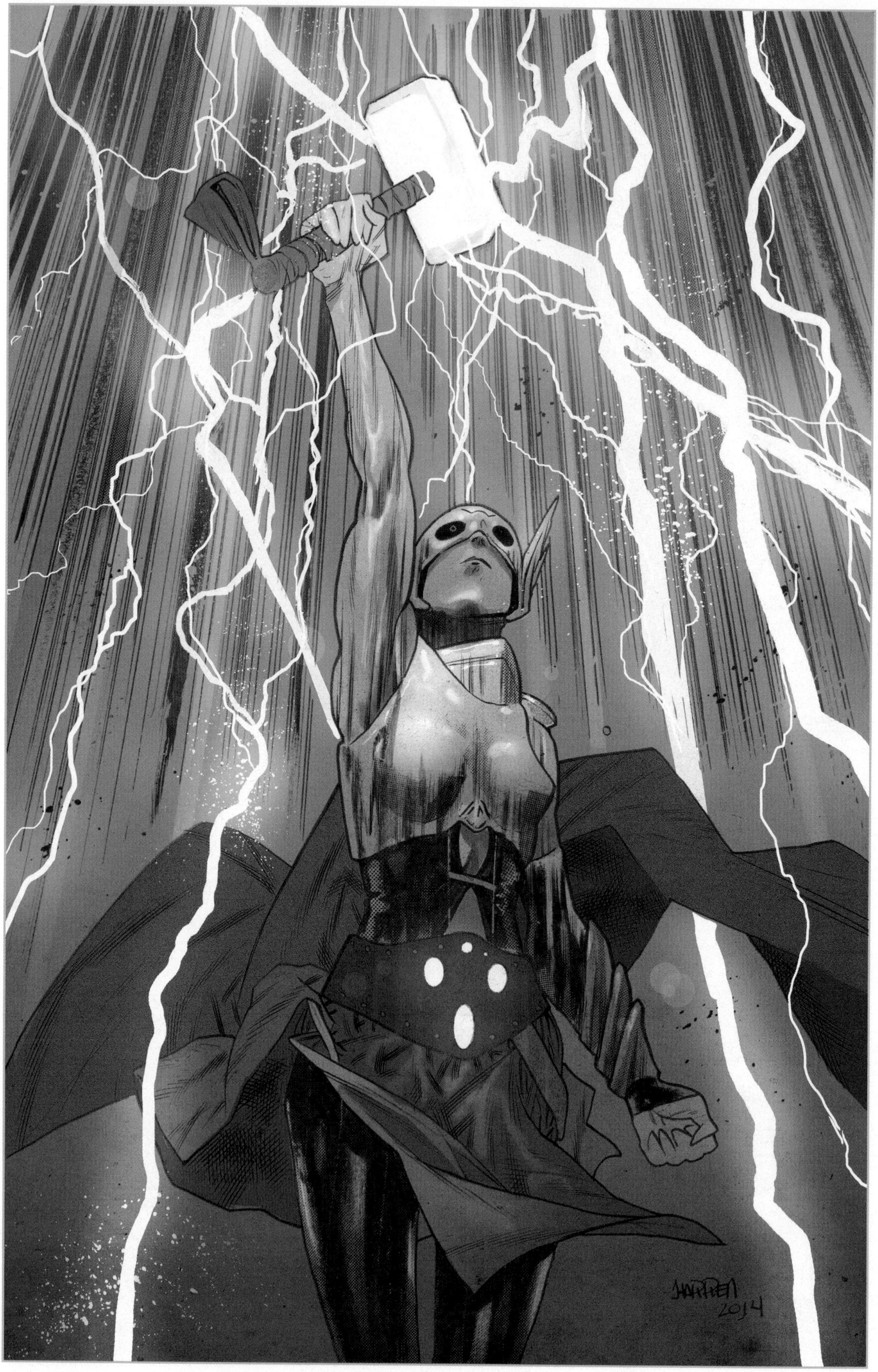
HARREN
2014

THOR # 3 VARIANT
BY **JAMES HARREN**

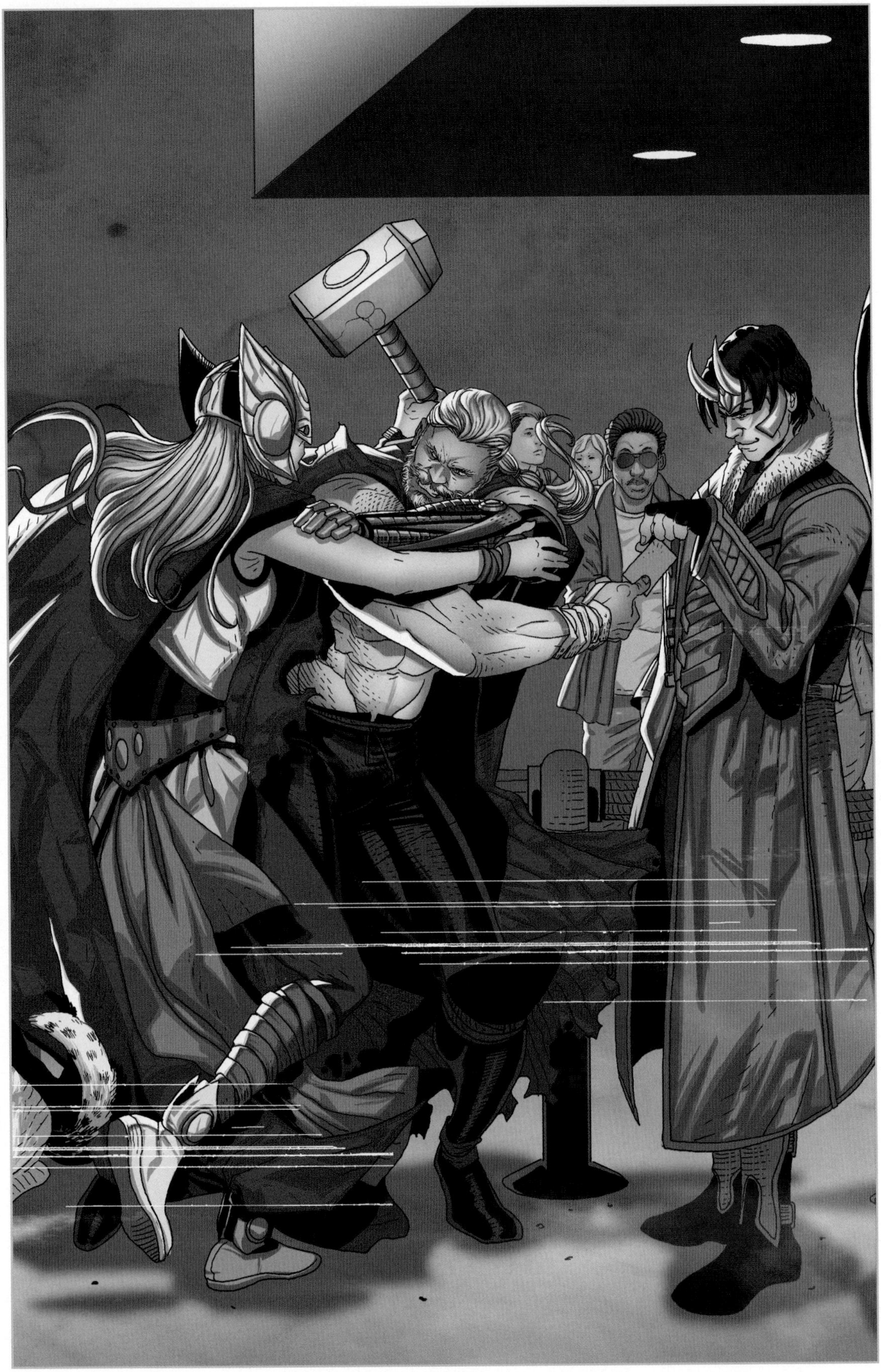

THOR # 4 WELCOME HOME VARIANT
BY **SALVADOR LARROCA & ISRAEL SILVA**

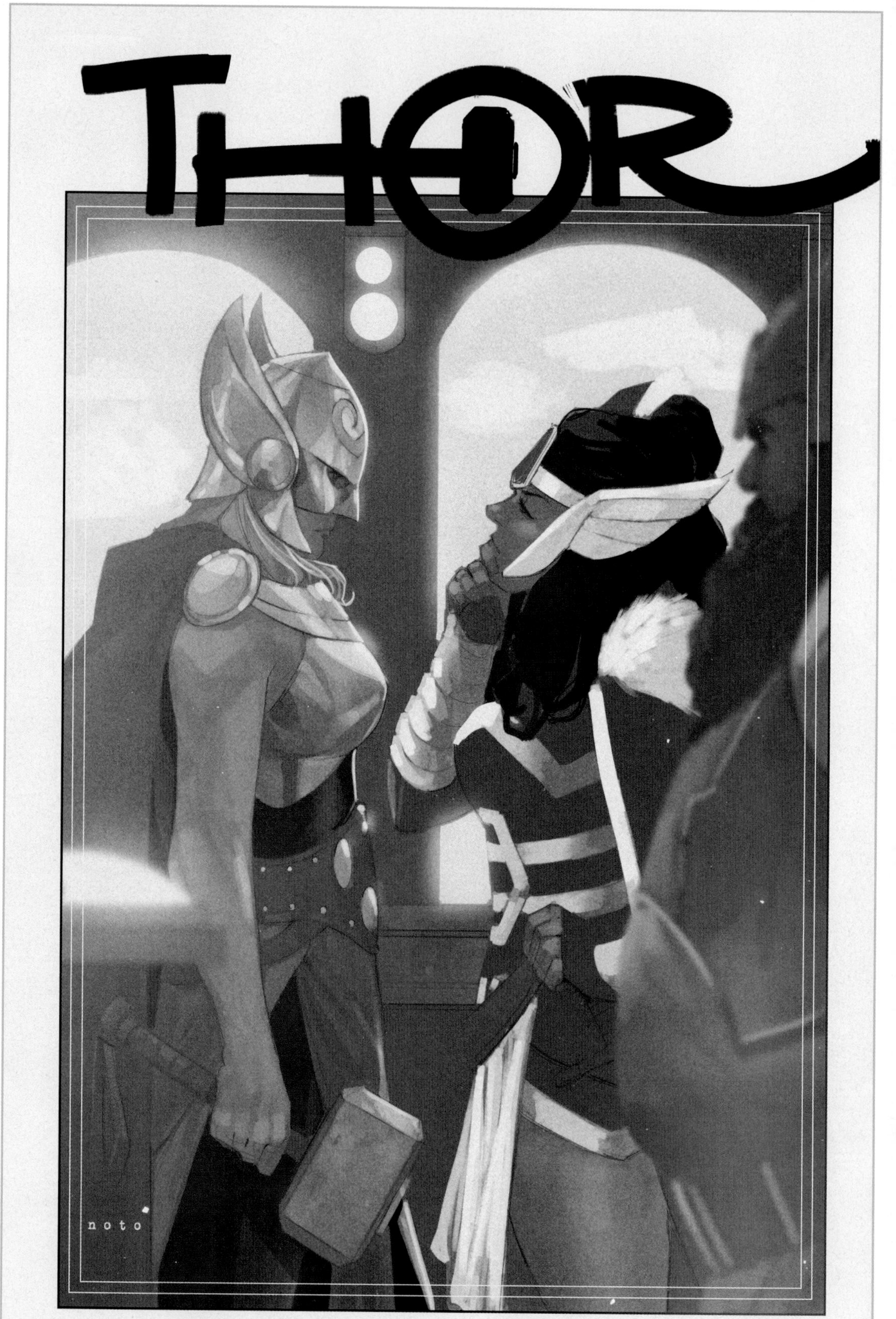
THOR
noto

THOR # 5 VARIANT
BY **PHIL NOTO**

CHARACTER DESIGNS
BY RUSSELL DAUTERMAN

THOR

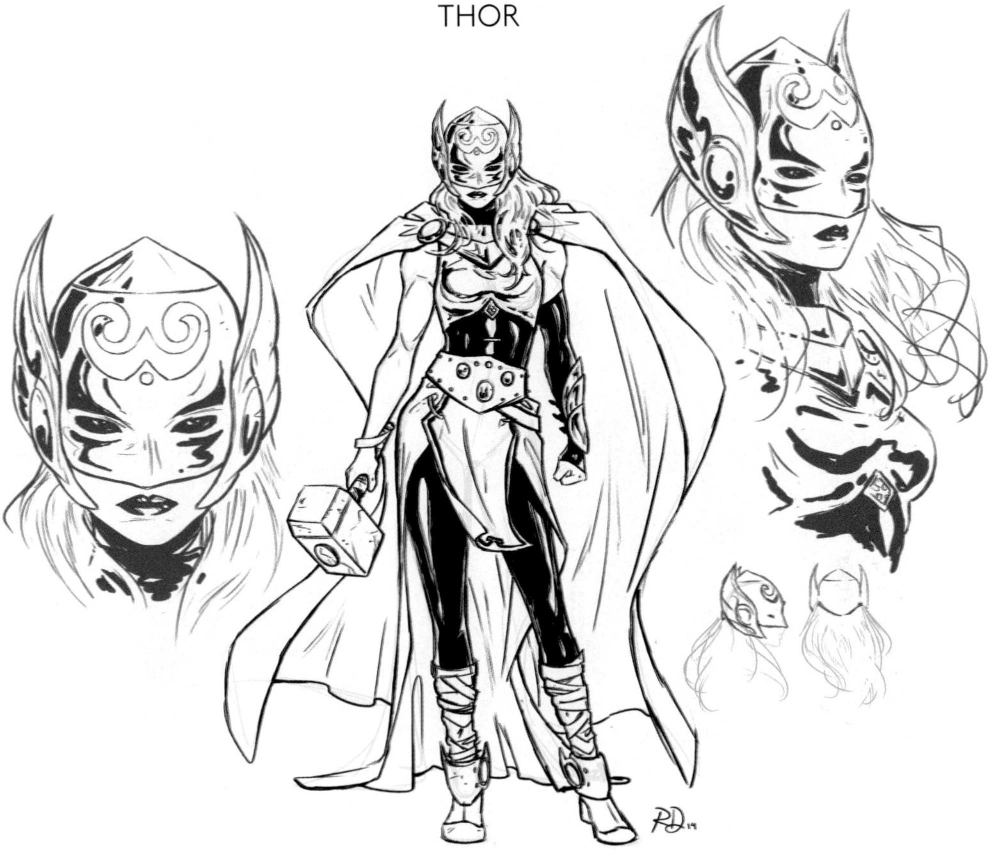

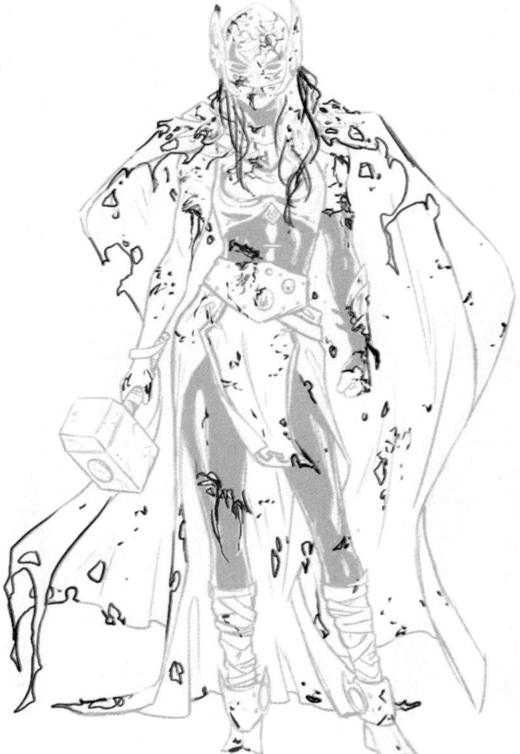

BATTLE DAMAGE

ODINSON

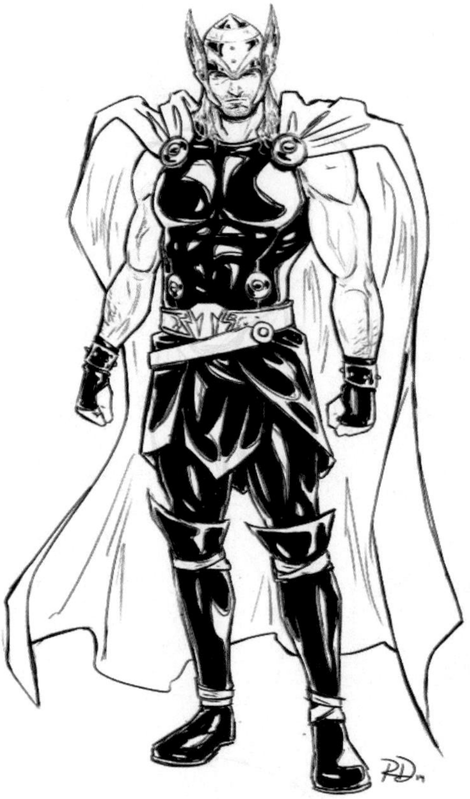

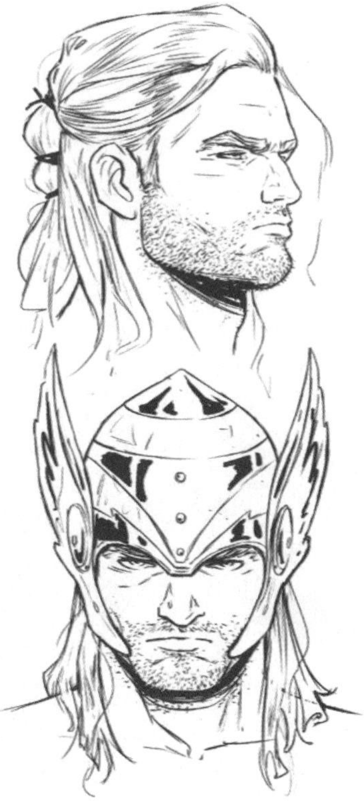

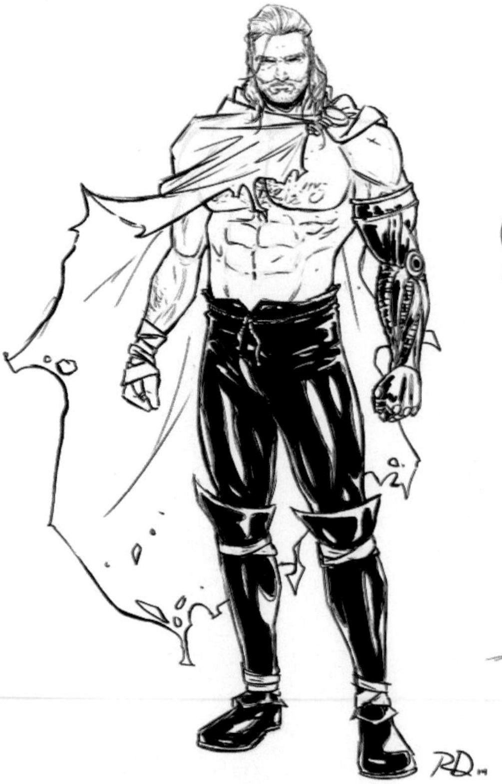

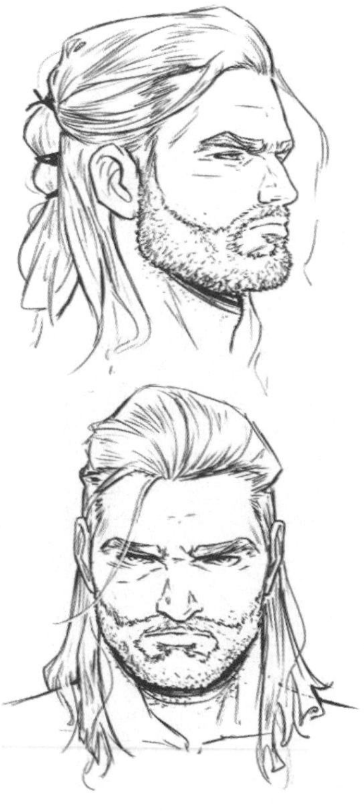

ODIN & FREYJA

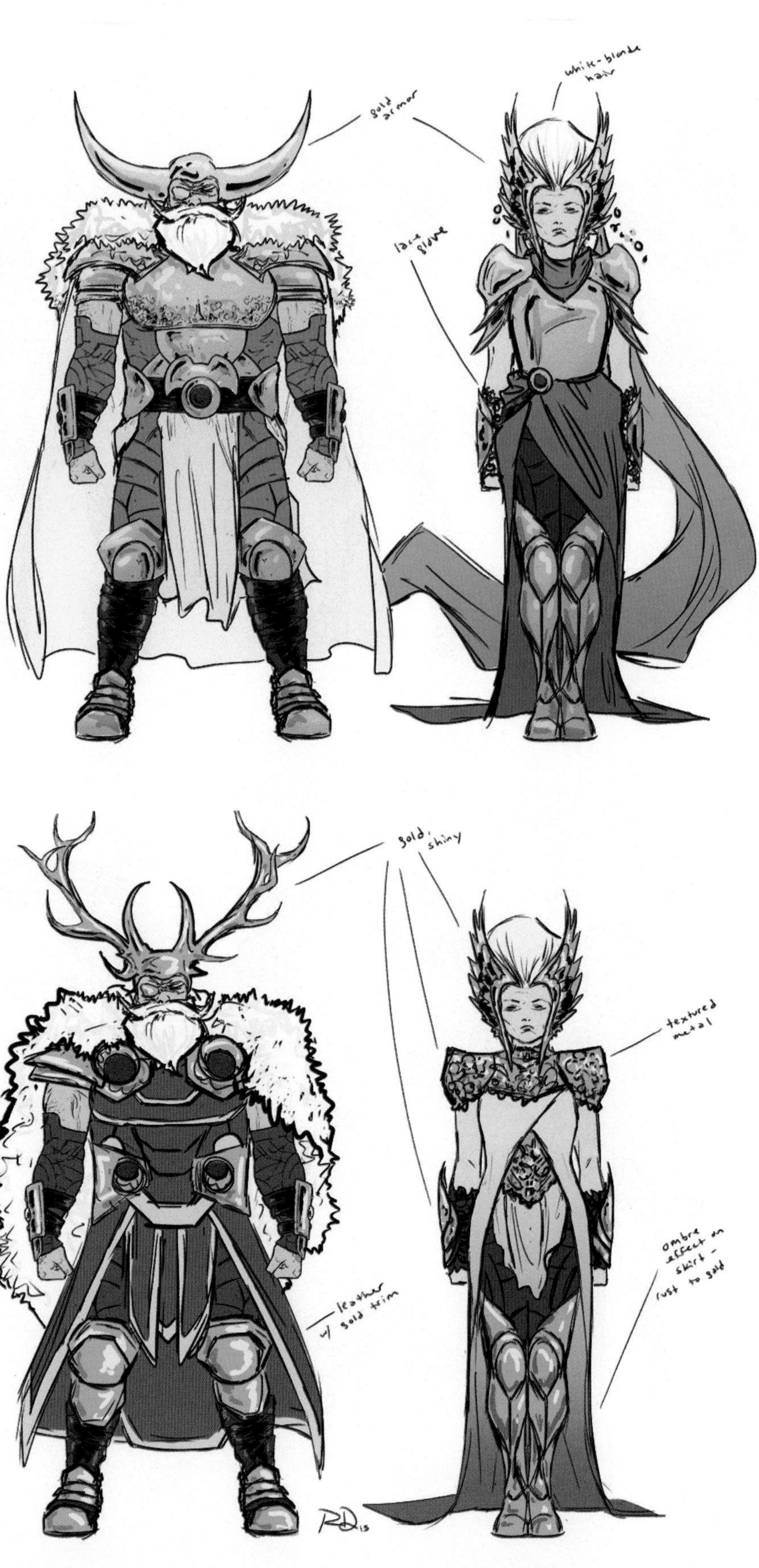
gold armor
white-blonde hair
lace glove
gold, shiny
textured metal
leather w/ gold trim
ombre affect on skirt - rust to gold

MALEKITH

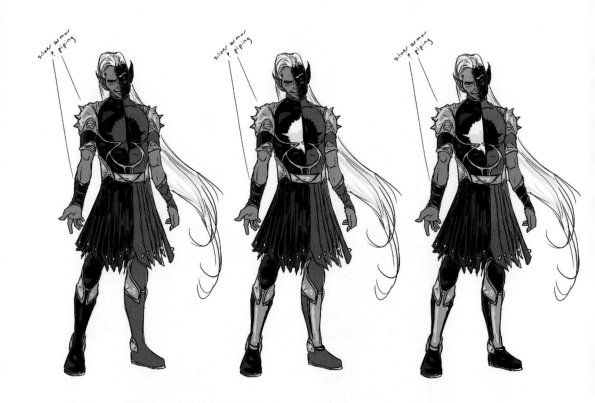

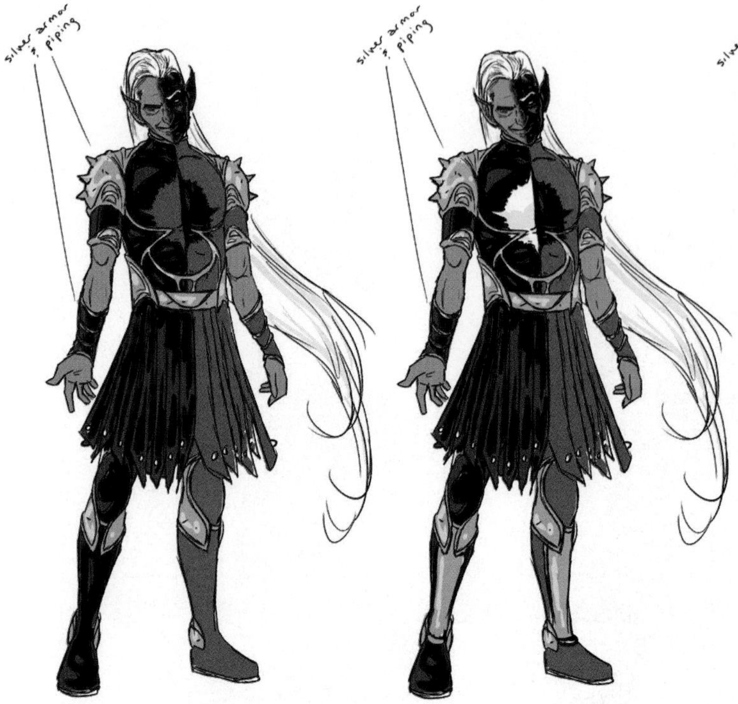
silver armor & piping
silver armor & piping
silver armor & piping

ROZ SOLOMON

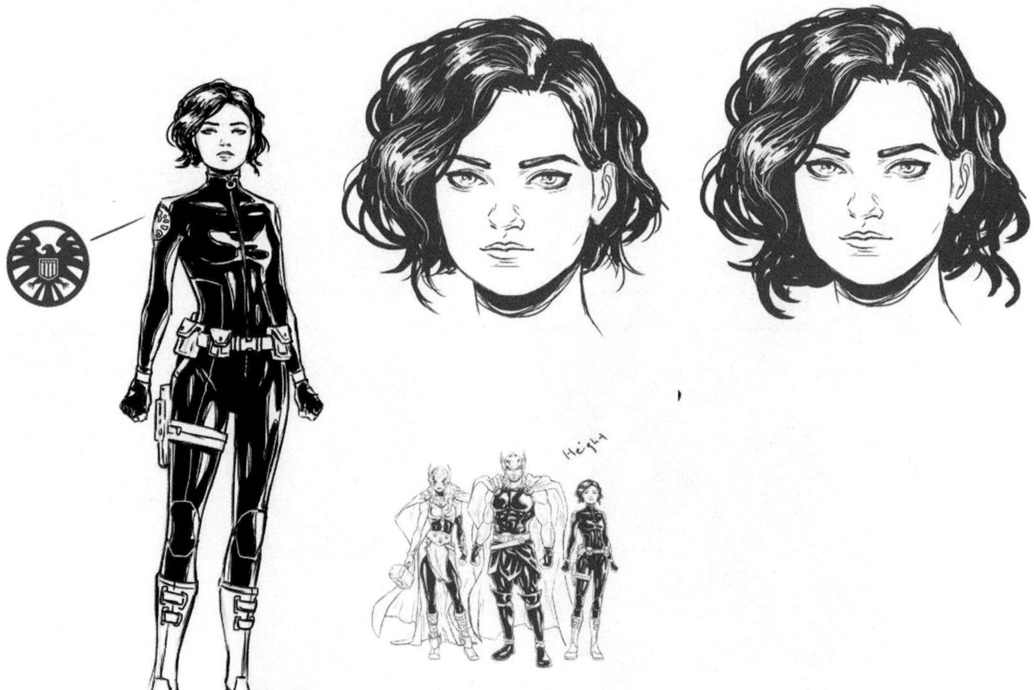
Height

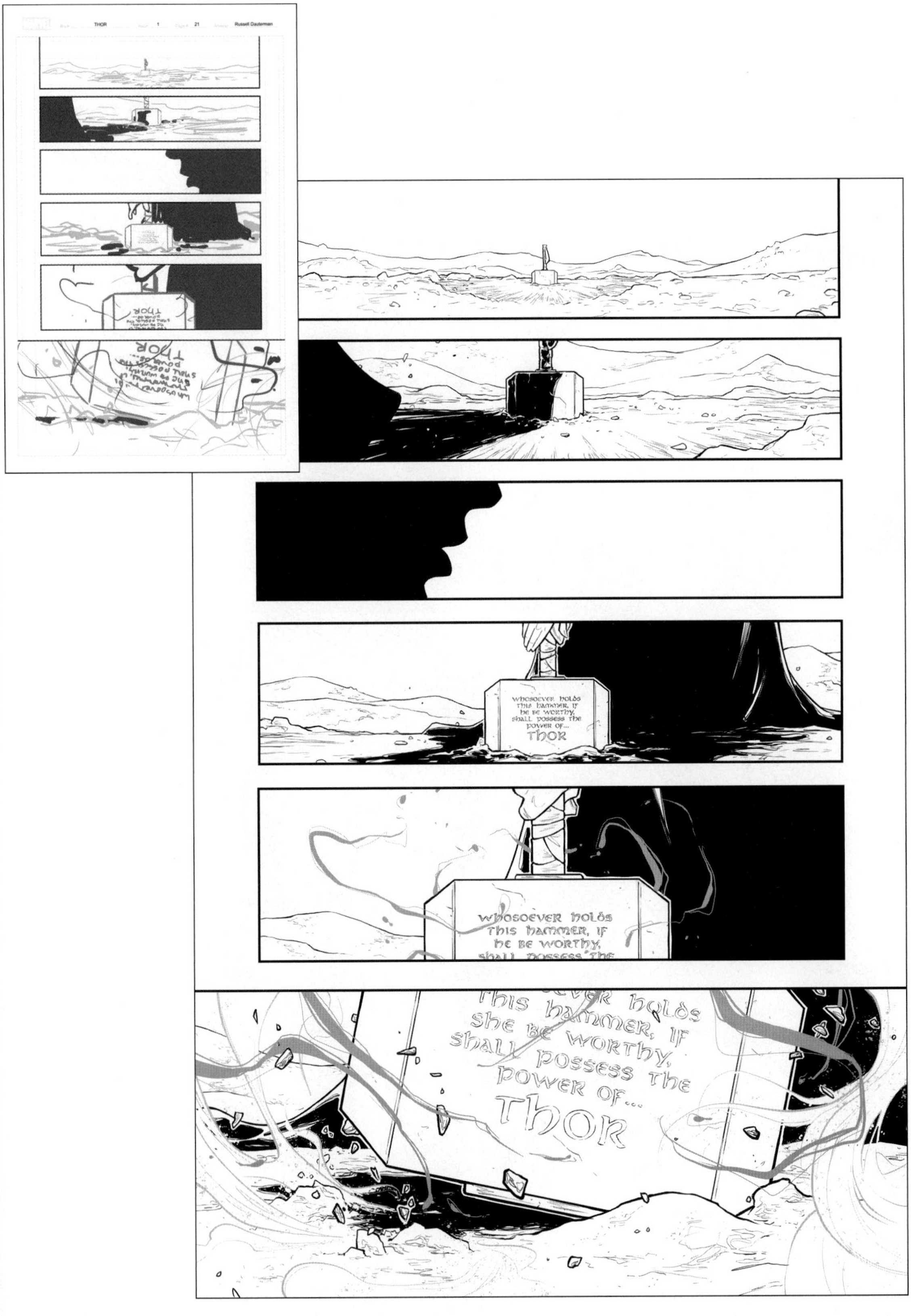

THOR
1
21
Russell Dauterman
whosoever holds
this hammer, if
he be worthy,
shall possess the
power of...
THOR
whosoever holds
this hammer, if
he be worthy,
this hammer, if
she be worthy,
shall possess the
power of...
THOR

#1 PAGE 21, LAYOUTS AND INKS

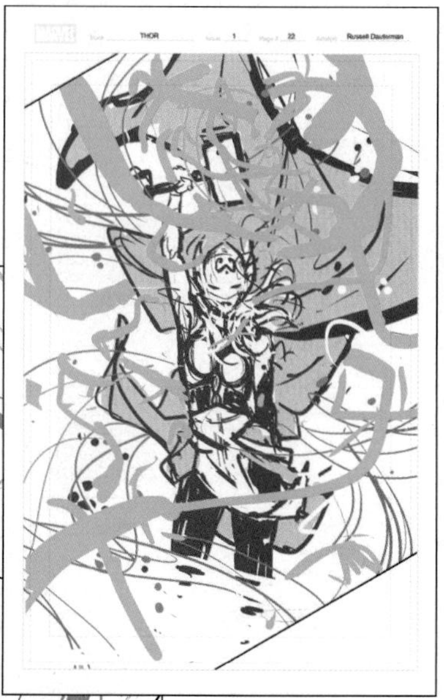

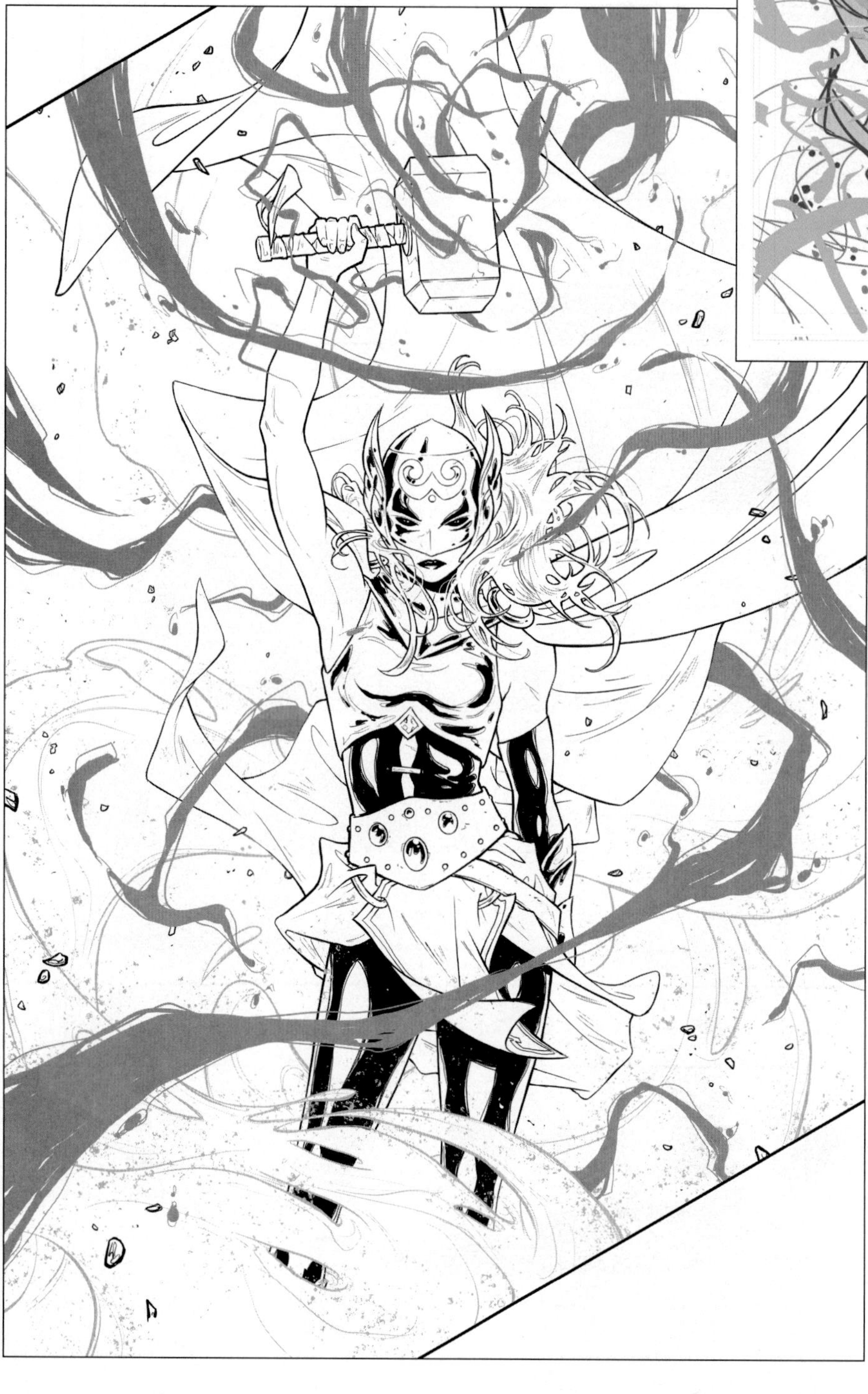

#1 PAGE 22, LAYOUTS AND INKS

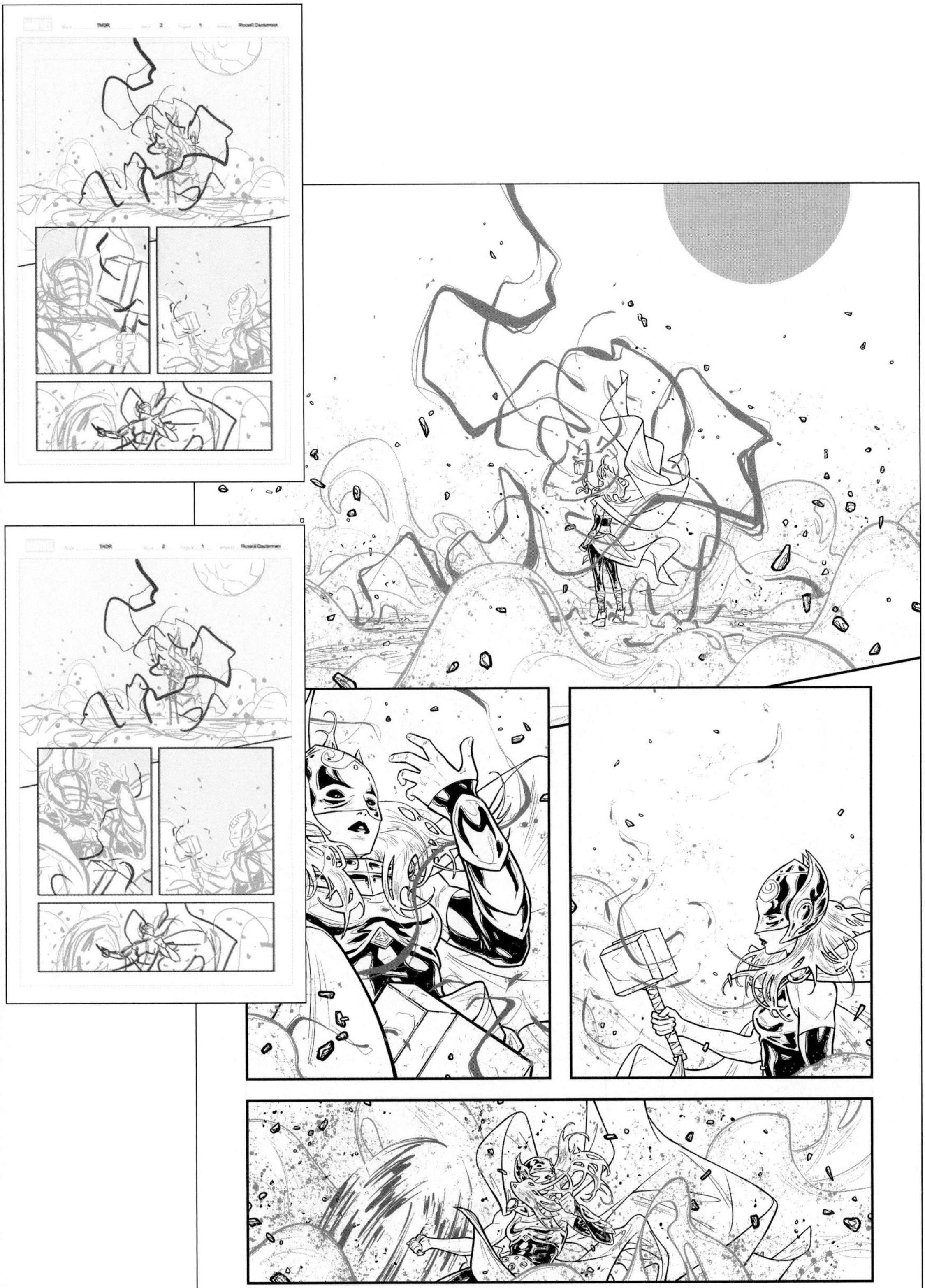

#2 PAGE 1, LAYOUTS AND INKS

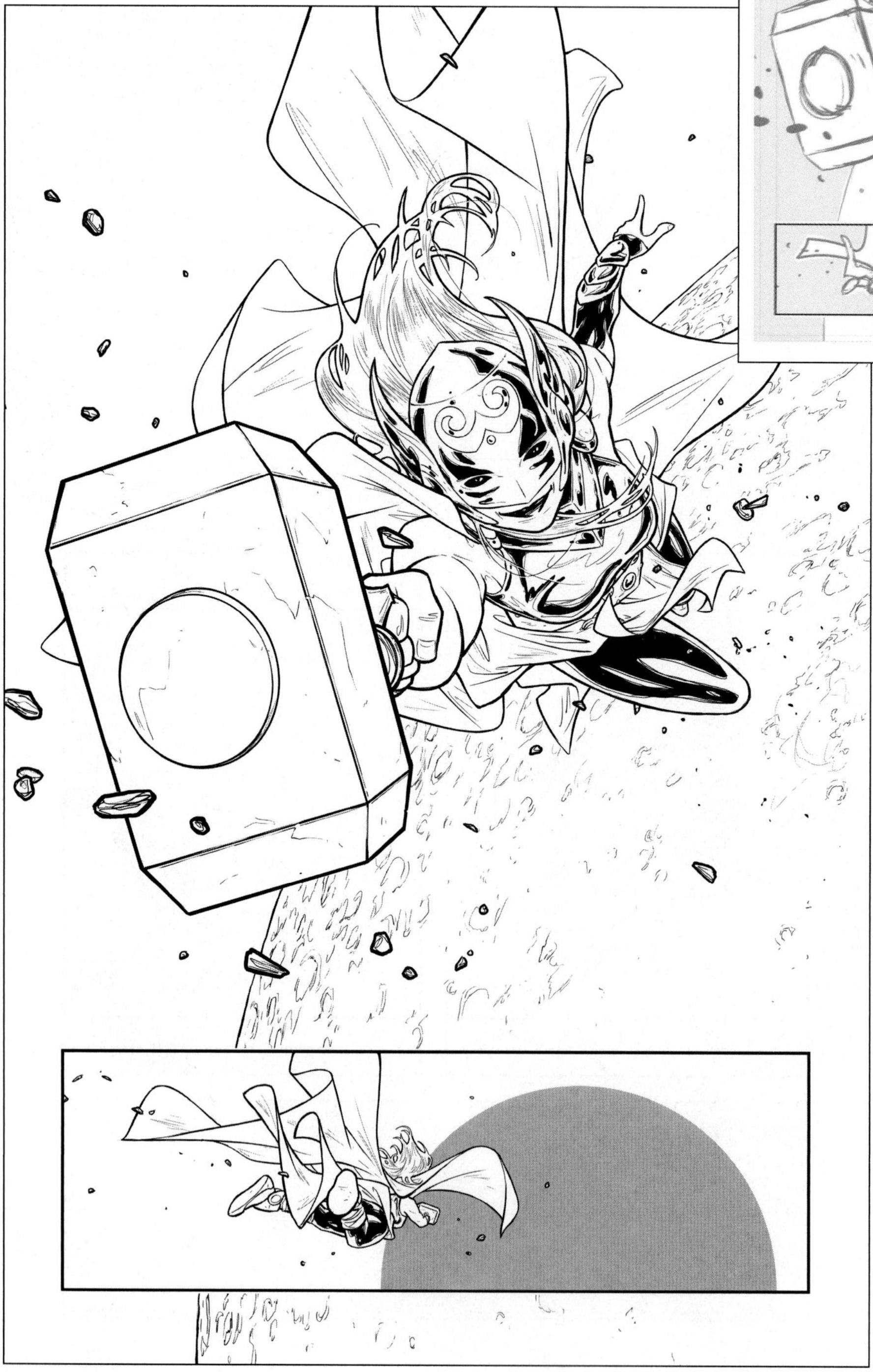

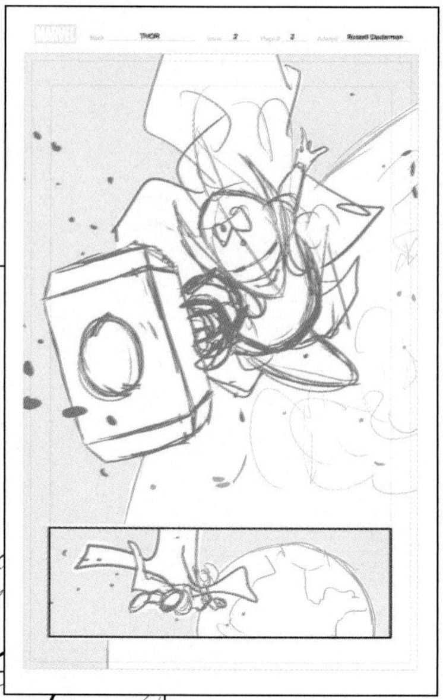

#2 PAGE 2, LAYOUTS AND INKS

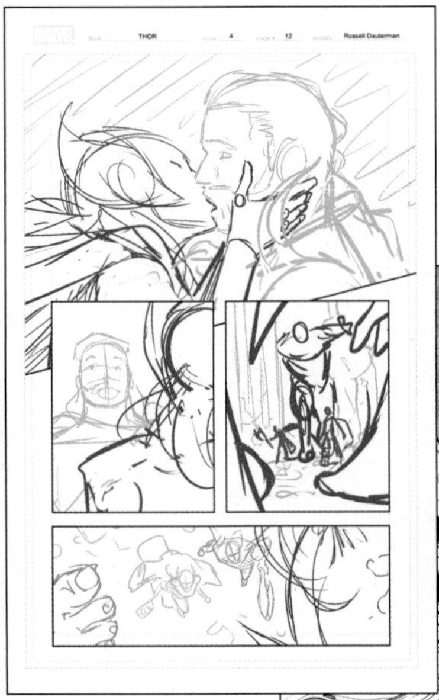
THOR
4
12
Russell Dauterman

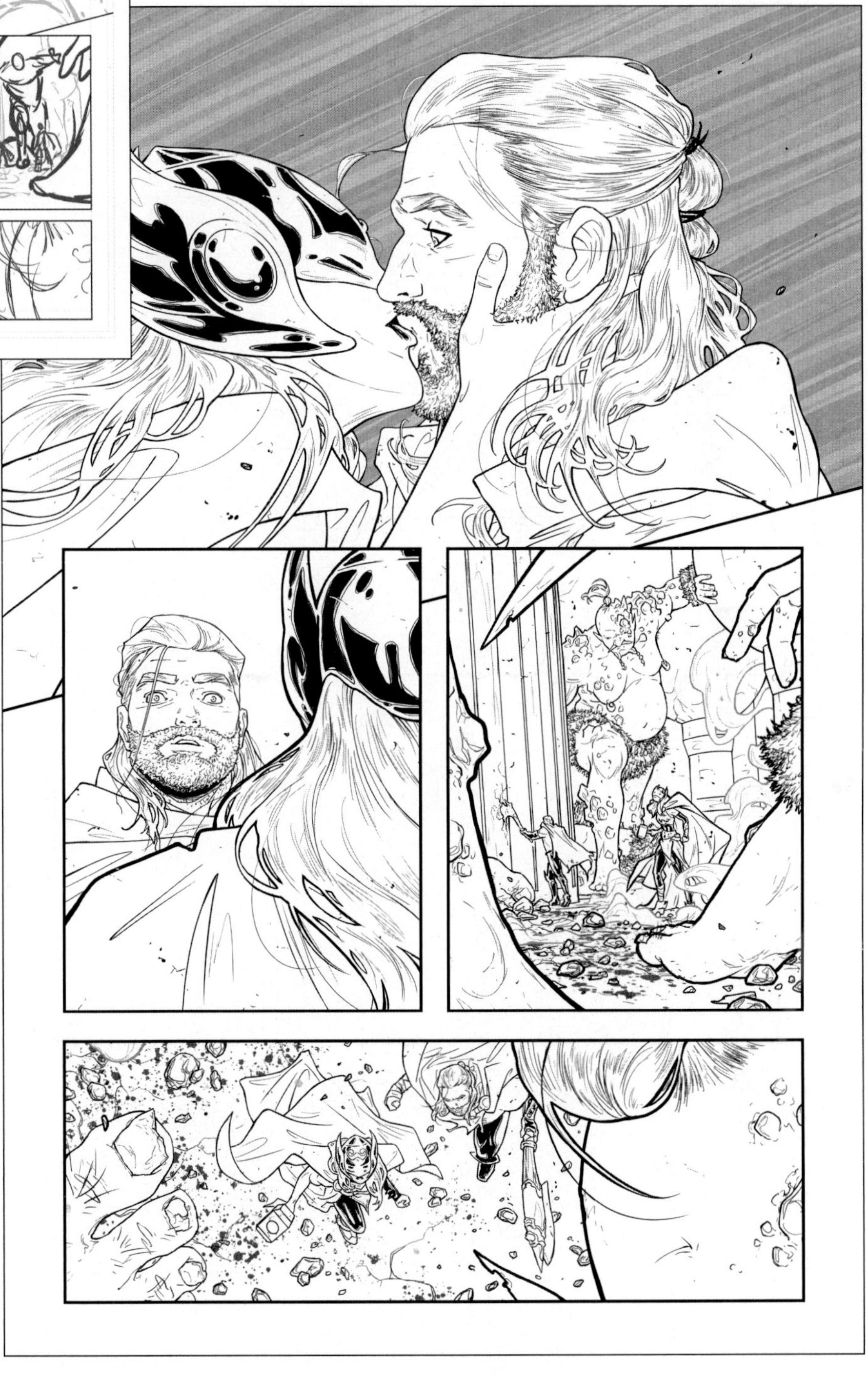

#4 PAGE 12, LAYOUTS AND INKS

ART PROCESS
BY JORGE MOLINA

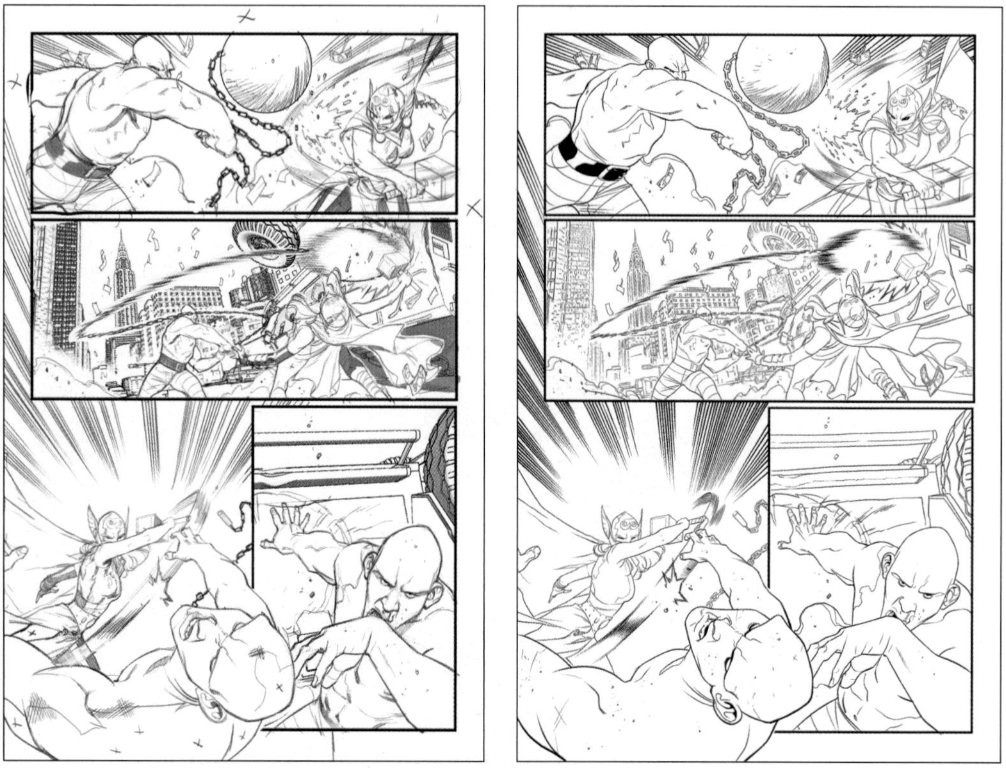

#5 PAGE 4, PENCILS AND INKS

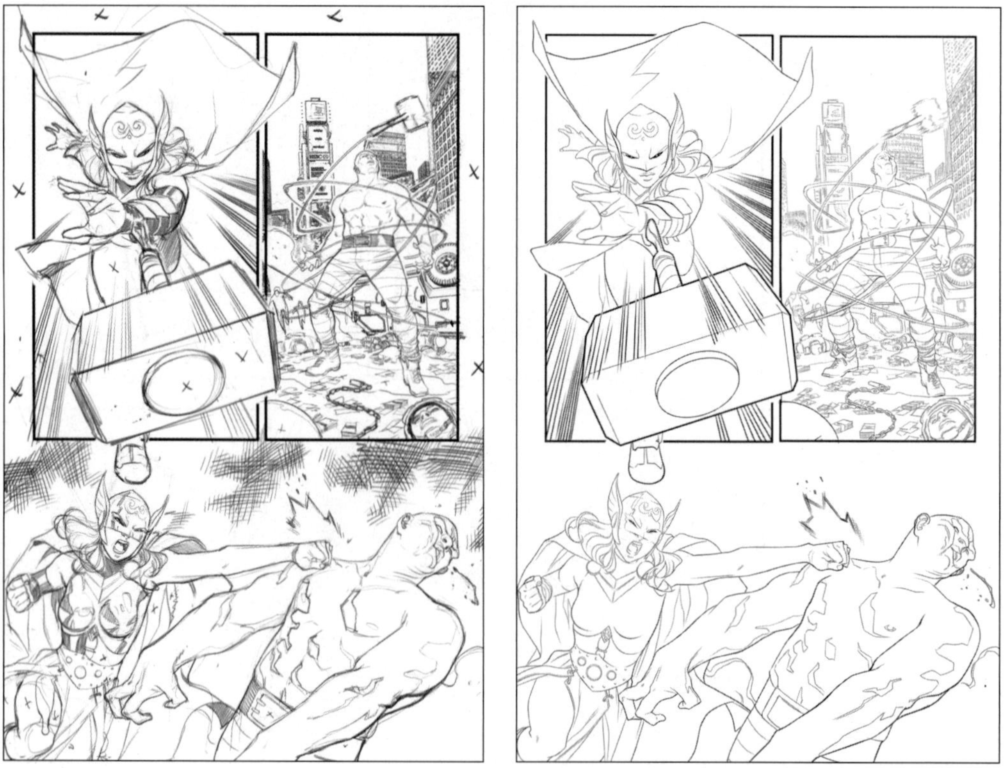

#5 PAGE 5, PENCILS AND INKS

MARVEL AR AUGMENTED REALITY

MARVEL AUGMENTED REALITY (AR) ENHANCES AND CHANGES THE WAY YOU EXPERIENCE COMICS!

TO ACCESS THE FREE MARVEL AR CONTENT IN THIS BOOK*:

1. **Locate the AR logo within the comic.**
2. **Go to Marvel.com/AR in your web browser.**
3. **Search by series title to find the corresponding AR.**
4. **Enjoy Marvel AR!**

*All AR content that appears in this book has been archived and will be available only at Marvel.com/AR – no longer in the Marvel AR App. Content subject to change and availability.

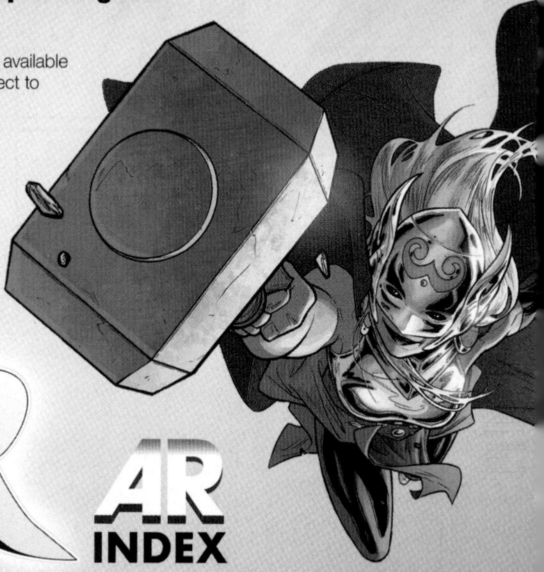

THOR AR INDEX

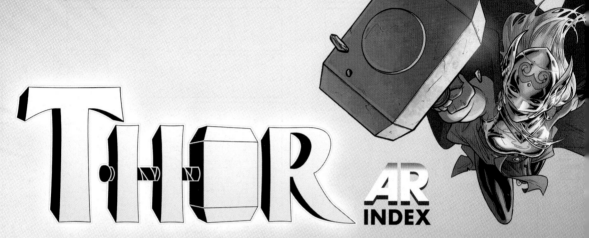

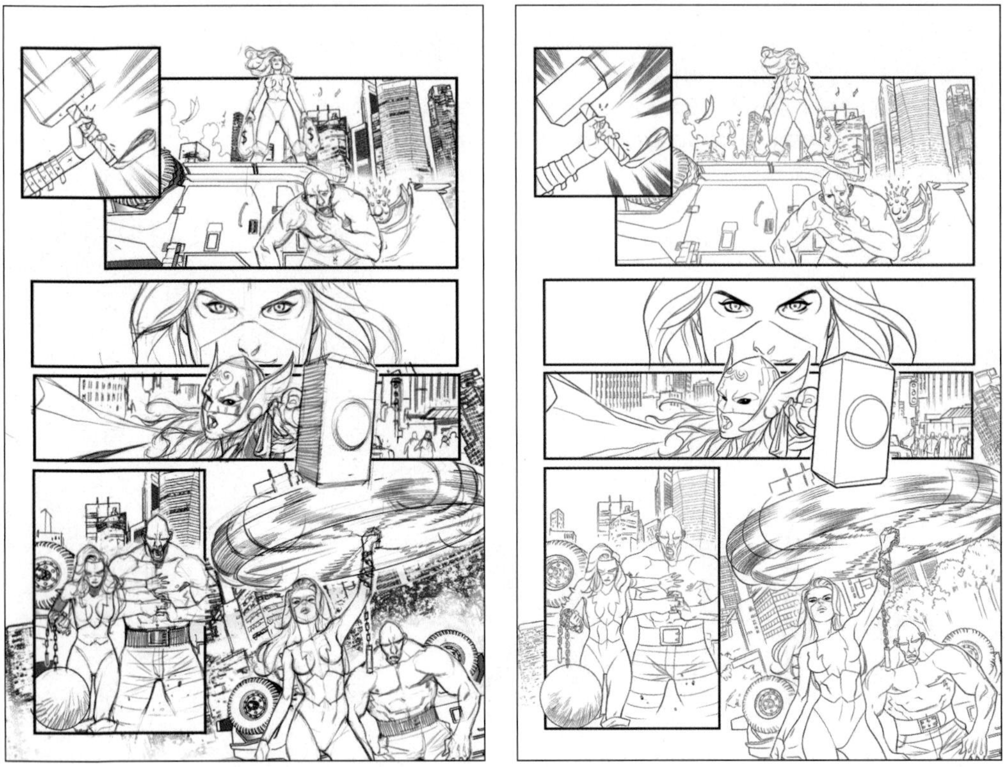

#5 PAGE 6, PENCILS AND INKS

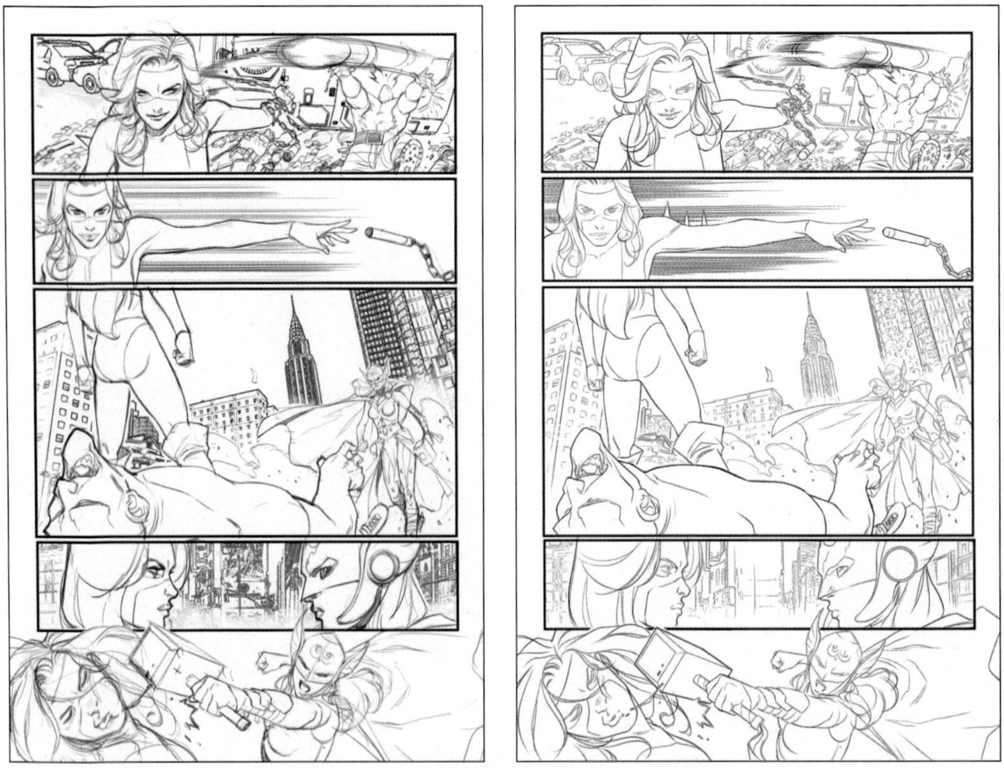

#5 PAGE 7, PENCILS AND INKS